Microsoft Rebooted

Microsoft Rebooted

How Bill Gates and Steve Ballmer
Reinvented Their Company

ROBERT SLATER

Portfolio

PORTFOLIO
Published by the Penguin Group
Penguin Group (USA) Inc., 375 Hudson Street, New York, New York 10014, U.S.A.
Penguin Books Ltd, 80 Strand, London WC2R 0RL, England
Penguin Books Australia Ltd, 250 Camberwell Road, Camberwell, Victoria 3124, Australia
Penguin Books Canada Ltd, 10 Alcorn Avenue, Toronto, Ontario, Canada M4V 3B2
Penguin Books India (P) Ltd, 11 Community Centre, Panchsheel Park, New Delhi—110 017,
   India
Penguin Group (NZ), Cnr Airborne and Rosedale Roads, Albany, Auckland 1310,
   New Zealand
Penguin Books (South Africa) (Pty) Ltd, 24 Sturdee Avenue, Rosebank, Johannesburg 2196,
   South Africa

Penguin Books Ltd, Registered Offices:
80 Strand, London WC2R 0RL, England

First published in 2004 by Portfolio,
a member of Penguin Group (USA) Inc.

10 9 8 7 6 5 4 3 2 1

LIBRARY OF CONGRESS CATALOGING-IN-PUBLICATION DATA

Slater, Robert, 1943–
   Microsoft rebooted : how Bill Gates and Steve Ballmer reinvented their company / Robert
Slater.
      p.   cm.
   Includes bibliographical references and index.
   ISBN 1-59184-039-2
   1. Microsoft Corporation. 2. Computer software industry—United States. 3. Gates, Bill,
1955–. 4. Ballmer, Steven Anthony. I. Title.

   HD9696.63.U64M5376 2004
   338.7'610053'0973—dc22

                                                                                    2004044522

This book is printed on acid-free paper. ∞

Printed in the United States of America

I dedicate this book to our three grandchildren—Edo Shalom, Maya Dorian, and Shai Natan—who, as every grandparent must feel, give new meaning and new joy to one's life. They are learning how to use a computer long before their grandfather did, and in no small way, they have Bill Gates to thank for that.

Acknowledgments

I have been thinking about writing a book on Bill Gates and Microsoft for a very long time. As part of the research I conducted for *Portraits in Silicon* (MIT Press, 1987), a book about computer pioneers and developers, I interviewed a young man who twelve years earlier had founded a company that had become the most outstanding software enterprise in the world. His name is Bill Gates and the company, Microsoft. It occurred to me soon after the book was published that Gates and his company would make a superb topic for a future book. He had, after all, almost singularly brought about the personal computer revolution. And, at the time, no one had told his story in book form. I wanted to be the first to do it. I took the idea to publishers, but they suggested that Gates was not well known enough to warrant such book-length treatment. I remember replying to one of them, "Well, he will be." I was right. Gates, of course, became widely known, especially after 1992, when he was named for the first time as the richest man in the world. Books on him followed, many of them negative. Meanwhile, I wrote a series of books on other business leaders, always wondering if there was a way to return to my idea of doing a book on Gates and Microsoft. I still believed that he was an intriguing figure, indeed one of the most intriguing of our era. Few others have had such an impact on society and few have become as controversial.

Then, in the early 2000s, my editor at Portfolio (The Penguin Group), Adrian Zackheim, and I began talking about my doing just such a book; it was around the time that Microsoft was trying to extricate itself from the greatest crisis it had faced: the lengthy antitrust trial that the Department of Justice had brought against it. Once the trial ended in November 2002 and Microsoft and the DOJ reached a settlement, Adrian and I returned to the subject of a Gates/Microsoft book; only, by then, Steve Ballmer had become the CEO and was as important to the Microsoft story as was Gates. We agreed early in 2003 that I would write a book about Microsoft as it was emerging from the agonizing previous four years of the trial, but the book would be about both Gates and Ballmer, not just Gates. That is how *Microsoft Rebooted: How Bill Gates and Steve Ballmer Reinvented Their Company* came into being.

I hoped to interview Microsoft officials, including Gates and Ballmer, and to talk with outsiders as well, people who had some connection to the Microsoft story. As I began my interviews in Redmond, Washington, Microsoft's headquarters, Microsoft's public relations people let me know that the company sharply limited the access of authors to its officials; but it had responded positively in my case because Steve Ballmer had enjoyed reading my 1998 book, *Jack Welch and the GE Way*, on the former GE chairman and CEO Jack Welch.

Having access to both Gates and Ballmer of course added immeasurably to the project. During my interview with Gates, I asked him mostly about the business side of Microsoft, much less about the technology. In most of his interviews he was asked exclusively about Microsoft's technology. But I was writing a business book and I wanted to hear his views on the way he had run Microsoft from 1975 to 2000, and what he thought about the way Ballmer had reshaped the business side of the company. As is evident in the book, Gates was much more eager to talk about his conduct of Microsoft than about the latest reforms. In my interview with Ballmer, we talked mostly about those reforms. It was no surprise that Ballmer was quite comfortable talking about his role in recasting Microsoft.

I thank Bill Gates and Steve Ballmer for the opportunity to talk not only with them but also with many other Microsoft employees, including a large number of its senior executives.

I also want to thank the people at Waggener Edstrom Strategic Communications, which handles Microsoft's public relations, for guiding me through the company on my many visits to Redmond. Pam Edstrom, the head of Waggener Edstrom, spoke to me a number of times, giving me the benefit of her long experience in dealing with Microsoft's public relations efforts. Corey duBrowa, senior vice president at Waggener Edstrom, organized my interviews with Gates and Ballmer and the other senior executives and offered some valuable insights into the company as well. Laurie Rieger was my main contact in both the interview and fact-checking phases. I am especially grateful for her friendly and extremely efficient efforts on behalf of the project. Jim Bak helped me to get started with interviews at Microsoft.

I also want to thank the people at the Bill and Melinda Gates Foundation in Seattle, especially Bill Gates Sr. and Joe Cerrell.

I would like to thank those who granted me interviews, some of whom agreed to see me more than once: Jim Allchin, Robert Bach, Brendan Barnicle, Christopher A. Bartlett, Eric Benhamou, Dan Bricklin, James I. Cash Jr., Scott Charney, Jonathan Cluts, John G. Connors, Dwight B. Davis, Ken DiPietro, John Eng, Bob Frankston, Michael Gartenberg, Mark B. Gruenberg, Anoop Gupta, Amir Hartman, Peter Haynes, John Heilemann, Robert J. Herbold, Elijah Hurwitz, Kevin Johnson, George Kelly, Alan D. Levy, Daniel T. Ling, Kai-Fu Lee, Kornel Marton, Mich Matthews, Craig Mundie, Mike Murray, Nathan Myhrvold, Scott Oki, John O'Rourke, Pamela S. Passman, Lew Platt, Jeff Raikes, Rick Rashid, Peter Rinearson, Robert S. Rosenschein, Rick Sherlund, Jon Shirley, Charles Simonyi, Bradford L. Smith, David Smith, Mary Snapp, Steven Sinofsky, Gary Starkweather, Deborah Willingham, Andy Wilson, David B. Yoffie, Mark J. Zbikowski, and a number of others who asked not to be identified.

I wish to thank Michael Gartenberg and Richard Sherlund for looking through the manuscript and helping me to clarify a number of key points in the text.

It has been a pleasure for me to continue to write books for Adrian Zackheim and his Portfolio imprint at the Penguin Group. I have learned a great deal from him. I appreciate his guidance in making this the best book possible. I'm also grateful to be working with the others at the Portfolio team: Will Weisser, Mark Ippoliti, Allison Sweet, and Jennifer Pare.

Finally, I thank the people who really made this book possible: my family, especially my wife, Elinor. As she always does, she created the best possible atmosphere for an author, enabling me to sit for hours in front of a computer and to travel to Seattle and elsewhere frequently in the knowledge that we were in many ways doing this book together. A professional editor of long standing, she read and edited the manuscript, making numerous improvements.

Contents

Part V
The Rebooting of Microsoft

Microsoft Rebooted

PART I

The Four-Year Crisis

1

A Surreal Halloween

October 31, 2002. The atmosphere that afternoon at Microsoft's main campus in the Seattle suburb of Redmond was surreal. It was Halloween and the costumed children of employees roamed the corridors trick-or-treating. Then word began to spread among the adults of a sudden, new development in "the DOJ trial," and suddenly employees huddled in groups of twos and threes to vacuum up every fresh detail. Inches below them, but seemingly worlds apart, delighted children giggled and gazed curiously at one anothers' costumes, oblivious to the nerve-wracking drama affecting their parents.

For the adults, the dreaded moment was imminent. It had been four years and five and a half months since the U.S. government had brought its antitrust suit against Microsoft. And Microsoft's legal team had just learned that U.S. District Judge Colleen Kollar-Kotelly planned to issue her fateful decision at 1:00 P.M. Eastern time the next day.

The question before Judge Kollar-Kotelly was whether to accept or reject a settlement hammered out a year earlier by Microsoft and the U.S. government along with nine states. Already, the courts had found that Microsoft had used its monopoly status in the operating software business to force companies to do business with it. Already, one court had ordered Microsoft to be split in two; but a higher court had then shelved that notion forever, or so it had seemed at the time. Nine other states not party to the proposed settlement were asking the U.S. district judge to impose harsher penalties on the company; Microsoft's worst fear was that the judge might use their recommendations as a springboard for eviscerating the software titan.

Before the crisis, the company had risen to become the most valuable company in America. Just sixteen days earlier, Microsoft's market capitalization had reached $265.1 billion, passing General Electric to gain the top spot. In 1999, Microsoft had become the first company to exceed $500 billion in market value. Its cofounder, chairman, and CEO, Bill Gates, had become unquestionably the best known business figure of the era. Blocking out the deafening giggles of the small children, Gates's executives worried that nothing less than the future of the most visible, most profitable, and most controversial high-tech enterprise in the world was on the line. Tomorrow would certainly be a historic turning point for Microsoft.

Although the Microsoft Windows operating system along with its productivity software was running on more than 90 percent of home and business computers, an outraged Gates had continuously insisted that his company was no monopoly. He further argued that, despite what the Government had charged, his company had broken no law. Brimming with confidence that Microsoft would be exonerated, he refused to talk settlement of the case for most of the trial. (But eventually realizing how much the trial had damaged Microsoft's reputation, Gates buckled ignominiously and the November 2, 2001, settlement was to follow.) Now, on October 31, 2002, the question in the minds of those Microsoft executives hovering over their costumed children was whether Judge Kollar-Kotelly would ratify the settlement. For her to reject the settlement would mean that Microsoft's nightmare would continue and might get worse.

The fifty-nine-year-old judge had been appointed to the bench by President Bill Clinton and had a reputation as a meticulous jurist. She had replaced U.S. District Judge Thomas Penfield Jackson as the judge handling the case; upon taking over, she immediately urged the sides to get into settlement discussions. Asking few questions, she had given little insight into her leanings during public arguments.

In agreeing to the settlement, Microsoft had affirmed that it would not participate in exclusive deals that could harm its competitors, and it would not offer different contract terms to different computer manufacturers. With the settlement terms in place, Microsoft had already begun to comply with other terms by distributing technical data and releasing an update to Windows XP that permitted the removal of Microsoft icons from that operating system.

The Inner Sanctum

As adults and children frolicked noisily in the corridors, Brad Smith, Microsoft's senior vice president for law and corporate affairs, was meeting around a conference table with twenty colleagues on the fifth floor of Building 34, headquarters for Bill Gates and other members of Microsoft's senior echelon. Smith always seemed to have a smile on his face. He was normally sociable and talkative, but not now. Now he was sober and without the usual smile. He looked nervous and worried. Not far away from Smith's gathering were the offices of Bill Gates and Steve Ballmer. This was the inner sanctum of Microsoft, where almost no one treaded uninvited.

Inside those offices were Ballmer and Gates, two men whose lives had been upended by the trial and who had high hopes that the end was in sight. They too had solemn looks and they too were more edgy than usual. Nearly two years earlier, they had taken on new roles in the company, but the trial had been a large reason why they had still not fully adjusted to those new roles. Back then, Ballmer had, with Gates's approval, replaced the cofounder as CEO; and Gates had begun to devote himself full-time to overseeing the company's technology as chief software architect.

By now, Brad Smith and his associates had learned that the antitrust case was to be resolved the next day. Suddenly the jaunty laughter subsided. Scooping up their notebooks, they hustled out of the conference room to consider postverdict scenarios. Suddenly stern-faced executives reviewed the previous four years of courtroom wrangling and tried to make a quick assessment. They knew their assessments were beside the point. The betting, unfortunately for Microsoft, favored a harsh decision.

Smith thought the whole scene outside the conference room door was bizarre. Stepping into the corridor and locating his wife and two costumed children, he spotted Steve Ballmer with his wife and three children. Ballmer, with his oval bald head and bulky, seemingly towering frame, was always easy to recognize. He had just lost fifty pounds, but no one would accuse him of looking gaunt. Smith gazed intently at the CEO's countenance, hoping to see Ballmer's thin lips curl up in a smile, but they did not.

He's frowning, Smith thought. *This is not a good sign.*

A smile or the lack of one became the key measurement for Microsoft's future.

Brad Smith wondered if tomorrow would bring smiles.

For Bill Gates, the Government's antitrust suit had been a disastrous ordeal. It had been his personal hell. News reports surfaced that Microsoft's cofounder had broken down in front of the Microsoft board of directors, but senior executives called such reports "overblown." Whatever the case, he could have ended the nightmare much sooner by negotiating a settlement. But he had chosen to endure it. He did so—he felt in the strongest possible terms—in order to save Microsoft from being torn to shreds, one shred at a time, by jealous, unimaginative, and rapacious rivals. He had no doubt that he could outlast them, and so he had been willing to take his chances with the courts. He had never admitted to being distracted, let alone overwhelmed, by *United States v. Microsoft*. But, severe distraction it had certainly been. In his own view, Gates had spent far too much time and energy on legal strategies—time and energy that could have been employed much more productively to monitor Microsoft's technology program. For those who cared deeply about Gates, the trial had been an agony. His father, Bill Gates Sr., admitted to feeling "a sense of relief after what he went through." It was no wonder.

Recasting His Image

In the early part of his career, Bill Gates had been in the media's eyes, the supernova of the technology world. He had been the boy genius of technology, creator of the company admiringly dubbed the smartest in the world. As the person who in the 1970s had almost single-handedly created the personal computer revolution, and as the wealthiest man alive during the 1990s, he had become a household name. Many had paid him the rare compliment of being the Henry Ford, the John D. Rockefeller, or the Thomas Edison of his age. At one stage in 1999, worth more than $100 billion, he was richer than many countries. He and Microsoft had sat on top of the heap and nothing seemed likely to budge them from that spot, but then, when evidence piled up of Microsoft's alleged unsavory business practices and the media gleefully applied such terms as *predator* and *monopolist* to Gates, his near-perfect image became badly tarnished. Shockingly, Gates could no longer count on history treating him with great reverence.

The verdict on whether he was supernova or predator remained unclear as *Time* magazine's 1993 profile of him suggested: "Though Gates is famous for his lack of pretension, his habit of flying in coach class, and his easy accessibility, he can also be brash, imperious, and brutally blunt." Five years later, the same magazine acknowledged that the verdict had still not come in on him: "[T]he real battle seems to be between two warring views of Gates. Is he the brilliant innovator who has brought the wonders of the information age to millions of satisfied customers? Or is he the rapacious capitalist leveraging his software monopoly to crush competitors?"

At a certain point during the trial, he began to disgorge himself of billions of dollars of his net worth, in the process creating the richest foundation in the world. Undoubtedly, he was deeply moved by the plight of millions of poor people and wanted to help them. And there seemed little reason to doubt his assertion that he was giving away most of his fortune to keep his children from having to bear the burden of living with inherited billions. What he did not say, however, what he could not say, was that emerging as the world's most generous philanthropist would help recast his image, an image shattered into a thousand tiny pieces by the daily barrage of trial-related verbal abuse heaped upon his persona.

Because the Bill and Melinda Gates Foundation's largesse had the undeniable effect of saving thousands of lives, its creation led some to suggest that Bill Gates might become better known for his philanthropy than for his pioneering work in the development of personal computer software. From such utterings, Gates hoped to repair his reputation. He hated being called a devil. He loved being known as a savior.

The judge's decision the next day, November 1, 2002, if it went the right way for Gates, would help him erase or at least bring to a halt the constant battering against him and against Microsoft. Hence, her decision was crucial to their futures. It seemed ironic that Gates would worry how history would judge him. He had, after all, despite his relative youth (he had turned forty-seven three days earlier), already made more of a mark on this planet than most others had.

Though he had clearly made that mark, he was so fanatically devoted to building what he called "magical software" that any thought of his departing Microsoft seemed unimaginable. Consequently, long after many of his contemporary founders of companies, especially wealthy founders, had drifted away from their businesses, Gates remained in charge of Microsoft. He had never quite adjusted to having all that wealth and he certainly had no interest in using that wealth to retire to some island. He had, however, easily adjusted to ruling the software world, and he had no desire to give up the crown.

His Worst Crisis

His climb to the top had not been easy. The trial had not been his first crisis, only his worst. Confronting much larger, much more powerful rivals, he had forced himself to read the burgeoning computer market carefully, trying to spot emerging trends. When he did, unlike far more conservative business leaders, he was prepared to shift the company's product strategy on a dime, reorganizing whole divisions overnight. He lived in fear that another company was secretly devising its own product strategy that would bring Microsoft to its knees. With little choice in his mind, he raised paranoia to a new art form in the business world.

That paranoia led Gates to turn the reinventing of his company into one of Microsoft's core competencies, suddenly dropping the MS-DOS operating system in favor of Windows and shifting personnel from other projects to Internet work overnight. "It is deep in the culture that success is never guaranteed," observed Pam Edstrom, explaining Bill Gates's paranoia and his reinventing strategies in one neat sentence. She joined Microsoft back in 1982 with the task of handling the company's public relations (in 2003 she was still running its PR through her own agency, Waggener Edstrom).

To Bob Herbold, the company's executive vice president, Gates's savvy and guts reflected in his reinventing strategies were all the more remarkable after Herbold's twenty-six years at Procter & Gamble. Perhaps because of the slower innovation rate of the consumer products industry, or perhaps because P&G had been so bureaucratically entrenched, nothing happened fast at his former employer. But Gates was able to move with the speed of lightning. Herbold remembered vividly, "After the launch of Windows 95, I was at a board meeting and Bill explained how, in the next two or three weeks, he was going to take hundreds of people from existing divisions and quickly define a new product division to jump on a new opportunity—very impressive." Impressive, yes; but the reinventing strategy was risky as well. Gates knew the risks were high. He always felt like he was in a fight for his life.

. . .

Now, on October 31, 2002, by his own personal choice, he was in another fight for his life. It was in fact *the* fight of his life. He hoped for a positive decision, one that would give him a welcome sense of closure to the four-year trauma and that would permit Steve Ballmer and himself the freedom to devote their full energies to the company. For all sorts of reasons, of which the trial was only one, Microsoft had not been running up to speed for a while. The company's annual growth rate, as high as 49 percent in 1996, had slipped tellingly to a mere 12 percent this year as its annual revenue stood for the fiscal year ending the previous June 30 at $28.37 billion.

Despite valiant efforts, the company remained a one- or, at best, a two-product firm (Windows and Office), and only three of its seven business segments (Client, Information worker, and the Server platforms) were showing profits. It seemed a minor miracle that the company was doing that well for the place was in turmoil. Senior executives were jumping ship. Morale among the rank and file was at an all-time low. Once they had boasted to friends and relatives that they worked at Microsoft. Now they kept it a secret, uneager to enter conversations about which of the allegations were actually true. No longer could they at least take solace in holding highly valued stock options in the company; the stock market had taken a plunge and the options were of far less value.

November 1, 2002, 8:30 A.M. Microsoft's attorneys and public relations executives gathered in a theater on the Redmond campus at Microsoft's studio a few blocks from Building 34. The studio lacked windows. Some in the room felt under siege, and not just because of the windowless room.

Gates and Ballmer were there and for the next ninety minutes the lawyers walked them through postverdict scenarios over scrambled eggs and bacon. The food gave the room a partylike atmosphere. But this was no party.

We Will Not Gloat

By 10:00 A.M. the two Microsoft leaders had left. Brad Smith stayed behind to talk with the public relations executives. He placed phone calls to the attorneys general of states involved in the case. "Whatever happens," he told one of them, Tom Miller, the Iowa attorney general, "we are committed to trying to develop an ability to work together. If it's good news, we won't gloat. If it's bad news, we won't complain about you to the press." (Miller had been coordinating the legal strategy against Microsoft for the states since the start of the case.) Most in the room believed that the news would be bad. The gloom was contagious. The company had been forced to take one body blow after another during the trial. Faces grew longer and longer.

Suddenly, it was only fifteen minutes before the announcement was due, 12:45 P.M. The Microsoft legal and public relations team began gathering in the company board room in Building 34. Down the hall Bill Gates and Steve Ballmer and another half dozen executives were meeting in a conference room near the CEO's office. Brad Smith walked quietly into that conference room to inform Gates and Ballmer that once he had learned details of the judgment from Microsoft's lawyers in Washington, D.C., he would quickly walk back down the hall and notify them.

A Good Day

Brad Smith returned to the company board room and sat down with other attorneys for the final vigil. Then precisely at 1:00 P.M., the phone rang in the board room. He picked it up. On the other end of the line, calling on a cell phone, was one of Microsoft's attorneys in Washington, D.C. Adding to the tension, Microsoft's chief counsel had trouble hearing the voice in Washington. Between the crackles on the line, Brad Smith strained to hear the fateful news. Finally, the reception improved once the attorney was outside. Now Smith could understand every word. To anyone else who had not followed the trial, the language would have seemed arcane. But Brad Smith could recite the trial record in his sleep. He listened for certain key phrases that indicated the judge had agreed to the settlement. When he heard them, he allowed himself a brief sigh of relief. Microsoft had by no means won the case; but it had not lost, either.

For all intents and purposes the case was over. It had not been the resounding victory Bill Gates had hoped for. There would be scar tissue. But the ratified settlement undoubtedly had constituted the best that a company as assaulted and bloodied as Microsoft could have expected. The Government had been able to impose important restraints on the company. But the good news was that Microsoft would not be split in two. The judicial edict calling for the breakup of the company had been overruled some time earlier; but who could be certain, if the case had continued, that another judge might not reverse again and order a dismantling of the company? Knowing all this, no one around Brad Smith's conference table screamed for joy. They all sat quietly, hanging on every word coming in through the phone. Eventually, the news sunk in. Microsoft could continue more or less as it had been. Here and there someone broke out in a quiet smile, perhaps sensing that it was too early to look too happy.

Now it was time for Brad Smith to deliver the news to Gates and Ballmer. He was thrilled to carry this kind of announcement, having dwelled far too long on what it would be like to transmit a negative outcome to the gathering. As he reached the conference room door, Smith could feel everyone's eyes on him. He knew that if he broke into legalese off the bat, he would confuse too many listeners. But he did not want to say simply, "We won," which he was all too aware would be oversimplifying things. Conscious of how important it was to get to the point at once, he searched for just the right phrase, something that would resonate with the crowd.

Suddenly, he thought back to the trial and an image stuck in his mind of Microsoft spokesperson Mark Murray on the courthouse steps. Briefing reporters, as he did every day, Murray was saying, "This is another good day for Microsoft." Within Microsoft, Murray's phrase had been greeted with a kind of gallows humor and whenever bad news broke in the trial someone was sure to utter, "Oh, another good day for Microsoft."

With that phrase ringing in his mind, Brad Smith looked around the room and blurted out, "This *is* a good day for Microsoft."

At first, there was silence. Some had questioning looks on their faces. A few broke into smiles at once but were not sure the smiles were in place. Then everyone saw the smile on Brad Smith's face and everyone understood. The place erupted in cheers. Steve Ballmer turned to Bill Gates, patting the cofounder on his back. For the first time in years, the people who were running Microsoft had something to shout about.

All of the above drama serves as the backdrop for *Microsoft Rebooted: How Bill Gates and Steve Ballmer Reinvented Their Company.*

But this is not a book about the trial, though the trial is a key part of the drama of this book; it is the catalyst for what will come, the major turning point that forces the company to deal with issues smoldering under the surface even before the trial. Though few at Microsoft like to hear it said, the trial is the occasion for much of what was to happen at Microsoft in 2002 and 2003.

The book has as its focus those two years, centering on what occurred at Microsoft and how Bill Gates and Steve Ballmer were attempting to change the face of their company during that period. It is therefore not a history of the company, even though some of that history emerges here and there in order to help the reader understand the way the company is currently changing. Nor is the book meant to be, by any means, a cobiography of Bill Gates and Steve Ballmer, though their personal lives are very much a part of this story and the change in their personalities over the years bears crucially on the book's main themes.

Finally, although Microsoft is known far more for its technology than for its business processes, the book does not offer detailed explanations of the company's various software products; those products appear in the narrative only as they relate to Microsoft's business side.

What the book *is* about is the attempt, still in progress, of both Gates and Ballmer to transform Microsoft into a completely different company from the one it had been prior to and during the trial. In the book we look at the main players, Gates and Ballmer; we examine how each in his own way contributed to the changes that would occur; and we make some assessment toward the end of how the revamping is progressing. But before moving too far along, we have to examine why Microsoft chose to act in the immediate wake of the trial, and not long before.

What Would Consumers Do?

Judge Kollar-Kotelly's judgment of November 2002 had ended the legal cloud hanging over Microsoft, but her seal of approval on the settlement had by no means returned the company's once-lofty image to what it once had been. Indeed, all of the assaults and allegations remained like a festering wound and it would take far more than the end of the courtroom battle to heal the wound.

Too many of Microsoft's critics had felt vindicated by the courtroom testimony; too many had been dismayed at the settlement, believing that it lacked the necessary teeth to curtail the predator. And too many had been distraught at the failure of Microsoft to admit to any wrongdoing before, during, and after the settlement. In short, the end of the trial meant that Microsoft could move forward in more or less the same configuration as in the past. Even if the settlement had imposed new restraints on the company, making it easier for consumers to choose non-Microsoft products, those same consumers could continue to purchase Microsoft products.

The question of how consumers would react to the more constrained Microsoft would take some time. A more burning question had to do with whether all of the other groups in the outside world, including its shareholders, Wall Street, the high-tech community, the federal government, and the media, would continue to keep Microsoft embattled, or whether those groups could be persuaded to drop their weapons.

Until now, although some of these groups had certainly tried their best, they had not brought Microsoft down. They had not induced the company's millions of customers to turn away from Microsoft products. But they had shown that they could seriously impair the company's ability to concentrate on building and distributing great products. Until now they had proved a serious distraction.

But what might happen in the future? If any of these elements stepped up their battles with Microsoft, at some point consumers just might stand up and take notice; consumers might begin to regard Microsoft as the enemy. They might decide to boycott its products. Until now, the company had been delighted to discover that its consumers had remained loyal to the company and to its products. Some 600 million people were using Microsoft's Windows operating system; and 400 million were using its productivity package of applications known as Office, which in 2003 was bringing in almost one-third of the company's sales and profits.

Even if they had not been madly in love with those products and had groused about the products' quality, customers had not defected because of the allegations. Still, Microsoft feared that eventually the negative effects of the trial would affect customer loyalty to its products.

Was there something Microsoft could do to prevent that from happening? The answer was yes. It could work hard to improve its reputation among the high-tech community, the government, the media, and the like. It could labor vigorously to show these critical factors in the external world that Microsoft had turned over a new leaf; that it was no longer a monopolistic predator; that it was, in effect, a new company, a kinder and gentler company.

Would this be a smart move on Microsoft's part? Of course it would. But too many employees wondered why it was necessary to repair the company's reputation. The mere suggestion that Microsoft was interested in repairing its image smacked of heresy. After all, this was a company that had bathed itself in innocence, and that had acted as if the whole world had been wrong and that it had been right.

Don't Blame the Trial

To get around the point, once it was decided that changes would be made, Microsoft executives argued imaginatively that factors other than the trial had caused the reforms. Some, like Microsoft board member Jon Shirley, saw the trial as an important role in curbing some of the excessive zeal that had existed before the proceedings: "The trial matured people; it's certainly caused a tempering, not of enthusiasm, but in the way that you compete; the way you talk to your customers; it's not the wild wooly West when Microsoft was a tiny little company." Shirley was the company's chief operating officer from 1983 to 1990; prior to that he had been with Tandy Corporation for twenty-five years, last as vice president for computer merchandising.

But the preponderance of Microsoft executives pointed to those other factors as far more important in explaining the need for the reforms. That rationalization proved useful because it kept those executives who had all along insisted upon the company's innocence from having to explain later why, if the company had committed no misdeed, reform was even necessary. Time after time, Microsoft executives insisted that the changes had to do with the sheer size of the company (numbering then around fifty thousand employees), with the souring of the American economy, with the slow-down in Microsoft's phenomenal growth rates, and with the dot-com revolution—anything but the trial.

Whatever the cause of the reform, some, most likely a tiny minority, had wanted these changes for quite some time. But their plaintive cries were drowned out by those who thought Microsoft had been doing just fine. When the company was founded in 1975, as a new start-up, its culture was anchored in certain traits that came in time to define how all start-ups should behave. Aggressiveness, competitiveness, a lack of discipline—these were the qualities that had launched Microsoft into the heavens. When that tiny minority preached reforms that would make these traits less crucial to the company's culture, almost no one listened. The majority clung to these trappings of a start-up and refused to let them go. No one had the foresight, no one could quite believe that these same qualities that had propelled Microsoft into the strato-sphere, if not tamed, might land it in legal entanglements. And yet that is precisely what had happened. Hence, the delay in taming those traits, the delay in putting its start-up mode to rest, had kept the company from imposing the kind of order that should have kept it out of the courtroom.

With the trial behind it, Microsoft faced a monumentally important choice:

It could hew to the start-up mode. It could keep proclaiming its in-nocence of any wrongdoing. In doing so, it would be saying, "We're simply not going to change the way we do business." In short, the company could do nothing.

Or it could shed its start-up trappings, play down its professions of innocence, and act as if the company needed to change its ways. To abandon its start-up mode characterized by all that zeal without ad-mitting to any wrongdoings might not get Microsoft too far. But com-pany executives were finally coming around to the view that the trial had been a turning point, it had been an eye-opener. One of those ex-ecutives acknowledged that the trial, if not the main driver of the com-pany's rebooting, had certainly been a distraction and a serious impediment: "Trying to get our message across had become a lot harder for a time because people kept saying, 'Aren't you that well-known felon?' Everything was seen through the lens of the trial." In the end, executives took a key decision. Changes would have to be made. Mi-crosoft would continue to admit to no wrongdoing; but it would, at long last, put an end to its start-up mode.

What was required at this crucial crossroads in Microsoft's history was not the launching of a new operating system or new software application; it was, at bottom, something far more fundamental to the enterprise: a complete revamping of the way the company did business.

Even if Bill Gates and Steve Ballmer were to decide to recast Microsoft so totally, nothing would be guaranteed. No matter how much kinder or gentler Microsoft became, no way existed of ensuring that the public would forgive and forget. One thing was certain: Microsoft was in for a long journey and this was only the start.

Even as the ink was drying on the settlement agreement, Gates and Ballmer (Gates grudgingly, Ballmer far more enthusiastically) decided to reinvent their company. To be sure, reorganizations had taken place at Microsoft before, but they would seem cosmetic compared to what the two leaders had in store. Gates and Ballmer planned to reshape the most fundamental pillars of the company, starting with their own leadership; then, the structure of its businesses; next, the kind of people it hired; and finally, its world-famous culture.

Carrying the Torch

Steve Ballmer was left to carry the reform torch mostly on his own. While playing his part in carrying out the reforms, Bill Gates said very little in public about the importance of those reforms. He may well have felt that by transforming itself, Microsoft was all but acknowledging its guilt of the various transgressions alleged by the Government.

In the end, Gates played a major role in the reinventing of Microsoft; but what he did was far more passive than what Ballmer did. While it may seem contradictory to assert that Gates played a major role and was at the same time passive, no contradiction exists. For without adopting that passive role, the reinventing of the company would not have taken place.

. . .

In the making of the new Microsoft, by far the most important changes came in the leadership sphere.

Bill Gates had ruled Microsoft essentially as a one-man show from its founding in 1975 until the start of 2000. He had been its chief technologist, chief executive officer, chief financial officer, and chief operating officer, all wrapped into one. Because Gates had personally created the Microsoft culture that had yielded such great numbers, no one quarreled with his leadership. It was simply a given that Bill Gates would rule Microsoft for as long as he wished. And it was widely assumed that only Gates would decide how and when to yield some or all of his power.

Undoubtedly Gates would have yielded very little power if he had had his way. But as time went on, he realized that one-man management at the top of a company that was adding thousands of employees year after year made less and less sense. He had to decide how to allocate his time better. He had to give up some of that power. But it was frustrating to contemplate such a change.

And yet, as the company grew in leaps and bounds during the 1990s, Gates understood that he had to spend less time on business questions and more on the company's technology program. Over the years he had delegated various business tasks to others; yet he had never really relinquished the ultimate decision making over how the business should be run. But all of that was before the trial.

It was the advent of the trial that triggered in Gates's mind a fateful decision. Rather than have others perform certain business tasks, as he had in the past, he would now relinquish almost all of the decision making on business issues to a single figure. He would attribute that decision to all sorts of things: The company was growing too large for him to make all the decisions; he wanted to focus on technology, and leave the business side to someone else; the trial had been consuming much of his time. But perhaps the most important reason was one that he could not mention: his finally acknowledging that the company had to change its cultural direction.

It had to cease behaving like a start-up.

The best place to start was for him to cede a good deal of power to someone else. In yielding that power, he would become less visible and less of a target for outsiders. It was not a decision he wanted to make; but it was one that he realized had to be made. It would be his way of trying to save the company.

The New CEO

In July 1998, Gates appointed Ballmer Microsoft's new president; but Gates still clung to a good deal of the decision-making authority. Then in January 2000, Gates relinquished almost all of the operational decision making by turning over the CEO duties to Ballmer.

Gates remained chairman and created a new post for himself, chief software architect. He said he wanted to devote more time and energy to overseeing the company's product strategies and development—and no doubt he did. But the main effect of the change in leadership was to make Gates a more secondary figure around Microsoft. That gave Steve Ballmer the opportunity to take in some of the limelight, to acquire his own set of credentials as the primary Microsoft leader, and, ultimately, to steer the company in a new direction. To many it would seem that Gates and Ballmer had worked out a unique kind of comanagement for the two of them. And in some ways they did comanage. But there was no mistaking the new reality: By and large, Steve Ballmer—not Bill Gates—was now in charge of Microsoft.

Critical decisions had to be taken as well with respect to the way Microsoft would be organized in the future. For a long time the company had been organized around a hub-and-spoke system with Gates the hub and other executives the spokes. When Ballmer rose to a senior position within the company, he became a second hub. When Microsoft was small, the system worked well. Gates showed that he could multitask at a dizzying speed, making decisions on business and technology without consulting too many others. But as the company grew, too many decisions had to be taken for just one person to handle.

In appointing Ballmer CEO, Gates had indicated that he thought the hub-and-spoke system had run its course. But all Gates was doing was getting rid of one hub (himself), while keeping the other hub (Ballmer) in place—which was not much of a change. Ballmer understood all this and knew that much more was needed to bring new efficiencies and discipline to the company. And so he chose to restructure the company's businesses into seven more market-oriented segments, empowering the heads of these business segments with sweeping powers over budgets, personnel, and products. This new attempt at decentralizing authority was aimed at making these businesses accountable for their operations and enabling them to apply their resources more effectively to get close to customers.

Crucial decisions were required as well with respect to the company's culture. Gates firmly believed that the only way to have Microsoft operate at full throttle was to create and nurture a culture that in effect mimicked his behavior style. He did that brilliantly in Microsoft's early years, invoking aggressiveness and competitiveness as the culture's key elements.

To promote a new Microsoft to outsiders, Ballmer knew that he had to modify the culture in important ways. Certain features, however, did not need scrapping: Employees in 2003 were still expected to exhibit a passion for technology plus a willingness to work hard, to persevere, and to be self-critical.

Cleverly, Ballmer never spoke openly about the need to drop aggressiveness and competitiveness from the culture. Those traits were so ingrained in the culture that it would have been difficult to argue so enthusiastically for them for twenty-seven years and then drop them as if they had been worthless. What Ballmer really wanted Microsoft employees to do was to abandon the attitude of winning at any cost. But he did not want to say that, either. No one at Microsoft, Ballmer included, liked to tell employees to stop trying to win.

And so, rather than concentrate on what Microsoft employees *should not* do, Ballmer explained what new ways of thinking they needed to inculcate into their behavior to adapt to the new culture. Without relating to the question of whether Microsoft had engaged in any wrongdoing in the past, Ballmer made it clear that an excessive zeal had permeated the culture and gotten the company into one legal tiff after another. The excessive zeal had to be tamed. But Ballmer didn't want to put things in the negative. Instead, he insisted that in all of the ways that they practiced business from now on, Microsoft employees would be expected to be open and respectful. He wanted the company as well to seem less secretive, less mysterious, and more communicative and above board. "Providing value to customers," Gates and Ballmer wrote to shareholders in 2003, "means not only building great products, but also listening carefully to customers, responding quickly, and being more transparent and accountable." It was as if Microsoft's leadership were saying, "We've always thought of ourselves as good guys. We don't think we did anything wrong. But all of you think we're not that great. So now we have to convince you that we *truly* are good guys."

The changes at Microsoft could only occur if the company were to hire the right kind of people. For quite some time, the company was interested in finding first and foremost the best and the brightest. At the same time it was hoped that the new hire exhibited a passion for technology, a willingness to work hard, a good deal of persistence, and a readiness to undergo self-examination. In order to carry out his reforms, Ballmer wanted a different kind of new hire in 2003. He still expected job candidates to possess all the character traits mentioned above. But now he wanted them to have as well an appreciation for and a willingness to carry out the new company values that he was starting to articulate. In short, he wanted job candidates to be aggressive, but he also wanted them to be open and respectful toward all those external elements that were collectively determining the company's image.

A Painful Decision

Throughout these pages we ask and try to answer why it was that the smartest company in the world needed such a far-reaching overhaul. We go behind the scenes to take a look at how and why Microsoft put the reforms in place. As we look at those reforms, we keep a focus on the two business leaders who in one way or another are carrying out those changes: Bill Gates and Steve Ballmer.

The stakes for the company were enormous. Microsoft continued to have more impact on consumers than almost all companies in the world. Only Coca-Cola had greater brand recognition around the globe. Coupled with that, no other company had as its chairman anyone who came close to the worldwide recognition that Bill Gates enjoyed. And yet, even as it emerged from the trial pretty much intact, it was still trying to put to rest a whole set of public perceptions that threatened to keep the company from making a full recovery. Bill Gates and Steve Ballmer could have chosen to bury their heads in the sand. They could have decided that it was simply too hard, or too complicated, or not that necessary, to reshape their company. But they chose to go ahead. We will spend most of the rest of the book digging deeply into how they proceeded. But before we go into greater depth on the reshaping of Microsoft, we first take a close look at the event that was both the company's greatest agony and the catalyst for its rebirth—*United States v. Microsoft.*

2

The Lawyer Gates for the Defense

When the actual launching of the U.S. government's antitrust suit against Microsoft occurred in May 1998, it hardly seemed explosive or overwhelmingly dramatic; for the Government had been investigating the company for much of the past decade on antitrust matters. In the run-up to the launching, it seemed that the Government and Microsoft's rivals were simply putting the usual pressure on Microsoft. It was, in Bill Gates's view, just another attempt by his competitors to even the playing field in a contest that Microsoft had won time and time again. There was no reason to sweat.

Every now and again some government regulatory agency went after the company, but by and large, Microsoft had escaped serious punishment. By 1991, Microsoft's Windows was running 90 percent of the world's personal computers. The Government engaged in legal probes against the company for abusing such a monopoly. Microsoft's arch-rival Scott McNealy (the head of Sun Microsystems, a provider of industrial-strength hardware, software, and services for the Internet) tweaked Gates by telling a U.S. Senate antitrust hearing, "The only thing that I'd rather own than Windows is English. Because then I could charge you $249 for the right to speak it, and I could charge you an upgrade fee when I add new letters."

Gates's close friend Warren Buffett saw nothing nefarious in Microsoft when the two met for the first time in 1990, as the investor explained to *Fortune*: "I am no antitrust scholar . . . [Bill is] a terrific teacher. He spent six or seven hours explaining Microsoft to me. Here I am the world's biggest dummy on technology, and he explained it to me pretty darn well. When he got through with it, I bought a hundred shares of stock so I could keep track of it. That shows two things: One is that I've got an IQ of about 50, and the second is that I didn't think he had any monopoly."

In 1994, Microsoft agreed to settle a Department of Justice case by making it easier for personal computer manufacturers to use its rivals' software. It signed a consent decree that forbade it from using its operating system dominance to smother competition. Still, Microsoft's competitors did not let up, claiming that the software titan had achieved and then abused its monopoly status by forcing others to do business with it. For his part, Gates claimed that Microsoft's business practices were no more pernicious than those of many other companies. But government regulators continued to believe that if Microsoft could be shown to be a monopoly—and there would be no trouble proving that—the same business practices when employed by other nonmonopolies legally would become illegal in Microsoft's case.

Gray and Subjective

For the life of him, Gates failed to understand why people complained that he sold so much software. Was there really something wrong with that?

What was Microsoft supposed to do: fail to improve its products, thus giving its competitors an edge? How did any of that make sense? Others at Microsoft were bemused. "There's no day that a bell rings," asserted Microsoft board member Jon Shirley, "and says you've now achieved what the Government thinks is a monopoly position so you have to change the way you behave. You don't know when you've reached that point other than the Government saying it, at which point it is all over for you. It was very hard for us to understand just what it was that the Government thought we had done and what we were supposed to do."

Others, however, understood all too well that Microsoft was playing hardball. Lew Platt is the former Hewlett-Packard chairman and CEO and, since December 2003, the nonexecutive chairman of Boeing. "Possibly," he said, "they were naïve and didn't think these practices would attract attention and eventually get them into trouble. Frankly, they did a lot of that stuff. They had some pretty predatory practices. Sure, I encountered them directly."

Platt noted when he held discussions with Microsoft about how products would be priced to H-P, "It was made pretty clear we'd get better prices if we were fully supportive of their products. . . . If you were friendlier, you got better prices." Platt also noted that, according to the law, H-P should have been offered the same prices offered to other companies under the same conditions and at similar volumes.

Still, few within Microsoft imagined that the company carried any responsibility. "The image of our company that was presented in a court of law was very different from what we thought we were in many cases," said Jeff Raikes, who in 2003 was group vice president for business productivity services management. "Any time you get hit like that, you think, Wow, we're not who that picture presents. That was one of the toughest things for all of us in the last five years."

To Craig Mundie, a senior vice president and Microsoft's chief technology officer in 2003, it was the vagueness of the antitrust laws that encouraged Microsoft personnel to believe they were innocent of all charges. "Antitrust is among the most gray, subjective areas of the law, which is why people here can say we never believed we did it—and yet others, including the courts, say we did." Mundie joined Microsoft in 1992 to create and run the Consumer Platforms Division, which he formed to develop Microsoft's non-PC platform and service offerings.

To Gates, the whole point of antitrust law was to protect consumers and to make sure new products were created and were innovative. Nowhere was this working better, he argued, than in the personal computer industry. Microsoft was certainly creating innovative products.

He also firmly believed that the term *monopoly* did not apply to Microsoft. How, he asked time and time again, could Microsoft be a monopoly when it was forced to cut prices and to invest heavily in research and development? Why would it take such steps if it did not have serious competitors?

The Government, Gates told himself, had no real case. It would get nowhere. He was sure of it.

And yet the Government persisted. On May 18, 1998, when it brought its antitrust suit against Microsoft, the case appeared to focus largely on the browser issue. The then attorney general, Janet Reno, noted on the day the Government filed suit that it was charging "Microsoft with engaging in anticompetitive and exclusionary practices designed to maintain its monopoly in personal computer operating systems, and attempting to extend that monopoly to Internet browser software."

The Department of Justice alleged that Microsoft had engaged in the following anticompetitive practices:

- Misusing its Windows operating system monopoly by requiring computer manufacturers, as a condition of getting Windows, to adopt a uniform "boot up" or "first screen" sequence that promotes Microsoft products.
- Attempting to persuade Netscape, an Internet browser software competitor, not to compete with Microsoft, but to divide up the browser market between the two companies.
- Engaging in exclusionary contracts with providers of Internet and online services, and Internet content providers.
- Forcing computer manufacturers to purchase and install Microsoft's Internet browser as a condition of getting its Windows operating system. In short, Microsoft used its monopoly power to develop a chokehold on the browser software needed to access the Internet.

The Department of Justice complaint was saying that Microsoft, as a monopoly, held an unfair advantage over Netscape (which was *selling* its Internet browser) by integrating its Internet browser into its operating system, effectively giving the Microsoft browser away for free. Countering, Microsoft argued that, in offering its browser as part of its operating system, it was doing nothing different from all those situations where it had integrated new features into Windows. To Netscape, the evidence that Microsoft was the villain lay in the statistics: In January 1997, Netscape had nearly 77 percent of the browser market, compared to Microsoft's 20 percent. But soon after the trial had begun, in August 1998, Microsoft had surpassed Netscape, achieving 49 to 48 percent.

Why had Microsoft included a browser in its Windows operating system software? Gates explained that the idea was to avoid having software developers duplicate one another's work. All that Microsoft was doing was taking anything that was common in all its applications and putting those features in Windows. This meant, in the case of the browser, that it was not necessary to buy a separate piece of software to connect to the Internet.

But to Bill Gates the case went beyond Microsoft's right to integrate its browser into its Windows operating system. It was, in his view, in fact about Netscape's bold-faced attempt to capture the operating system market which Microsoft had owned for years. It was also about Microsoft's rivals harboring resentment against the company for being too successful. "We have people who think that we are more successful than any company should be," Gates said in the summer of 2003.

A Machiavellian Poker Game

Netscape openly acknowledged that it hoped its browser would serve as an operating system platform to run software applications. "In other words," conceded Gary Reback, the Netscape attorney who had convinced the Government to bring suit, "if Netscape is successful, you won't need Windows or a Microsoft operating system anymore." On the other hand, if Microsoft continued to embed its Internet browser into its operating system, maintaining its monopoly, Reback insisted that it would "go on to bundle in content, their Microsoft Network, financial transactions, travel services, everything. They have a game plan to monopolize every market they touch."

Gates, however, kept contending that Microsoft had done nothing wrong. "Should we improve our product, or go out of business? If improving a product based on customer input is willful maintenance of trying to stay in business and not have Netscape turn their browser into the most popular operating system, then I think that is what we are supposed to do."

Gates tried to exude confidence about Microsoft's prospects in the case; but underneath, he sensed that he was in a fight for his company's life—which, as it turned out, was true. He himself was in no small measure responsible for the heat generated by the trial. Rob Glaser, a former Microsoft executive who in 1995 founded RealNetworks, an Internet media delivery enterprise, observed after he left Microsoft that Gates is "pretty relentless. He's Darwinian. He doesn't look for win-win situations with others, but for ways to make others lose. Success is defined as flattening the competition, not creating excellence." Glaser noted that the "atmosphere [at Microsoft] was like a Machiavellian poker game where you'd hide things even if it would blindside people you were supposed to be working with." Glaser had worked closely with Gates from 1983 to 1993, becoming Microsoft's vice president of multimedia and consumer systems.

For his part, Gates shrugged off such criticism, wondering what being a zealot had to do with making great software: "If we weren't so ruthless, we'd be making more creative software? We'd rather kill a competitor than grow the market? Those are clear lies. Who grew this market? We did. Who survived companies like IBM, ten times our size, taking us on?"

The legal assaults against the company, both from rivals and from the Government, bewildered Microsoft's senior echelons. The founder of Microsoft's research arm and chief futurist, Nathan Myhrvold, balked at the Department of Justice's apparent view that the DOJ and the courts had the right to decide what new technology should go into a product: "Taken to an extreme limit, if this view prevails, then Microsoft should fire me. What use is technological innovation if we can't put it into our products? If it is wrong to invest in research and come up with great technology to put into a product, then how should the game be played?" (Myhrvold joined Microsoft as director of special projects in 1986 when Microsoft acquired Dynamical Systems, a software company that he had founded. He has worked with Professor Stephen Hawking on research in cosmology and holds a doctorate in theoretical and mathematical physics from Princeton University.)

What Gates and Myhrvold refused to grasp was that it was Microsoft's excessive zeal toward customers, and not its right to employ technological innovation, that lay at the heart of the allegations. Other business monopolies managed to avoid antitrust charges simply by avoiding unfair business practices. "Microsoft," said Mike Murray, the company's former head of human resources, "didn't realize that the rules of the [software] industry had changed and it took them many years to realize they couldn't be superaggressive." (Murray joined Microsoft in 1989 as general manager of the Network Business Unit, the predecessor to the Windows NT BackOffice product line. In 1992 he became Microsoft's first vice president of human resources.)

One such indication was Microsoft's continuing unwillingness to put in place an antitrust compliance program for Microsoft employees, something that most corporations did routinely. The program was designed to educate employees on what constituted fair and unfair business practices. Gates regarded such a policy as an intruder, one that was likely to impair the aggressiveness he expected from his sales force; one that was likely to make it harder for Microsoft to continue in its startup mode. Lew Platt said he was told that Microsoft eschewed such ethics training: "They were in fact more likely to say, 'Don't worry. We'll be strong and we'll take care of that if it becomes a problem.' So instead of giving that kind of ethics training, they cut people loose and let them run away on the fringes of ethical behavior. . . . They didn't talk about antitrust behavior because they were afraid their people would act differently. They wanted people to compete extraordinarily aggressively and if they got their feet across the line, they would deal with it."

Finally in the early 1990s, Microsoft instituted a policy requiring employees to receive training in their obligations under antitrust laws. But the policy arrived too late. Had it been introduced earlier, the Government might have had a much harder time compiling evidence of antitrust mischief within Microsoft.

Gates had always exhibited little concern that his company would incur the wrath of Government officials for antitrust violations. He knew that Washington, D.C., had little interest in small start-ups, as Microsoft appeared to be even into the early 1990s. He knew also that the media had been largely on the company's side, its coverage a blend of adulation and awe. The Government would not pick on a company so adored by the media, would it? He doubted it.

For its first seven years, Microsoft drew a pass from the media. Its first significant coverage came when Peter Rinearson, then a reporter for *The Seattle Times*, sat down on a Saturday afternoon with Gates and Microsoft cofounder Paul Allen in their primitive-looking offices in Bellevue, Washington. At the time Microsoft had 130 employees. When Rinearson's article, headlined "Riding the Big Computer Boom," appeared on Valentine's Day of 1982, the excited reporter and software chief visited a newsstand together to see the newspaper. The sense of wonder that Rinearson's article conveyed toward Microsoft became the model for media coverage of Microsoft for some time. It credited Gates and Allen with coming "as close as anyone in the world to a monopoly on a fast-growing field of computer programming. It is the system-software industry for microcomputers, a field no one even knew could exist until Gates and Allen proved it by writing a key program in late 1974 and early 1975." (Rinearson in 2003 was corporate vice president and a member of the five-person senior leadership team of Microsoft's Information Worker Business Unit, overseeing the unit's New Markets division. He won a Pulitzer Price in journalism and coauthored Bill Gates's first book, *The Road Ahead*.)

In subsequent media coverage, it became fashionable for reporters to fawn over Gates and the Microsoft coders as brilliant, carefree workaholics whose worst sins had been inviting strippers to their parties and skinny-dipping in Bill Gates's pool, and whose greatest virtue had been nearly single-handedly creating the personal computer software revolution.

Shy and awkward in public, unsure of what he should or should not say to the media, Gates chose to reside in a comfort zone of privacy that left many asking the same question that appeared with the photo in his high school yearbook, "Who is this man?" By the early 1980s, it was becoming evident that Gates possessed some remarkable skills, both as a computer genius and as a spokesperson for the burgeoning personal computer software industry. He alone seemed credible in discussing futurist visions for the industry. He had become far too much of a public relations asset for Microsoft to shield him from public view much longer.

A Boyish Grin and an Unruly Cowlick

In September 1982, when Pam Edstrom was hired as Microsoft's first public relations manager, she worked hard to turn Gates into the mouthpiece and the personification of the company. By 1984, Gates had won widespread media acceptance as the leading software figure of the age. But, by not building a strong lobbying presence in the nation's capital, Gates ultimately paid an extremely high price, allowing a vacuum to form that his rivals found easy to exploit. "Here was a way you could take on an incredibly popular, well-known figure and mop the floor with him," argued Myhrvold, "and no one would push back. With Microsoft, you could make tons of political hay at no cost."

As unenthusiastic as Gates was about a strong Washington, D.C., presence for Microsoft, he had seen even less reason to try to enhance the company's image with the mainstream media. When Microsoft executives sought his approval for publicity campaigns to boost the company's image in the mainstream media by seeking articles on others at Microsoft, Gates rejected such campaigns as distracting attention from the company's main message, trying to sell its technology.

While he focused on changing the world, the external world was taking increasing notice of both Microsoft and Gates. First, in 1986, when Bill Gates was thirty years old, the company went public, an event that quickly turned countless Microsoft employees into multi-millionaires and made Gates even wealthier than before. Then in 1992, Gates was declared the richest man alive. After that, the media focused less on Gates as a technology genius and more on his staggering fortune and the concomitant power he had accumulated over the personal computer industry. Gates was described less and less as the modern-day Edison or Rockefeller and increasingly as the devil incarnate, as Bill Gates the monopolist *cum* predator. As a result, he spent far too much of the 1990s, in his view, battling legal charges, spending as much time being the architect of his company's legal strategies as being the architect of its software.

His eagerness for privacy did not sit well with some Microsoft executives who, fearful that the media would interpret his introverted stance as arrogance, pleaded with him to make himself more available to the media. Because he seemed largely inaccessible (as late as 1997, *Time* insisted that very little was known about Gates personally), the media felt free to write whatever it wanted to about him. "Once he became a myth rather than an individual," said Nathan Myhrvold, "for journalists, he ceased to be Bill Gates the actual human being and became this mythic figure about which you could say whatever you wanted. It's wrong to say he brought [his poor media image] on himself, but it's equally wrong to say he bears no responsibility."

By the time Microsoft's rivals and the U.S. government banded together in the late 1990s to take on the software giant, the company's public relations battle was essentially lost. But it was not too late for Bill Gates to take the regulators seriously. His rivals had exploited the prevalent trust-busting mood to convince the federal government and a bunch of states to accumulate evidence against the software giant. That got Gates's attention. And, if he insisted that the company was blameless, others at Microsoft knew otherwise. "Undoubtedly," observed Nathan Myhrvold, "there were things Microsoft could have done differently that would have been far more politically correct. . . . Microsoft pushed too hard in many ways." There were, he acknowledged, a whole series of terms in Microsoft's contracts that others had found offensive. "Most of what the noise was about [in the Government's case] were statements such as, 'We'll license this, if you make us the exclusive or semiexclusive seller of software to you.' The phrases in those contracts were clearly stupid because they attracted lots of attention and they didn't get much business benefit." (As if to suggest how unnecessary those terms were, Myhrvold noted wryly that after the terms were removed from contracts, Microsoft's business did not collapse.)

Never Write That in an E-mail

Kornel Marton, a program manager for Microsoft Word in the 1990s, also thought Microsoft could have done things differently to avoid the trial. "The problem started with Netscape in 1994, and, frankly, it was all very orchestrated by the backers of Netscape who managed to goad some stupid Microsoft executives to do some silly things. . . . Microsoft had some people in the Windows division who were not really that smart, who did some really stupid things. Of course, we had a policy that we would try to drive WordPerfect [an early word processing program] out of business and clone its features, but you never wanted to write that in an e-mail. But there were people who wanted to advance at Microsoft by appearing to Bill and Steve to have bigger balls and so they wrote tough e-mails, things like, 'We should choke off the air supply of Netscape.'"

One sign of how serious Gates took the Government's case was his decision to engage himself 100 percent in the battle. He could have turned the whole case over to Microsoft's lawyers and spent most of his time on product strategies and development. But it was *his* company that was being called to account. It was *his* culture that had been challenged. He could not treat the case as some minor legal squabble.

He had, in addition, a special place in his heart for the law. His father is an attorney, and he himself had thought seriously about going to law school and becoming an attorney. However, if young Bill had harbored any thoughts of going into his father's law firm, he would have run into the firm's nepotism policy that would have barred his joining. Once at Microsoft, he made deal after deal, giving him an increasing understanding and appreciation of the law.

He decided to become the company's chief legal strategist, taking personal charge of *United States v. Microsoft.* He knew that he ran the risk of personalizing the trial, of allowing the case to turn into *U.S. Government v. Bill Gates.* But he refused to remain passive when his rivals and the media hurled arrow after arrow at him. He was all too aware of the Web sites that were dedicated to mocking him; he knew about the industry crowd who hated him; he knew too about the lawyers inside and outside of Government who had been lying in wait—sometimes for years—for this one big moment when the resources of the U.S. government and the states could be marshaled against him. He knew that the charges were baseless. He was not going to hide in a cave.

As part of the legal strategy, he wanted to make a big point that no one had been injured as a result of Microsoft's so-called predatory policies. He kept asking, "Where are the victims?"

Start with the consumers. Were they being hurt? Not in the least. Millions of people were buying his software. They could not be classified as victims.

How about Microsoft's competitors? Had he harmed any of them? The answer had to be no.

"So," he asked in conversation with Microsoft colleagues, "where are my victims? I want to meet my victims. Who are the guys I victimized? Where are all these people I drove out of business? Larry Ellison

[Chairman and CEO of the software firm Oracle]? Last time I checked, he was the second richest guy in the world. Scott McNealy? He's a billionaire. Jim Barksdale [at the time Netscape's CEO]? He walked away with a billion dollars. So where are the victims? Who was wronged? It's really not obvious."

Gates felt that *he* was the victim, not in the sense that he had built a fortune and then lost it; or that Microsoft had once been mighty but no longer was. Gates was still the richest man in the world. Microsoft's revenue in 1998 came to $15.26 billion and it was growing at a 30 percent clip over the previous two years. He was the victim, however, because he was Bill Gates, he was at the top of the heap, and therefore he was everyone's favorite target. He, of course, thought it highly unfair to attack him for being so successful; and even if Microsoft had engaged in some unfair business practices, he saw no reason to vilify him so ferociously. All such talk got his competitive streak going. He wanted to take his accusers on frontally.

Of course, Microsoft's competitors could "win" the case early just by forcing the company into a kind of paralysis by putting its business on hold throughout the legal proceedings. Other business leaders, facing the kind of legal entanglement that awaited Microsoft, might have understandably concluded that there was not much point in keeping the daily operations of the business going at the same pace and scope as before. Other leaders might have rationally decided that the smart thing to do was to freeze all major business decisions, avoid huge expenditures, and put off hiring—in effect, to put the company on a low flame until a legal outcome was in view.

Gates saw the flaws in that strategy immediately. He understood that shutting down the company temporarily gave his opponents a de facto triumph; it provided them with an advantage from which Microsoft might not recover. Accordingly, he passed word that, along with him, only a few senior executives would deal with the trial; all others were to carry on normally. "The key message that he we had during that period," recalled Kevin Johnson, senior vice president for Microsoft Americas in 2003, "was, 'We've got a small team of lawyers along with Bill. So you people don't have to be concerned about the trial. We have to stay focused on the customer and what we're doing to deliver value to the customer.'"

Of course, it was not possible to seal the company off from the legal battle as hermetically as Gates would have liked. A number of executives were called to testify; thousands of other employees pored through news accounts and held lengthy conversations with friends and relatives whose morbid curiosity led them to ask for inside information about the trial. As it became increasingly apparent that Microsoft's legal opponents wanted nothing less than to split the company in two, employees who had been asked by Gates to stay beyond the fray found themselves sucked into the whirling vortex, agonized, traumatized, all too painfully involved in the legal process.

Somehow, people *did* manage to do their work. Gates's strategy of keeping the company moving full-steam ahead paid off. "You would have thought the threat of splitting the company in two," said Mike Murray, "would have put everything on hold, but it didn't. It may have looked like things weren't going well, that it was going to be messy, but Microsoft grew revenue every year during the trial. That's remarkable." Indeed, from 1998 to 2002, the years of the trial, Microsoft's revenue went from $15.26 billion to $28.37 billion and its profits rose during the same period from $4.49 billion to $7.83 billion. In one further indication that Gates had not put the company on hold, its head count grew from 27,055 in 1998 to 50,621 in 2002. Microsoft's stock rose impressively during that period as well: from $21 a share in May 1998, when the trial began, to a high of 57.8 in December 1999 (the stock did fall off starting in April 2000, but then again so did every other stock).

It was also during the trial that Microsoft launched some of its most important products: Windows 98 on June 25, 1998; Windows 2000 on February 17, 2000; Office XP on May 31, 2001; and Windows XP on

October 25, 2001. Meanwhile, the company was busy developing such products as Xbox, the Microsoft games system, and software for various hand-held devices. Most impressively, the Windows operating system retained a 93 percent market share of the worldwide desktop computer market.

When interviewed in the summer of 2003, after the trial was over, Gates explained what had driven him to keep the company functioning during the legal proceedings: "It takes a lot of belief in what you're doing and the importance of what you're doing . . . to go through a tough challenge like that when it's start-ups over here, lawsuits over here, some of the growing pains of success over here." Some had suggested that Microsoft's optimal strategy would have been simply to take the blame for everything: "Why don't you do a *mea culpa* on everything? Say that start-ups are really the cool new future and the long-term stuff isn't good or that everything that you've been accused of, that there must be some element of truth in it." But that was not Gates's way. He had no desire to confess guilt. He had no desire to yield without a fight.

The Fight of His Life

To be sure, Gates knew that he was in the fight of his life. Sure, he had faced challenges before, but what had differentiated the trial from all of those challenges, Gates explained, had been a fundamental point: In the past when a challenge arose at Microsoft, the solution was evident and within the company's grasp, if it was creative enough, or spent enough money, or remained tenacious. The solution, said Gates, usually arose from the marketplace. "We always had challenges, but we sort of knew the framework."

Even when IBM, a company ten times Microsoft's size, brought all of its resources against the software start-up in earlier days, Gates knew the framework, saw the solution, and then had to figure out how to go after it. "That was an unbelievable challenge for the company . . . but we knew that would be decided by the developers and the customers, and we knew what we were good at, what would count on that one. And it was fun because we were kind of the underdog on the whole thing. And we lived that. Every day we woke up and thought about it and the guy on the other side didn't live it like we did. . . . We were moving faster, thinking faster than they were."

But the trial presented a whole new ball game for Microsoft. With respect to the legal problems, Gates noted that "it wasn't clear you could outthink the problem. Sure you could think, but you couldn't outthink it. . . . Had Netscape uncovered the secrets of the world and fifty other companies as well? Netscape kept saying they were moving on Internet time. Well, because we caught up with them and moved ahead of them, we must have been moving on some even faster time line than then they were."

To Gates, it was simply unthinkable to bring Microsoft to a halt during the trial. There was too much to do. And there were always competitors out there trying to undo you. "It's interesting in this business. Even when you do things well and you meet challenges and all these things where people said you could never do this, you never get to look back and say, 'I told you so,' because the next challenge is already in the dock by [that] time."

Microsoft, he observed, had bet heavily on a graphics user interface (GUI) as the new look of the personal computer's operating system and, by 1996, it had achieved great success with Windows, the embodiment of the GUI. But by 1996, the Internet had come along and Microsoft had to focus every minute on it. "So we never got a chance to say, 'Wow, graphics interface, our productivity office, [we] blazed new trails, gained market share on that'; but we were just into the Internet thing and then that came with its start-up phenomenon and then the trial got very intense. . . . [There is] plenty of challenge, which is why it's good we're not a culture that looks back and has to waste a lot of time celebrating what we have done well."

To Gates, it was essential to demonstrate that the tiny upstarts in Silicon Valley and elsewhere, including Netscape, could not triumph over Microsoft by running to the federal government with their complaints.

He would not buckle. He would not settle the case. It would have been far too costly to Microsoft's reputation. While Microsoft would never acknowledge guilt as part of a settlement, others would interpret Microsoft's settling as an admission of guilt; and so settling became an absolute nonstarter for Gates, a no-brainer. Settling meant allowing the Silicon Valley upstarts to nibble away at Microsoft's freedom to sell its products. Of all the decisions he would make in the antitrust case, none was more important to him than this one.

When word arrived that Microsoft was in the hot seat, Gates gathered his forces for a strategy meeting. Seated with his twelve-member Strategy Committee in a Microsoft conference room, Gates listened as lead company attorney William H. Neukom, speaking from Washington, D.C., through a speaker box, urged Gates to take the federal government's charges against Microsoft seriously. Of course, Gates was taking the charges seriously. But what Neukom meant was that Gates should take the charges seriously enough to settle.

Pointing his finger at the box, Gates replied, "You're going to have to fix it."

"Fix it" meant winning the case even if Microsoft would have to go to court; it did not mean settling. Others around the table saw only the dark side of a trial: It could go on indefinitely, the opponent in court was no less than the U.S. government, and the damage to Microsoft's reputation would be immense.

"Why not just settle?" some around the table asked in imploring tones.

Gates would have none of it.

Why not?

"Because," he said, in a phrase that Microsoft executives remembered long afterward, "legal trumps PR."

It made more sense to Gates for Microsoft to take a legal route than to try to finesse the allegations by some clever public relations spin. Were Microsoft to settle, it would pay a large fine, but much worse, others would regard the settlement as tantamount to its pleading guilty.

That's Not Chocolate Sundae

Gates did not want to leave even the impression that the company was admitting to wrongdoing. He wanted to beat back his foes once and for all, and put the whole set of allegations to rest. Even if it meant sitting in a courtroom for years, even if it meant the attacks on him and on Microsoft would continue unabated, he preferred that the case be adjudicated.

If the option of a quick settlement had been available to Gates, he would surely have been wise to have availed himself of such a strategy. Had the trial been brief, had Microsoft emerged from the courtroom battle without much scar tissue, a quick settlement would not have been required. But it was too late for Gates to duck out early. He had naïvely assumed that the Government and his rivals would never get into bed together; that he could ride out any and all criticism without having to resort to lengthy legal battles. Now he faced federal government prosecutors who were not eager to let Microsoft off the hook with an early settlement. They wanted their day in court. And their strategy paid off.

Even though the federal government did not officially win the case against the software giant, the daily assaults on the company had the effect of turning Microsoft into a loser. Toward the end, the company was in a state of shock, its legions demoralized, battered, and humbled, and its capacity to function effectively a very big question mark.

As for Gates, the trial was a grueling experience. It was not just that the media was covering the presumptive villain Microsoft every day in bold headlines. It was the sorrow and humiliation he felt at his own government suing him. "That's not chocolate sundae," his father said nearly a year after the trial began.

As the chairman and CEO of the company, Gates quickly became a central part of the case, though he naïvely assumed that he could keep the case from revolving around his persona. The Government's prosecuting team shrewdly made Gates and his behavior the centerpiece of its case—not the technology, which anyway was too complicated for the judges and for the media to absorb easily; and not other Microsoft executives, whose roles in the company's alleged shenanigans were probably not small, but who carried less voltage than the luminescent Mr. Gates.

Carefully scripting its case so that Gates's videotaped deposition became the signature piece of evidence of its case, the prosecutors never let the case focus only on browsers or operating systems or any other kind of software that would force eyes to glaze over.

Gates's deposition became the key element of the courtroom drama. Unfortunately for him, he became his own worst enemy during those twenty hours of interrogation spread over three days in August 1998.

Despite his own insistence that the slightest sign of accommodation would be interpreted as weakness, Gates could only have benefited from a modicum of humility when confronting the plaintiffs. At the least, he would have put them off their guard. But he had convinced himself that his best strategy was to look and sound tough and to treat the U.S. government as if it were a little boy too stupid to understand the software business. The strategy backfired. Belittling and demeaning the U.S. government simply did not fly.

His demeanor during the deposition was startling. He seemed at once disinterested and flippant. Rather than sounding like an authoritative, forceful spokesperson for the software industry, he appeared incapable of taking the offensive; indeed, he gave the impression of wanting to run away from the stand as quickly as possible.

Because the deposition had been videotaped, the plaintiffs were able to pick and choose the juiciest parts to display at the trial. Thus the videotape recorder became an unexpected ally for the Government, catching as it did every one of Gates's pauses, awkward silences, and defensive posturing. If the Government's task was to portray Gates as arrogant, unresponsive, prickly, evasive, and lacking in credibility, his videotaped presentation accomplished all of that and more.

At times, Gates appeared out of touch with reality. He acknowledged, for example, that when the Department of Justice had served him with the antitrust complaint, he had not bothered to read it. At other times, he was wily. His e-mails contained phrases that the plaintiffs considered smoking guns: "Do we have a clear plan on what we want Apple to do to undermine Sun?" and "I think there is a very powerful deal of some kind we could do with Netscape." On some occasions he was evasive, as when asked about the Apple–Sun e-mail. He could not recall sending the message and had no idea what he could have meant by it. Sometimes he simply lacked credibility, parsing fine distinctions (example: Microsoft's "deal" with Apple versus their "relationship").

To *Time* magazine, Gates's performance was just what the plaintiffs had hoped for: "He followed each question with a lengthy silence, denied knowledge of e-mails he had written and professed not to understand words like 'market share,' 'concerned' or 'ask.' He was, in other words, one of the most potent weapons in the Government's armory."

So smart-alecky had Gates appeared in his infamous deposition that some prayed that the court would break Microsoft up, if only as punishment for the way he acted there. As for Gates, he understandably hated much of what had happened during the deposition, the way the lawyers asked questions, the way they assumed he was automatically guilty. Publicly, however, he could not say any of this. He defended his deposition forcefully, insisting that he gave "totally truthful answers. I have a great memory. When [the Government's attorney David Boies] would ask imprecise questions I would simply point out to him the imprecise nature of the question." He admitted that "If I'd known that the video was going to be shown . . . I would have helped [Boies] do his job more because I do come off as a bit pedantic when he does a bad job asking questions. Still, there is no law in this land about being a little rude in a deposition." He had one other criticism of his performance: he wished he had smiled more.

The Government's strategy of making Gates the centerpiece of the trial and of relying on the videotaped deposition to put Microsoft on the ropes seemed flawless. And, had it not been for the strange behavior of U.S. District Judge Thomas Penfield Jackson, who presided over the case at that stage, *United States v. Microsoft* might have been a slam dunk for the Government.

Walking to Court

Jackson had arrived at the bench in 1982, a Reagan appointee who had once been a navy officer. Then sixty-five years old, he stayed fit by sometimes walking twenty blocks from his Georgetown home to the courthouse. He had been involved in legal cases against Microsoft dating back to 1995, when he approved the settlement in a Government lawsuit against the company. As he sat and listened to the testimony against Microsoft, he eventually could not contain himself. Shrugging off all notions of judicial restraint, he lost his temper toward witnesses, openly laughed at the Gates videotape, and granted media interviews, calling Microsoft trial attorney William Neukom dumb, terming the appeals court judges "supercilious," and accusing those judges of embellishing law "with unnecessary and, in many cases, superficial scholarship." Jackson reserved his sharpest language for Gates: "I think he has a Napoleonic concept of himself and his company, an arrogance that derives from power and unalloyed success, with no leavening hard experience, no reverses."

If the case had once seemed a slam dunk for the Government, Judge Jackson's caustic revelations, so out of turn that it was hard to understand what had prompted him to unleash his venom, offered Microsoft an easy lay-up. Until then Microsoft was battling the U.S. government and hoping that the judge would adjudicate the case in the company's favor after an impartial hearing of the facts. But now, thanks to his strange behavior, Judge Jackson had played beautifully into Microsoft's hands, offering its lawyers a strong case of judicial bias. The judge's interviews would prove costly to the Government.

The legal proceedings moved through their paces slowly. On November 5, 1999, Judge Jackson issued his initial findings of fact, asserting that Microsoft had indeed held monopoly power and had used it to harm consumers, rivals, and other companies. He ruled that Microsoft had used its monopoly powers to keep innovative products from reaching the market.

Seven months later, on June 7, 2000, the same judge ordered the breakup of Microsoft into two companies: one for operating systems and another for everything else. Though one school of thought held that Microsoft might actually benefit from being dismembered, that the two new companies would eventually emerge stronger than the single existing one, that was a distinctly minority view. The much more prevalent feeling was that the sundering would sharply impair Microsoft's ability to innovate.

That debate ended when, on June 28, 2001, a federal appeals court ruled that breaking up the company was excessive punishment. Jackson's conclusion that Microsoft had repeatedly abused its monopoly power was left standing. Chastising Jackson for criticizing Microsoft in media interviews, the same federal appeals court said another judge should hear the case. By this time, both sides appeared ready to move toward a settlement. It was then that Judge Kollar-Kotelly took over, promptly ordering the two sides to find a way to settle.

The President Steps In

But the greatest incentive for a settlement arose with the arrival of a new president of the United States, George W. Bush, who took office on January 20, 2001. Had the Democratic candidate for president, Al Gore, become president, it was taken for granted that the new Democratic administration would have insisted that the Department of Justice retry at least part of the case. But George Bush had made it clear that he liked Microsoft, liked big business, and had no desire to pursue antitrust cases. He wanted the Microsoft case dropped. With that, the new attorney general, John Ashcroft, declared the following September that his department no longer demanded the breakup of Microsoft.

The pressure to settle rose steadily. Adding to that pressure were the events of September 11, when the national mood became preoccupied with the fight against terrorism and had little time for corporate chicanery. By that time the U.S. economy had soured, although Microsoft was suffering much less than other enterprises. Why, some asked, would anyone want to punish one of the few companies that was hiring employees and contributing to the economy?

It was no surprise therefore when, on November 2, 2001, the Department of Justice reached a settlement with Microsoft. Nine states (Illinois, Kentucky, Louisiana, Maryland, Michigan, New York, North Carolina, Ohio, and Wisconsin) agreed to settle on substantially the same terms four days later. Nine others and the District of Columbia sued for tougher sanctions.

Thirteen months later, Judge Kollar-Kotelly affirmed the settlement, effectively bringing to an end the Microsoft trial. She rejected the contention of the still-suing nine states and the District of Columbia that Microsoft's actions warranted harsher sanctions. Many of these proposed harsher sanctions, the judge argued, were meant to benefit Microsoft's competitors, not consumers.

Still, Microsoft faced serious constraints. Under the terms of a consent decree that arose during the court battle and became part of the November 2002 decision, Microsoft had to permit end users and OEMs to enable or remove access to certain Windows components or competing software (e.g., Internet browsers, media players, instant messaging clients, e-mail clients) and designate a competing product to be invoked in place of that Microsoft software. Microsoft also had to disclose and license technical information relating to Windows. It had to make available on reasonable and nondiscriminatory terms the protocols implemented in certain Windows desktop operating system products and used to interoperate or communicate with Microsoft server operating system products.

In summary, it had to agree to halt its aggressive tactics against competitors and to refrain from retaliating against rivals whose products competed with Microsoft software, such as browsers. It also had to permit rivals to plug their products into Windows, and to disclose source code and new products to competitors.

To be sure, it was a very fortunate Microsoft that emerged from the trial; the legal situation had played out as best as the company could have hoped. Cynics suggested that it was not so much that Bill Gates and his colleagues had "won" the case, it was more that the Government had lost it on procedural grounds when Judge Jackson spoke to the press during the trial. Microsoft was adamant that it had beaten back most of the allegations made against it in the law suit. No one went public to dispute such statements. No one had the will or the energy. Still, Microsoft's critics had not gone away. If less vocal after the trial, they remained cynical that Microsoft would alter its business practices. They had no reason to believe that the trial had caused Microsoft to repent. Microsoft continued to suggest that it had nothing to repent for.

And yet there was a distinct movement within the company to take a new course. Whether it would actually go ahead and do that depended entirely on Bill Gates and Steve Ballmer. That is what made the new relationship they were carving out for themselves in the early 2000s so intriguing.

PART II

Emerging from the Crisis

3

The Most Unique Partnership
in Business

Few have thought of Bill Gates as anything other than a technology genius, yet he has been, in addition, one of the most successful business leaders of our era. His interest in business goes back to childhood. He read *Fortune* magazine in high school—one of only two students in his school who did so, he boasted years later. He possessed an entrepreneurial spirit from the start, running some computer-related businesses as a youngster, asking himself questions at that point that were normally posed in business school: What determines the value of a business? What makes someone buy from one company and not another? How is it decided to place one price on an item and not another?

No Appetite for Negotiations

With a strong interest in business, it was only natural that when Gates cofounded Microsoft in 1975, he chose not only to devote time to producing "magical" software but to micromanage the fledgling enterprise as well. Hiring people and developing them into top-notch employees was the part of business he liked the most. He had less appetite for closing deals and admitted to being "not particularly good at negotiation," though, ironically, his colleagues assumed that someone as tough-minded as he was in other areas automatically enjoyed the give and take of bargaining.

In Microsoft's earliest phase, Gates made all the decisions, large or small. He allowed no middle managers between him and his employees. Though only in his early twenties, Gates was Microsoft's chief decision maker, chief technologist, chief salesperson, chief cutter of deals, and chief visionary. Seven of the first twenty-six employees reported directly to him. In 1981, he even drove a potential hire, Charles Simonyi, to the airport to catch a plane. He also hired everyone, organized and ran every meeting, supervised every marketing campaign, and decided on every product. Since the company was small, he could do that then. No one thought of what he did as micromanaging in any kind of negative sense. Gates was simply managing. Yet he might as well have called the place Bill Gates Inc. "For many years," Bob Herbold noted, "Microsoft was a very small company run by one person in terms of strategic direction. Lots of companies hunger for the CEO to provide that direction. Lots of CEOs don't want to step on the toes of individual business units. They want the business units to run things."

By the early 1980s, with Microsoft growing nicely, Gates looked to reduce the operational burden without yielding any real power. Over time, he hired such people as Jon Shirley, Michael Hallman, and Bob Herbold to handle the business side, and all three men removed a considerable weight from Gates's shoulders. But Gates continued to make most of the company's major decisions, and that required a great deal of his time and energy.

Without being conscious of it, the young head of Microsoft organized the company into a hub-and-spoke style of management, where Gates was the hub and numerous other executives the spokes. The hub-and-spoke system proved successful throughout the 1980s and a good part of the 1990s. But by late 1997, with more than twenty-two thousand employees, with product teams that numbered in the hundreds, and with the company coming off a record-breaking 49 percent annual growth spurt the year before, Gates began to sense that he had truly taken on more than he could handle. Not only was he running Microsoft's day-to-day business, he was also directing the company's legal strategies in the walk-up to the Government's antitrust case and functioning as Microsoft's chief technology officer.

The time was approaching for Gates to think seriously of relinquishing some of that power. Thus it was that in May 1998, Gates elevated one of his closest colleagues, Steve Ballmer, to the post of president. Though Gates had deployed Jon Shirley and a few others to handle administrative chores in the past, he seemed to be grooming Ballmer for a kind of coleadership role at Microsoft.

Steve Ballmer was born near Detroit in March 1956, making him five months younger than Bill Gates. Ballmer's father was Swiss and dropped out of university in Switzerland; he spoke six languages and after World War II became a translator at the first Nuremberg trial. Later, making his way to America, he became a manager at the Ford Motor Company. Ballmer's mother was born in Detroit. Her father had been a cobbler in Russia who had immigrated to Detroit, where he owned an auto parts shop. From the time young Ballmer was eight years old, his father told him that he was destined for Harvard. A promising student, the youngster earned a scholarship to the Detroit Country Day School, where he played football, was a shot-putter on the track team, and managed the basketball team. He also received a perfect 800 score on the math SATs and served as class valedictorian. His father was right—he enrolled at Harvard, living down the hall from Bill Gates during their sophomore year. Gates often ran into Ballmer, a math and science student, at breakfast, where the two talked applied mathematics. They shared graduate-level math and economics courses.

The Odd Couple

They seemed an odd couple: Ballmer, solidly built, bordering on the chunky, with thinning hair, sociable, extroverted, the manager of the football team, and publisher of the university's literary magazine; Gates, lean, gawky, nerdish, with long, unruly hair and large, round black-rimmed glasses, a computer geek long before the phrase had come into vogue, a poker player enjoying the game in the early-morning hours almost nightly. A magazine article once compared Gates to the movies' Andy Hardy in physical appearance, but the Microsoft boss was no all-American teenager, as the Mickey Rooney character had been. Ballmer, for his part, looked like a cross between Hollywood mogul Barry Diller and former NFL quarterback Terry Bradshaw. Of the two—Ballmer and Gates—only one was destined to graduate. Ballmer earned his bachelor's degree in mathematics and economics in 1977; Gates dropped out at the end of his sophomore year.

Ballmer had been accepted to the Stanford Business School but deferred enrollment to work for the next two years as an assistant product manager for Procter & Gamble in Cincinnati, Ohio. There he learned brand management and handled the Duncan Hines Brownie Mix and Moist & Easy Snack Cake Mix accounts. He shared a cubicle with a young up-and-comer named Jeff Immelt, who in 2001 became chairman and CEO of General Electric upon Jack Welch's retirement.

Ballmer had lost touch with his college pal Bill Gates, who by then was running a tiny software company near Seattle. Soon after Ballmer had sought unsuccessfully to enter the film business, his Harvard buddy phoned; he had not forgotten their friendship or Ballmer's go-go personality. It was 1980 and Gates was eager to find someone he could trust to help him put some order into the chaotic, loosely run Microsoft. He needed a business manager. Ballmer seemed the ideal choice. But he had just finished his first year of business school and seemed intent on completing his studies. Inviting Ballmer to Seattle, Gates wined and dined his college friend, getting him together with his parents, Bill Sr. and Mary, and giving him a tour of the city.

This was not the way Microsoft recruited in later years; then the process became much more rigorous. No one got a tour of the city or a chance to meet Gates's parents. But at this stage, Gates eagerly wanted Ballmer, hoping he would drop out of business school at once.

Gates's pursuit of him put young Ballmer in a dilemma. He could remain in business school and please his father, who had not gone to college and was keen on his son's getting a business degree. Or he could pick up his friend's offer to become his assistant at a $50,000 annual salary and a 5 percent cut of the business.

Ballmer chose to go to work at Microsoft, concluding the deal with Gates, who was at that moment on a sailboat with friends, talking to him by ship-to-shore phone. Ballmer became employee number eleven.

Even more confrontational than his new boss, Ballmer got off to a rocky start as Microsoft's first business manager. The other employees quickly distanced themselves from him, resentful of his fat pay package despite his obvious handicaps: He could not program. He had spent all of one year at the Stanford Business School. He had joined the company largely because he and Gates had been Harvard buddies. The pièce de résistance came when Gates's confirming letter to Ballmer became public knowledge around the company. Why, employees asked each other, had Gates given Ballmer such a high salary? Why had he given him a 5 percent cut of the business?

Ballmer was too close to Gates for any of this to matter for very long. The two seemed inseparable. Not only did Ballmer use the end of a sofa in Gates's office as his own place of work, he also moved in with him. The two young men did have one verbal tiff that threatened to unglue their seemingly rock-solid bond, quarreling over the part of the business most precious to Gates: head count.

From day one of Microsoft, young Gates vowed that he would not hire beyond the company's financial capacity. But, trying to accommodate the young firm's growing workload, the new business manager wanted to double its size to thirty employees. Gates balked, decreeing that Ballmer start with hiring one good person; and then they would talk about hiring a second.

You're trying to bankrupt me, Gates shouted at Ballmer.

Frustrated and angry, Ballmer decided to find another place to stay. Eventually, thanks to Bill Gates Sr., the two men reconciled, and the new employees were hired. The friendship between Gates and Ballmer remained intact through the years; they were close enough that Ballmer was Gates's best man at the Microsoft chief's 1994 wedding; and Ballmer's three sons refer to their father's business colleague as "Uncle Bill."

In time, Microsoft employees regarded Ballmer as a welcome addition. Someone was truly needed to put order into a company that still did the books by ledger and had no budgets, no planning process, and no formal pricing strategies. Gates was pleased with his first major hire. He got what he had wanted, someone he could trust.

I Made the Decisions

In the ensuing years, Gates and Ballmer continued to work well together. At various times, Ballmer ran several Microsoft divisions, including operations, operating systems development, and sales and support. Ballmer was encouraged to come up with new ideas. He could question what Gates was doing at any time. But nothing could change the basic nature of the relationship: Gates was in charge and he was quite pleased to remain in charge. "Steve was supercritical, full of ideas, influencing everything we did—even technical things, how we would organize, what people we would pick. But I was the decision maker."

The Gates–Ballmer relationship became critical for Microsoft's future. Gates had worked closely with other colleagues; but with no one else had he been able to forge such a close working relationship. Choosing Ballmer to work for Microsoft, Gates said much later, was one of the best business decisions he had made. It was important to Gates to have someone such as Ballmer who was not only totally trustworthy, but who shared his vision and who was as committed to Microsoft's success as he was. Gates thought it a plus that Ballmer came with a somewhat different skill set than his, and that he could run ideas by him and get solid feedback. Gates concluded, "The benefit of sparking off somebody who's got that kind of brilliance is that it not only makes business more fun, but it really leads to a lot of success."

In time, Gates and Ballmer developed one of the most profitable business partnerships in American corporate life—and perhaps the most unique one as well. Rarely did two such strong-willed business personalities comanage a company with such effectiveness. Gates was present for Microsoft's creation; Ballmer arrived five years later. But the company was so small when Ballmer arrived that he seemed almost like a kind of cofounder. Elsewhere, high-tech company founders often burned out or voluntarily retired, allowing new professional management, possessing far greater business skills but much less technology know-how, to manage the enterprise. It was rare for founders to last too long as business leaders; it was just as rare to find successors who were adept at both business and technology.

Gates was the master technologist, but was adept at running a business as well; Ballmer had sharp business skills, but also understood and appreciated the technology. Both loved what they were doing and, despite accumulating vast amounts of wealth, showed no signs of retiring. Both men saw in Microsoft the start and finish of their careers. Neither had aspirations to hold public office or to join another firm. Both men could lash out at each other in private (never in public, of course) and then move on to other topics as if the tiff had never occurred. Microsoft was their pride and joy. Both men had helped to define and nurture the original culture; both had weathered the periodic crises; both had been responsible, to one degree or another, for the company's reaching such dizzying financial heights.

Within the Microsoft community, no one groused that Gates and Ballmer had hung around for so long. The small eight-member Microsoft board of directors (which in 2003 included Gates, Ballmer, and Jon Shirley) had no complaints. With Gates running the company and

Ballmer holding senior positions, Microsoft had turned numerous employees into multimillionaires; and even during the company's darkest moments in the Department of Justice trial, no evidence surfaced to suggest that the Microsoft board had become vexed with either of the two men.

It was not surprising that as the Microsoft trial was coming to a close toward the end of 2002, Bill Gates and Steve Ballmer remained at the helm. Both were relatively young, in their late forties. Both were getting more and more adjusted to their coleadership roles. As Gates and Ballmer seemed to fit more easily in those roles, others at Microsoft liked what they saw. Said Craig Mundie, who as the company's chief technology officer had worked closely with both men for years, "That combination has given us a chance to create a comanagement structure that is sustainable." At other companies such a sharing of power often led to deep mutual distrust, bruised egos, jealousy, and bitterness. "What's unique about us," observed Mundie, "is that this structure could persist as long as both of these guys want to work."

From their earliest days together at the company, Steve Ballmer had always seemed a right-hand man to Gates, carrying out a whole host of business chores. Gates not only was the more visible of the two, but for over two decades had been the only visible figure at Microsoft. As the arm twister, the coach, the chief tactician, Ballmer was by far the more emotional of the two, yet few saw that emotion outside the company. Some thought it slightly odd that Gates had elevated a feisty pugilist such as Ballmer to the post of president, especially as the appointment came in the midst of the Department of Justice trial, when Microsoft might have been better off projecting a more benign image. But Gates was grooming Ballmer for even bigger things to come.

And so no one was truly surprised in January 2000 when Steve Ballmer took up the post of chief executive officer at Microsoft. In some respects, there was nothing that new about the division of labor the two men had carved out for themselves that winter. Ballmer had, after all, been running the business side since 1998; in his case, the job description remained nearly the same. Gates always played a major role on the technology side. What Ballmer was supposed to gain from becoming CEO was a new authority, a new sense of respect from both within Microsoft and without; for as long as Bill Gates had been chairman and CEO, anyone else in the company, regardless of the lofty rank, would be treated merely as Gates's appendage.

Spreading His Wings

Now, Ballmer had a chance to spread his wings, to convince others in the software industry—as well as Wall Street, the media, and politicians in Washington, D.C.—that he was to be considered a coleader at Microsoft. It was asking a lot of Ballmer and of all those power elites, since Gates was not leaving the company. Indeed, he was retaining a certain part of the leadership even as he gave up a significant share of the power. He remained chairman of the board, and as such retained decision-making power over many of the governance issues the company faced. Still, by creating for himself a new position (chief software architect), Gates hoped to signal that he was once and for all distancing himself from Microsoft's day-to-day business operations and devoting himself as fully as possible to technology strategies. (One idea under consideration, but eventually rejected, was for Gates to move his office closer to the technology people so that he could distance himself from senior executives who were mostly involved in the business side. For the man who had built Microsoft from scratch that may have seemed like a little too much distancing.)

Much speculation surrounded the reasons for the Gates–Ballmer transition that winter of 2000. That Gates wanted to give himself over fully to technology seemed to some far too simplistic an explanation. Certainly Gates *was* needed to impose order on the proliferation of software projects within Microsoft. As a whole new array of computer devices required software, including hand-helds, cell phones, watches, and tablets, someone had to stay in touch with the various product development teams to ensure that no disconnects occurred among them, and to make sure that synergies among the teams were properly exploited.

And, to be sure, Gates had felt the tug of the business side pulling him further and further away from the product teams: "[B]y '99 a combination of that overload and some impact of the lawsuit going on . . . meant that I was enjoying my job less than I had in previous years. . . . I still . . . loved the job. It's just that I didn't feel like I was on top of everything as I like to [be]." He had always prided himself on being able to walk into a meeting, having had ample time to prepare for it. Without the time to prepare, all he could do was show up and listen. He preferred having the chance to come up with his own ideas. For that he needed time.

The conventional wisdom within Microsoft was that the transition from Gates to Ballmer had become inevitable given the company's remarkable growth during the 1990s. The company had become far too complicated and multifaceted for even someone as talented as Bill Gates to run on his own. The statistics illustrated how far Microsoft had come in the previous seven years alone. In 1993, it had $3.79 billion in revenues, $953 million in profit, and 14,430 employees. In 2000, revenues had soared to $22.96 billion, profits to $9.4 billion, and the headcount to 39,170. Between 1999 and 2000 alone, the company had taken on nearly 8,000 new employees.

Planning to Retire?

And yet, cynics grew convinced that a hidden agenda lay at the core of the power shift. One theory had Gates elevating Ballmer as part of an overall plan to ease himself out of the company. It did not seem implausible that the wealthiest man alive just might want to get away from the daily grind, given how much of a strain the Microsoft trial had become. Gates certainly appeared frustrated and overwrought by the trial's increasingly negative effects: the hemorrhaging of senior executives, the dazed, embarrassed employees, the front-page headlines.

Given all this, was a Bill Gates retirement really so unlikely?

But, more practical minds chalked up the Ballmer appointment to a new twist in the trial that required a calmer, less emotional mind at the helm. The Government, some theorized, was secretly planning to press for the breakup of the company. Microsoft therefore had little choice but to seek a quick settlement. Better a clever, less emotional deal maker such as Ballmer in charge at this critical time than someone who blindly believed his company had done no wrong. So the thinking went.

Yet, another, far more compelling reason for the leadership change existed, one that was far too delicate for Microsoft executives to acknowledge in public.

It was that, in stepping down as CEO, Gates would become a less visible figure, hence less of a promising target for the company's detractors. No longer would the company's competitors have a whipping boy in their struggles to debilitate Microsoft. Gates was no longer the chief spokesperson, the voice of the company. Steve Ballmer was. Microsoft's image would be automatically less strident, more businesslike. By becoming less visible, Gates was paving the way for a new Microsoft under new leadership to come forward.

Abandoning power did not come easy to Bill Gates. Prime ministers and American presidents left office, if not cheerfully, then at least gracefully, knowing they were bound by electoral rules. Kings, however, abandoned their monarchies rarely, enjoying jobs for life, bound by no rules at all. By early 2000, Bill Gates was a king—a king far too young to abdicate, yet far too controversial to cling to monarchical authority. When he and I met in the summer of 2003, I saw the strain on Gates's face and heard the crack in his voice when he spoke of the relatively new Ballmer era at Microsoft. For years it had never occurred to him that writers might, while he was still at the company, be able to compare a Gates era to what would come afterward. Such comparisons, he imagined, would come only decades after he had left the company or even later perhaps. He seemed to worry about what comparisons the writers might draw between the two eras.

Yet the transition did make certain sense to him. He could shift into high gear on the technology side. He could ease the way for Steve Ballmer to orchestrate a settlement of the DOJ case, which was by then even in his judgment the optimal outcome for Microsoft. He could even see the logic of propelling Ballmer into a more visible role at Microsoft. But none of that stopped him from feeling a sense of awkwardness, discomfort, and longing for what had been. He had liked Bill Gates Inc. As the company's biggest asset, and an icon on top of that, he had led the company to greatness. Around Microsoft he had been revered. And yet, with Steve Ballmer Inc. in the making, he could be quickly forgotten. Relegated to a secondary position, he might become less and less appreciated. He never came out and said as much in public; but he came pretty close.

A More Visible Steve Ballmer

Gates was being unusually harsh on himself. Few others at Microsoft appeared ready to forget him that quickly. The mere suggestion that he was becoming less visible raised hackles. It became important to provide evidence that Gates was still very much a central figure. Company spokespeople pointed out that, as chief software architect, Gates was still the bearer of the company's technology vision. As the symbol of the mightiest software giant on the planet, he continued to keynote major high-tech conferences. He still hosted the majority of the company's product launches, as he did in the fall of 2003 when Microsoft launched Office 2003. It was not that Gates had become less visible, executives indicated; it was simply that Ballmer had become more visible.

In his new role as CEO Ballmer began handling the various management-oriented initiatives that Gates had dealt with in the past. He was presiding over the seven new business segments. He was holding forth on the business strategy part of shareholder and analysts meetings. And, he was becoming the voice of the company on all operational matters. The new Gates–Ballmer leadership was on display on July 24, 2003, at the annual Microsoft analysts meeting on the Redmond campus. In the past, the analysts hung on every word that Gates uttered. They still did. During the lunch, analysts crowded around a table where Gates was answering questions. What *was* new was the fuss made over Steve Ballmer during the cocktail hour. This time Ballmer was creating his own center of attention. Wherever he stood, a crowd of analysts surrounded him and peppered him with questions. To the analysts, Bill Gates was still a voice of the company, but now so was Steve Ballmer.

Gates and Ballmer seemed more like brothers than business partners. They fought like brothers, finished each other's sentences, and anticipated the other's thinking. Most important, they had a deep admiration for the others' special skill sets. Ballmer appeared truly awe-stricken at Gates's grasp of technology; Gates, in turn, spoke of Ballmer's business skills only in superlatives. But in a number of other ways they seemed less like brothers.

In public, Ballmer was the more expressive and therefore the more memorable. Gates kept his emotions wrapped up in a private box; Ballmer walked onstage as if on a caffeine high. In their public speeches, one was salesman, the other nerd. Ballmer pounded his fists on the lectern, repeated certain phrases for emphasis three or four times. "Work it, work it, work it," he told Microsoft engineers, pushing to make their products better than rivals. To another crowd he shouted, "Windows! Windows! Windows!"—damaging his vocal chords so much that he required surgery.

Emerging from a Cake

For Microsoft's twenty-fifth anniversary, Ballmer popped out of a cake. On another occasion he ran back and forth across a stage, arms flailing, as if he were trying to lift himself off the ground. Sometimes he became imprudent, such as the time in 1999 when he catastrophically asserted that Internet stocks—including Microsoft's—were overvalued. Microsoft's stock immediately plummeted but soon recovered. Two years earlier, replying to a reporter's question, he embarrassingly suggested, "To heck with Janet Reno," the then U.S. attorney general who had been investigating Microsoft for alleged antitrust violations. Ballmer was never boring onstage.

Gates might have been, had he not become, even when in his twenties, the world's most authoritative voice on personal computer software and its future—so authoritative that each year starting in 1983 he was invited to be the keynote speaker at the Comdex technology trade show in Las Vegas, the high-tech industry's most prestigious event.

During his public appearances Gates offered few memorable phrases, no emotional outbursts, no remarks that he came to regret. A Gates speech was crammed with facts and observations, brief forays into computer history, and countless demonstrations of Microsoft products. He never repeated a phrase three or four straight times; but he did speak in a sophisticated computerese language that only aficionados understood. In that sense, while he often spoke to thousands in an audience, Gates always seemed to be speaking to a tiny set of high priests.

Ballmer took on broader slices of the public—and just about everyone understood him and was amused by him.

One came from the technology world, the other from the business world. That difference showed up in their personalities.

Technology evoked specifics: the exact number of bits and bytes, the precise speed of a computer, and so on. Business employed rhetoric that was imprecise and vague. Paradoxically, in their evaluations of people and events, Gates the technologist tended to be vague and imprecise; Ballmer the business figure preferred to be blunt and clear-cut. "In general," Ballmer explained, "I see the world black and white and Bill sees gray. I tend to want to say 'Good' [or] 'Bad.' Bill will more often say, 'It's got these good points and these bad points.'"

These differences showed up when they decided on promotions and demotions. "I will say this person is good or bad," Ballmer indicated.

"I will categorize much more radically than Bill will. He will say, 'Yeah, the guy is underperforming, but he's got these good characteristics.'"

Ballmer, in his own view, paled in comparison to Gates when it came to seeing the forest for the trees, the forest being the big concepts, the trees being the details. "Bill sees forest *and* trees. I tend to see the forest and have a hard time with [the trees]. People will tell you that I'm good at details. I'm not bad at details . . . but I don't have the mental capacity Bill does. He builds a model, a checklist of questions to ask. It's just a marvel to watch him build these checklists in his mind on a problem."

But it was their knowledge of the details of technology that separated the two men the most. Gates began as a programmer and evolved into the supreme technologist. Ballmer never studied computer science and never really programmed: "If I say I wrote four programs when I was in high school, that would probably be too many."

If Gates loved technology, Ballmer got excited about business processes. Ballmer said of Gates, "He doesn't mind management process, but he doesn't gravitate to it." Ballmer liked to solve business problems by scheduling a meeting with certain people, fixing an agenda, then meeting every few weeks, but "that's not where Bill evolves to naturally," Ballmer explained. "He evolves much more naturally to 'I can help figure that out. I'll just get a few people in the room and we'll figure it out.'"

More Anal Compulsive

Summing up their office routines, Ballmer called himself "much more anal compulsive," but both were compulsive about not wasting time. Each year they reviewed each other's schedules with an eye to overlap, hoping to make their time more efficient the next year.

The two were in touch all the time, either at widely attended meetings or in weekly one-on-one sessions. Ballmer was keener to get together in person than Gates. From 1998, when Ballmer became president, the two had offices close together. They tried to hold hour-long chats once a week, but met only about twenty times a year one-on-one because of their travels. Both preferred e-mail to simply dropping in on the other. "Bill's not a dropper-inner," observed Ballmer. "I'm more of a dropper-inner, but maybe once a month." It was Gates's habit to send Ballmer ten to fifteen e-mails over a normal weekend and by Monday Gates would have Ballmer's replies.

If they differed in their knowledge of technology, and in the way they sized up people and situations, they did share one feature of their lives: their incredible wealth. Gates, of course, was the wealthier of the two. But Ballmer was no slouch. According to the *Forbes* list of the four hundred richest people in America for 2003, Gates was first with $46 billion, while Ballmer was eleventh with $12.2 billion. There was far more equivalency in their yearly salaries. In 2003, Ballmer was paid a $551,667 salary as well as a $313,447 bonus; Gates that same year was paid the same salary and the same bonus as Ballmer. Eventually Gates announced that he would give away much of his fortune for good causes. A great deal is known about how that fortune gets distributed because Gates has been so public with those details. Ballmer, on the other hand, has kept his own philanthropy a totally private matter.

As the two men learned to adjust to their new coleadership roles, Gates had to cope with less authority, and Ballmer had to learn how and when to exercise the new power given to him. Getting there for both men had not been easy, as Craig Mundie noted. "It didn't fall in our laps. It took a conscious decision on Bill's part and real work on the management side to work into this structure and make it operational."

With Gates remaining a central pivot at Microsoft, inside and outside the company many wondered whether Ballmer would have the patience to listen to others, to delegate authority, to decentralize, which was something the place clearly needed. In short, would he be able to take over?

Ballmer never had any doubt that Gates wanted him to be the CEO, but neither of them, Ballmer acknowledged, had any appreciation of what the new titles would do to the relationship they had forged over the years. "It was fairly clear," Ballmer commented, "shortly thereafter that neither he nor I really understood what [the shift in power] meant, how were we really going to change our working dynamic. And it probably took us, again, almost a year to really sort that through."

Who's Driving This Car?

In corporate life often the same person holds both the chairmanship and the CEO post to avoid confusion and disagreement over lines of authority. Yet, even after the Gates–Ballmer transition, Gates remained the company's chairman and its largest shareholder. So, from the start, Ballmer was under some constraint. For both men, it was figuring out *when* one should exercise authority that caused the most strain. "We were both kind of frustrated with each other in terms of, well, who's driving this car," admitted Gates, referring to those first days after the transition. In some ways, the two men grew into their jobs; in other ways, they continued to grope with those lines of authority. In September 2003, during the fourth year of the new division of labor, Ballmer told me candidly, "It is an evolution and it's still—truthfully—still evolving."

Craig Mundie worked closely with both men after the transition and sensed how hard it was for Ballmer to run the company: "Steve had never been CEO of anything. It takes a while to learn what it really means to fly this plane by yourself. Here you had a little bit more baggage. Dad hadn't died. He is still around. It was a big risk that the company took, and Bill consciously took his partner Steve and turned over the formal responsibility of CEO over a relatively short period of time. Steve had to learn how to be a CEO and he had to do it while essentially Bill had not retired. Now he's trying to be CEO in an environment where there's a shared responsibility for Microsoft."

At times Ballmer wondered to himself if he should simply demonstrate his authority to show that he was comfortable being in charge. But he decided to start off slowly, spending the first three months

doing little more than talking to the company's one hundred most senior technical and product people. Meanwhile, Gates kept his antenna
alert. "Even though Steve is really running it all, Bill knows what's
going on everyplace," said Gates's close friend, investor Warren Buffett. "No sparrow falls, or even thinks about falling, at Microsoft without him knowing about it." Some disagreements surfaced behind
closed doors. Ballmer, it was said, was less excited than Gates about
Microsoft's large investments in telecommunications companies and
its costly plunge into the video game business.

Anoop Gupta, Microsoft's corporate vice president for real-time
collaboration, became Bill Gates's technical assistant in October 2001,
eighteen months after the transition. Before Gupta arrived at Microsoft in July 1997, he had been an associate professor of computer
science at Stanford University for eleven years. Before becoming
Gates's TA, Gupta had worked for four years at Microsoft Research,
where he led the Collaboration and Multimedia Group.

He observed the two leaders up close, sensing that neither one had
clear ideas about the boundaries of their leadership. "When I took
over," said Gupta, "Bill and Steve were still figuring it out. It was as if
they were asking all the time, 'What are you doing? What am I doing?'
Bill felt that he was giving away control of certain things he used to
control and manage. He felt less important." Gupta recalled being at a
business plan review meeting with Ballmer and Gates when Ballmer
had to step out for a five-minute break to make a phone call. "Now
you can talk about the unimportant stuff," Gates quipped to the others
in the room, prompting Gupta to say later, "Maybe he was joking;
maybe he wasn't."

Gupta suggested that eventually the two men found a new comfort
level when sitting in at meetings together. "Bill might go ballistic in a
meeting, but Steve came in to calm the situation; Steve balances Bill
out and the other way around. They play off each other really well.
Steve can't get into the technology, but he brings a lot of value to technology discussions because he's not so closely involved, and he has

a sense of the market and of the customer. Both jump in. It's wonderful, like having two CEOs. There is much deep trust."

As time wore on, the two men eased into a more sharply defined division of labor. They learned instinctively when to defer to the other. For his part, Steve Ballmer was responsible for setting the business vision and for running the company in general, or, as he put it, "Making sure we really are doing a good job of having management process, people, and organization. Do we have the right people in the right jobs?" While Bill Gates still offered input, Ballmer now made the final decisions. For example, if Microsoft was about to hire a senior technologist, Gates weighed in with his opinion but could not, as in the past, expect to have veto power. He was similarly restrained when it came to sales and marketing issues. Clearly, Ballmer gave Gates preferential treatment. "I always want to know what things are important to Bill and that he really wants funded." On product development decisions, Gates's opinions always carried the day. "If Bill says we need to do it," said Ballmer, "we do it."

Gates held sway over all technology issues; this included research and development, and any key business strategies rooted in technology such as intellectual property and antitrust issues. Gates continued to travel and speak for the company, but he did so in a more limited, choosier way. If the customer was big enough, he paid a visit. But he left the CEOs mostly to Ballmer and tried to spend his own time with chief technology officers and information technology personnel.

Despite the early rough spots for him, the media recognized Ballmer's new key role in the company. *BusinessWeek* named him one of its top twenty-five managers of the year for 2002, crediting him with playing a large role in Microsoft's success at a time when most other high-tech firms were getting weaker. Under CEO Ballmer, revenues had grown 16 percent in 2000, 10 percent in 2001, and 12 percent in 2002. The company was growing at a slower pace than previously, but no one blamed Ballmer personally. Many other reasons were cited, including the fact that Microsoft had reached a certain peak in its growth pattern and that the economy had gone through a very bad patch in those years.

Steve Ballmer understood that he would have to take the lead in the making of the new Microsoft. He understood that, whatever the truth of the antitrust allegations, Microsoft had to change. "We may think of ourselves still as young upstarts coming up, struggling every day, [but] that's not how the world thinks of us; that's not how our customers think of us."

Bill Gates knew that the Government's antitrust law suit against Microsoft had defined the company for far too long; it was, as he put it, "kind of a cloud over everything we did because of the uncertainty it created." But he knew that, if anyone was going to lead the battle for reform at Microsoft, it would have to be Ballmer. Gates had become far too identified with Microsoft as the aggressive, competitive start-up, however long in the tooth.

Both men in public expressed astonishment that anyone could think of Microsoft in any other terms but saintly, but Ballmer seemed more sensitive to the glaring public perception of the company and of Gates as some kind of corporate monster. That alone made Ballmer much more equipped to take on the task of transforming the company's sagging public image.

And indeed, as the reform campaign got under way, Ballmer led the fight; Gates receded into the background, hardly mentioning the vast changes that Ballmer was engineering. "Steve's personality and background as a sales guy," said Microsoft executive Mary Snapp, "make him the one to evangelize and deliver the message in a way and with skill sets that would be harder for Bill to do." As corporate vice president and deputy general counsel, Snapp oversees Microsoft's compliance with the Government's antitrust decree. Craig Mundie, the company's chief technology officer, thought it significant that Ballmer quickly grasped the new reality that begged for Microsoft to reform. It was not easy, Mundie argued, "because you know what reality is, but whatever perception is in the outside world *is* reality. You can yell and scream, but that doesn't always prevail."

January 2003. The Microsoft trial was over. The two company leaders could now exploit their new roles more fully. For the first time Gates felt able to devote most of his efforts to the technology side. Ballmer had gotten past the kinks and could now think about playing an even bigger leadership role. Both men faced hard choices at the start of 2003. With the trial over, they had for the first time an opportunity to take the company down a new path. For both men, turning over a new leaf would not be easy. Were they up to it?

4

Putting the Start-up to Bed

The key message that Microsoft wanted to project in those first moments after the trial was its readiness to take a new path. Gates and Ballmer scheduled a news conference soon after the judge's decision, their first opportunity to set a new tone and to make it clear that both were behind a reinventing of Microsoft.

The men onstage at that news conference were determined not to act as if they had somehow emerged triumphant. Nor did they want to appear as losers. It was important to set a humble tone immediately. Gates spoke first, reading a prepared statement: "We believe that today's ruling, largely affirming the settlement we reached with the Department of Justice and the nine states, represents a fair resolution of this case."

To Gates and the others, the case was over. The court had given Microsoft a chance to begin anew. And Gates talked as if he had gotten the message. "This settlement puts new responsibilities on Microsoft, and we accept them. We recognize that we will be closely scrutinized by the Government and our competitors. We will devote the time, energy, and resources needed to meet these new rules. I am personally committed to full compliance."

He did not gloat, but he did take great satisfaction in the decision because "while putting new responsibilities on Microsoft, this settlement also gives us the freedom to keep on innovating for our customers.

The next few years will be an incredibly exciting time for our industry as Microsoft and many other companies work to develop technology for an increasingly digital world."

As part of complying with the new rules, Microsoft appointed an Antitrust Compliance Committee on November 5, 2002, and charged it with overseeing the performance of the compliance officer, who in turn had been mandated to develop and supervise Microsoft's internal programs and processes to ensure compliance with the settlement. The compliance officer was required to maintain a record of complaints received and actions taken by Microsoft and to report credible evidence of violations of the settlement.

No one had ever articulated in public the remarkable comparisons one could find between Microsoft at the end of 2002 and IBM two decades earlier; but the difficult days that IBM faced as it emerged from its own lengthy antitrust trial with the Department of Justice in the early 1980s had to be on the minds of Gates, Ballmer, and anyone else concerned with Microsoft's fate.

In much the same way that Microsoft had become a monopoly in personal computing operating systems and personal productivity software (word processing, spreadsheets, etc.), IBM had decades earlier done very well from its monopoly in mainframe hardware and software. And just as Microsoft was facing an assault from a free operating system (Linux) in the early 2000s, IBM had faced competition back then from computers that used low-cost microprocessor technology.

It quickly became apparent to Gates and Ballmer that the way to avoid the same kind of devastating losses that IBM faced in the early 1990s as it emerged from *its* trial was to take some radical steps. IBM had waited a long twelve years—until 1993—to turn the company around, appointing Lou Gerstner, and giving him broad authority to impose new discipline within Big Blue. The Microsoft leadership team felt that it did not have the luxury of waiting a whole decade to begin its reforms.

. . .

Twelve days after the trial ended, Steve Ballmer sent a companywide memo, attempting to establish a new tone that he hoped employees would adopt. Through the memo, he wanted, he said, to pass on his ideas about how Microsoft would be "forging a new relationship with our customers, our partners, the industry and governments around the world. I believe we are creating an entirely new Microsoft." The U.S. District Court's judgment required Microsoft to make certain changes, some of which the company had already begun to implement. He spelled these out:

- "We are restricted in how we negotiate with computer manufacturers. We now operate based on a transparent and uniform price list for the Windows operating systems.
- We are required to make design changes in the Windows user interface so that access to certain Microsoft features can be removed to give prominence to competitor products instead.
- We have identified nearly 300 internal Windows interfaces and have disclosed these (at no charge) to competitors and others in the industry so that they can use these to interoperate with Windows.
- We have made available for license the protocols that the Windows desktop operating system uses to communicate with our Windows server operating system. Competing server software vendors can acquire up to 113 protocols under this program."

He acknowledged that many people had asked him what Microsoft had learned from the ordeal of the trial. "We learned that we needed to take a different perspective on being a good industry leader. Frankly, part of the problem was that, even five years ago, we still tended to think of ourselves as the small start-up company that we were not so long ago. Today we recognize that our decisions have an impact on many other technology companies. We have an important leadership role to play in our industry, and we must play by new rules—both legally and as determined by industry trends."

He gave some examples: Recognizing that Microsoft needed to support industry cooperation in new, creative ways, it had started to develop standards based on Extensible Markup Language, or XML, which had become the universal way for computers to talk with one another across the Internet. It had begun as well to try to do a better job of industry partnership in developing security solutions based on industry standards, enhancing security for the entire technology industry and its customers.

The new Microsoft planned to cooperate more with national and local governments and international organizations. One way was to cooperate with governments in fighting identity theft, cybercrime, and attacks on the Internet. Microsoft's goal, Ballmer noted, had shifted from putting a PC in every home and on every desk to one that called for making great software that helped people and businesses realize their potential. The mission has shifted slightly because of new opportunities for Microsoft's software to go from running just PCs to connecting people to all the information they needed—at home, at work, and in the classroom.

The key sentence in the memo had to do with the way Microsoft planned to deal with the outside world: "We're committed to being upfront about what we are doing and who it affects, open in communicating about every aspect of our business, and sensitive to the new issues of corporate governance that have become increasingly important to market confidence. . . . We are renewing our commitment to improve our communications with partners and customers."

That was Steve Ballmer's pledge in November 2002. Gates felt a need back then to project a kinder, gentler Microsoft, not because of any of the trial issues, but more because he now realized that he had been naïve in assuming that Microsoft could foster a positive image among the politicians without establishing a firm presence in Washington, D.C.

Gates now felt he should have been looking out for the company's image a long while ago. "There's no need to go back to anything particular that happened relative to the lawsuit and prove that we were right or anything like that," said Gates. "Independent of the lawsuit, when you have our level of success where you are playing the central role in the technology that is going to change people's lives, there is a need to reach out and remind people, 'Hey, we're people here who want this software to work in a way that helps you out, preserves your privacy. We want this software to be available to kids in schools, kids in libraries.'

"There is a huge responsibility to reach out, to be part of a broader dialogue; to reach out to Washington, D.C., and be part of the spam dialogue; to reach out to Brussels and share what we see coming down there. So in terms of the company being kinder and gentler—yeah, kind and gentle—that's always been . . . ever since we have been really successful, that's been very important. We get smarter about how to do it partly by making mistakes. We have the resources and the cleverness to look at those mistakes.

"In the early days of the company I was very proud that we had no lobbyists ever, no PACs [political action committees]," Gates noted. "I had to spend more time in capitals of other countries than our capital. And, what a testament that was to America. You could build a company with great success without involvement in political activities of any kind. Well, at a certain point that was nice, but then when we got to a certain size that was a naïve approach and it became important to have smart people in D.C. who were sharing what was going on with technology and be there to listen if people were developing concerns: was Microsoft thinking through the issues? And so that was a mistake. It is a mistake that has led us to have a good presence in D.C. and a good dialogue. Then people say, 'Oh, you're trying to get political influence.' No, we are trying to be part of a dialogue." Microsoft hired a lobbyist in Washington, D.C., only in March 1995; by January 2004, it had thirteen lobbyists in the nation's capital and another seven in state capitals.

It was one of those unusual times when Gates articulated a wish to make Microsoft seem more open, more involved in the external world. In various ways he played an important role in helping the company turn over a new leaf, but he spent far less time in public than Steve Ballmer did evangelizing the need for Microsoft to be more open and communicative. "Steve more than anyone else, but both Steve and Bill encouraged people to set aside whether the trial was unfair," said Microsoft's chief counsel, Brad Smith. "They encouraged people to ask, 'What can we learn from the trial? How do we turn it into a positive force, rather than a negative one?'" The fact was that Ballmer did most of the encouraging in public. Gates was in some ways just as active as Ballmer in reinventing the company. But Gates did not spend much time in public putting those activities into the context of the new reforms. That was all left to Steve Ballmer. But Gates played a large part in the reinventing of the company. The first big initiative he took in that respect had to do with trying to improve the performance of computers.

Becoming More Attuned to Customers

Bill Gates decided that he needed a bold, new companywide initiative that would somehow send a message that Microsoft was trying to reform itself. He cleverly understood that he could not make a grand public announcement that Microsoft was trotting out a major new initiative in order to create a kinder, gentler Microsoft. It was far too early for Microsoft to appear to make promises of this nature. Such an announcement would have been greeted with the utmost cynicism.

And so when Gates rolled out his Trustworthy Computing initiative early in 2003, he and Microsoft's image spinners promoted it as helping Microsoft become more attuned to its customers and more attuned to the outside world in general. Specifically, the initiative was meant to show how sensitive Microsoft planned to be toward its customers' problems with its software. Through it Microsoft planned to build more reliability into its products, to become more trustworthy.

Trying to improve its relationship with customers was a good place for the reinventing to start. For all the isolation Microsoft had felt during the trial, its customers and partners had come to exhibit an increasing dependence on the company. In ways that had not been true in earlier years, whole companies, not just millions of individual customers, now felt inextricably bound up and reliant upon the reliability of Microsoft's products. Customers had far greater expectations and demands than ever, insisting that Microsoft's operating systems and productivity applications work without crashing and without slowing down or paralyzing the operations of these companies.

In preparing the initiative, Gates worked closely with Craig Mundie, who said he "believed that our products would be more and more recognized as infrastructure for society at large and, as with any critical infrastructure, more and more would be demanded of us with respect to trustworthiness. The world depends on that infrastructure and won't tolerate it going away or being flaky."

Perhaps customers should not have raised the bar so high. Perhaps it was unfair to allow Microsoft so little margin for error. But they did raise the bar; they no longer would tolerate fault-filled software. Better than most, Gates understood the growing burden this put on his company: "When computer systems aren't perfectly reliable, who are you going to think needs to do much more about that? Naturally, you'll think about Microsoft."

And so Bill Gates latched on to those seemingly disparate complaints about Microsoft's products—they were not secure enough; they were too vulnerable to viruses and so on; they were not reliable enough; they were crashing too often—and announced in a memo distributed to employees on January 15, 2002, that he planned to deal with all those complaints in the new Trustworthy Computing initiative.

In the memo, Gates announced that Trustworthy Computing had become "the highest priority for all the work we are doing." It meant that "customers will always be able to rely on these systems to be available and to secure their information. Trustworthy Computing is computing that is as available, reliable and secure as electricity, water services and telephony."

People no longer worried about electricity or water services being available. As for the telephone, it was simply assumed that service would be both available and secure. However, Gates observed, "Computing falls well short of this, ranging from the individual user who isn't willing to add a new application because it might destabilize their system, to a corporation that moves slowly to embrace e-business because today's platforms don't make the grade. The events of last year [2001]—from September's terrorist attacks to a number of malicious and highly publicized computer viruses—reminded every one of us how important it is to ensure the integrity and security of our critical infrastructure, whether it's the airlines or computer systems."

Gates said Trustworthy Computing would occur under the following conditions:

> Availability: Our products should always be available when our customers need them. System outages should become a thing of the past because of a software architecture that supports redundancy and automatic recovery. Self-management should allow for service resumption without user intervention in almost every case.

> Security: The data our software and services store on behalf of our customers should be protected from harm and used or modified only in appropriate ways. Security models should be easy for developers to understand and build into their applications.

> Privacy: Users should be in control of how their data is used. Policies for information use should be clear to the user. Users should be in control of when and if they receive information to make best use of their time. It should be easy for users to specify appropriate use of their information including controlling the use of e-mail they send.

To show how much importance he attached to the initiative, Gates selected one of the biggest experts in the computer security field, a man named Scott Charney, to become Microsoft's chief Trustworthy Computing strategist. Besides overseeing the Trustworthy Computing initiative, Charney was put in charge of the company's Security Strategies Group, which worked with product teams and others at Microsoft to advance the development of secure products and services. Before joining Microsoft, Charney had served as chief of the Computer Crime and Intellectual Property Section in the Criminal Division of the U.S. Department of Justice. As the leading federal prosecutor for computer crimes, he had helped prosecute nearly every major hacker case in the United States from 1991 to 1999.

"Part of the initiative," he observed, "is to develop products and services where people say, 'I trust Microsoft.' We want people to trust us. People trust banks. We have to be able to say at some point, 'You can trust us to keep your machine running, reliable, and secure when you're doing transactions. You can trust us to respect you, give you control over data, and have transparent business practices, so you know what we do. When your system crashes, it's called 'the Blue Screen of Death.' That's not good when that phrase becomes a phrase in the dictionary. We want to get to the point where people say, 'I trust them.' "

In his January 15, 2002, memo Gates sought to get across a far broader message than simply the need for secure and reliable products. "There are many changes Microsoft needs to make as a company to ensure and keep our customers' trust at every level—from the way we develop software, to our support efforts, to our operational and business practices. As software has become ever more complex, interdependent and interconnected, our reputation as a company has in turn become more vulnerable. Flaws in a single Microsoft product, service or policy not only affect the quality of our platform and services overall, but also our customers' view of us as a company." In other words, as people become more comfortable using Microsoft's products, they will develop a more positive attitude toward the company and the way it does business.

A Little Less Zeal

Such thoughts did not arise in Gates's mind in earlier years when the start-up mentality dictated that growth and earnings were the key performance metrics and the *only* way to tell whether customers had a positive attitude toward the company. As long as Microsoft piled in one great feature after another into its software, customers would flock to its products.

Gates was now reconsidering such attitudes.

In promoting Trustworthy Computing, he was prepared to step back a little from the utter zeal he had always promoted as part of the Microsoft culture. "In the past, we've made our software and services more compelling for users by adding new features and functionality, and by making our platform richly extensible. We've done a terrific job at that, but all those great features won't matter unless customers trust our software. So now, when we face a choice between adding features and resolving security issues, we need to choose security.

"Our products should emphasize security right out of the box, and we must constantly refine and improve that security as threats evolve. A good example of this is the changes we made in Outlook to avoid e-mail–borne viruses. If we discover a risk that a feature could compromise someone's privacy, that problem gets solved first. If there is any way we can better protect important data and minimize downtime, we should focus on this." These were new thoughts for Bill Gates, as he grudgingly sought to put his start-up to bed.

Part of the aura of the earlier start-up phase had been a certain mystery surrounding Microsoft. Through Trustworthy Computing, Gates was shedding some of that mystery. In a memo dated July 18, 2002, this one to Microsoft customers, Gates explained that the new initiative was "part of our commitment to ensuring that Microsoft is more open about communicating who we are and what we are doing."

To underscore the importance of the new initiative, Gates noted that earlier in 2002 he had put on hold the work of more than 8,500 Microsoft programmers while the company conducted an intensive security analysis of millions of lines of Windows source code. All Windows programmers plus several thousand other programmers had been given special training in writing secure software. He had estimated that the stand-down would last a month but it took two, and cost Microsoft $100 million.

On November 19, 2003, Charney testified before the Subcommittee on Commerce, Trade and Consumer Protection of the House Committee on Energy and Commerce, updating the Congressional subcommittee on the initiative. He noted that Microsoft had enhanced the training of its developers to put security at the heart of the software design and development process. Moreover, all new software releases and service packs were now subject to an enhanced security release process which had already resulted in a notable decline of vulnerabilities in some of the company's server software. "This effort, which can cost hundreds of millions of dollars and delay the software's release to the market, is a critical step in improving software security and reliability," he stated.

Vulnerabilities were decreasing. For example, Charney mentioned that in the first ninety days of Windows Server 2003, the company reported and patched three critical or important security vulnerabilities and six total in the first 180 days. In contrast, with Windows Server 2000, Microsoft had found eight critical or important vulnerabilities in the first 90 days, and twenty-one in the first 180 days.

Considering how much hope Bill Gates, Craig Mundie, and Scott Charney were placing on Trustworthy Computing, it was intriguing to discover that the company had decided to keep the initiative in low profile at first. Charney explained that Microsoft knew it was dealing with a cynical, skeptical public and for that reason it seemed prudent to avoid boasting about the program until it proved itself. "Until we can show this initiative makes a huge difference, we shouldn't be trumpeting it. At the end of the day, the best thing is to let the results speak for themselves."

If Trustworthy Computing was the opening shot of the company's new reform program, it was by no means the only element. Steve Ballmer began to address the business aspects of those reforms. On March 21, 2002, he presided over a retreat for the company's executive staff at the Sun River Resort in Sun River, Oregon. Executives present were supposed to settle on the nuts and bolts of the reforms.

Returning from the Sun River retreat, Ballmer spent the next few months drafting a document that laid the groundwork for the changes he wanted to implement. The document was significant as a further indication of Ballmer's building a new authority for himself. Not only was he setting his own stamp on the company; more important, he was putting Microsoft on a new course, with a new mission, with more sharply defined values. In that memo, distributed on June 6, 2002, Ballmer wrote in part:

> Simply put, our mission is to ***enable people and businesses throughout the world to realize their full potential***. Today, we use software to help people get there. Over time, this will evolve to be a combination of software and software services. But our mission is not just about building great technology. It's also about who we are as a company and as individuals, how we manage our business internally, and how we think about and work with partners and customers.
>
> As an industry leader, we have a unique role in the world—unique in the contribution we make and the responsibility that comes with that. Customers expect us to hit a very high bar in terms of product and support quality, delivering on our commitments, and providing excellent customer-focused decision making. Our industry wants us to be more actively engaged and open about who we are, and about our roadmap for the future. Our pending settlement with the DOJ adds new responsibilities that we must deliver on. We are committed to working with the DOJ and other government agencies to ensure the settlement is a success and that our relationship is positive and constructive going forward.

Explaining just what Ballmer meant, a Microsoft public relations manager noted, "You still want to be competitive and have that drive, that's what made the company great, but you have to evolve, you have to understand your place in the market, and in the industry, and that means you have to be a better partner with the Dells and Compaqs, the software partners, the development community, customers; you just can't ram products down their throats, you have to understand their business and what their problems are."

The events of the previous four years, Ballmer noted in that memo, and the changes in the industry, made this a good time for Microsoft to take stock of itself. It was also a good time to understand how others perceived the company "and to think about how we can do a better job explaining who we are and what matters to us." No single sentence better summarized Microsoft's new mission.

Explaining Itself Better

Even as it was redefining its mission with regard to its product strategy (to enable people and businesses throughout the world to realize their full potential), it was mandating its own employees with an even more crucial mission that went far beyond the way Microsoft developed product strategy. That broader mission required Microsoft to explain itself better to the outside world. "Many of us," Ballmer wrote in that same memo, "feel a disconnect in the way we see ourselves and our mission and motives, and the way we are portrayed, and only we can change that."

This was a startling acknowledgment.

During the trial and even for some time afterward, many in the company believed that there was nothing Microsoft needed to do, or could do, to change, since all the accusations leveled at it had been untrue. What Ballmer now was saying was, in effect, let's not dwell on what we did or did not do, let's simply assume that we have an image problem, a serious one, and let's try to correct it. In other words, let's act as if the accusations are true and then see what kind of changes we have to make in that light.

Steve Ballmer understood how crucial it was to redefine the company's mission and to articulate in clear fashion what the company's values were going to be. In the past, the company's mission had been, as some would say in retrospect, rather bombastic. It was to put a computer on every desk and in every home. It was not a mission for the faint of heart or for the laid-back. The mission required workaholics whose mantra was not "Let's spend the weekend with the family," but rather "We are going to win!"

Over time, Microsoft tried to soften the more grandiose elements of the original vision by coming up with "Empowering people through great software—any time, any place and on any device." That new vision was meant to capture the changing computer environment, but the emphasis was still on the product.

But, at the March 2002 retreat Ballmer and the executive staff concluded that it was time for the company's mission to go beyond simply what it wanted for its products. "[O]ur mission is not just about building great technology," Ballmer wrote in the memo that followed the retreat. "It's also about who we are as a company and as individuals, how we manage our business internally, and how we think about and work with partners and customers."

This was the crucial change for Microsoft. Reinventing at the company had always been about changes in its products. Now, reinventing meant changing the entire company. Those words—who we are as a company, how we manage our business internally, how we think about and work with outsiders—formed the core goal of the rebooting process. They were a signal that Microsoft was going to spend as much time, if not more, on getting its house in order as on the developing of great products.

By focusing the mission around the company and not on its products, those words were signaling as well that Microsoft felt a need to stifle parts of its start-up atmosphere in favor of creating a more grown-up, mature company.

The Sun River Resort Retreat became Steve Ballmer's call to action. Microsoft's troops had to pause and give new thought to each aspect of their work. It was Ballmer's own personal responsibility—and he recognized this—to make sure all the parts of the business worked together. He knew the place had been too centralized, and he planned to fix that. He wanted the company's products to excel—not only because they should, but because in doing so they would meet with the approval of Microsoft's customers. It was on customers that Ballmer wanted to focus the company's new outreach initiative.

Ballmer and others stressed that despite the damaging effects of the trial, Microsoft knew that it must not stop innovating. In fact, the trial, in their view, basically sanctioned Microsoft's right to keep on innovating. Customers wanted and expected that from the company. In sharpening its focus on customers, Microsoft intended to be more open with them, to show a bit more humility, but, as Brad Smith, the company's general counsel and senior vice president for law and corporate affairs, explained, "We are going to continue to innovate, but we will do it in a legally and socially responsible way."

In the past, Microsoft had developed its products pretty much in a vacuum. Now it planned to take a whole new set of factors into account.

First and foremost were the legal sensitivities. Gates and Ballmer planned to ensure that Microsoft stayed on the right side of the law. Again, Brad Smith: "You have to look at the legal standards articulated by the court. Do we meet [them] with this new feature? That's the first test." Second, the broader impact of Microsoft's products on others had to be taken into account. "How are they going to feel about this feature?" Brad Smith asked. "We've got to be honest and forthright with people about what we do. We've got to communicate that early, clearly, candidly so that other people know our view on where we're going and they don't feel blindsided about what we're doing. But we've got to continue innovating. It would be a great shame if the lesson of the lawsuit was that we should no longer push the edge of the envelope in terms of consumer advances."

To that end, Microsoft's executives promised themselves that they were not going to behave the way IBM did after its lengthy antitrust case and send an attorney to every meeting with an OEM. "We're going to have people read the consent decree," said Microsoft board member Jon Shirley, "but we're not going to assign a lawyer to make sure they implement it."

Within days of the trial's end, Microsoft sent a message to the world. The timing was impeccable. Just six days after the judge's decision, here was Bill Gates rolling out a brand new product that carried the highly significant message that Microsoft had not been weakened by the trial. Indeed, the company was saying that it was as strong as ever. It was continuing to innovate.

On November 7, 2002, Gates launched the new Tablet PC operating system software. The tablet technology had been one of Gates's big dreams—in effect, replacing pen and paper with an electronic tablet and stylus. Some computer makers had tried pen-based computing in the past (most notably Apple Computer with its Newton), but had failed. Gates had persisted; he had enjoyed mailing magazine articles to investor Warren Buffett, jotting notes in the margin; but Gates looked forward to the day when he and Buffett would be free of such old-fashioned ways. With the new Tablet PC, Gates called up articles from the Web, scrawled thoughts on the screen with a digital pen, and e-mailed them off to Buffett, saving time, energy, and effort. To launch the product, Microsoft had to overcome problems that had dogged pen computing: poor screen resolution, short battery life, and seriously inaccurate software for deciphering handwriting. But in time it overcame those problems.

Microsoft developed the design specifications, but PC makers were to sell the piece of hardware. Gates concluded that, despite earlier failed attempts, it was now possible to create what he called "digital ink"—with one's handwriting superimposed on a document on the screen. Digital ink could then be integrated easily into instant-message programs, allowing people to exchange handwritten notes or drawings via their computers.

The Tablet PC became such a personal quest for Gates that his aides felt additional pressure to deliver on the product. Though he carried the Tablet PC with him to meetings, Gates took a while to develop total trust in it; he brought note pads along for note taking at first.

Some had been skeptical about the prospects for sales, saying that no clear market demand existed for the new technology. Predictions were that only a few hundred thousand Tablet PCs would be sold the first year, partly because of the sour economy and partly because the user interface was not that easy to navigate. Microsoft had spent $400 million on the technology and planned to spend $70 million more marketing the Tablet PC. Still Gates predicted optimistically that at least a half million would be sold in the first year. Nearly a year later, Microsoft was on track to meet Gates's predictions.

By early 2003, numerous Microsoft employees were using the Tablets during meetings. Gates explained how it was going. "We've got a wireless network, so if you sit in a meeting here, if you're allowed to bring your computer (which some meetings we say that's OK, some meetings we say it's not OK), if the meeting is not that interesting, you can sit down, look up your electronic mail, see what's out there on the Internet, make sure your schedule for the weekend looks good, use your time in a much more effective way."

Just ten days after launching the Tablet, Gates was making his annual pilgrimage to Las Vegas to give the high-tech world's equivalent of the president of the United States' State of the Union speech. For anyone plugged into high tech, the annual Gates speech to Comdex had become the obligatory way of learning what Bill Gates's latest thoughts were on the state of the high-tech world and, perhaps no less interesting, what he had to say about the state of Microsoft. For Gates, Comdex was a highlight of his year. He loved the audience, loved the platform it gave him, loved the chance to talk about new ideas in technology. To him, the speech was so significant that he went through a full-blown rehearsal hours before the speech was to be delivered.

Deeply Digital

As Gates prepared himself for his November 2002 Comdex appearance, he looked forward to standing before a major audience for the first time with the burden of the trial behind him. Now he could look forward to a future that contained a new kind of clarity for Microsoft. He could speak to a high-tech audience confident that Microsoft would not be constrained from putting forward a whole array of new products. As he began to speak, he exhibited a mixture of self-confidence and excitement that had not been heard for a while.

He spoke with great passion about what he liked to call the Digital Decade, the idea that a whole variety of high tech scenarios would occur between then and 2009 and would become commonplace. That is, that the "advances in chips and connectivity, and the devices themselves will make so many things common sense to be done in digital form, whether it's sending a phone bill to a company, whether it's analyzing sales results or taking notes, organizing your music, sharing your family memories with other people."

Over the next decade much hard work would have to be done to nurture the Digital Decade: "Deep architecture, new tools, many of these requiring literally tens of billions of dollars to be spent, and collaboration across literally thousands of companies. And I say that this is the task that we're all engaged in." He would not have felt comfortable making that statement until getting over the legal hump sixteen days earlier.

He quickly got around to delineating the state of the high-tech world and, inferentially, suggesting how and where Microsoft would fit into that world. "During the course of the Digital Decade, we'll think about personal computing in a different way. It's not just sitting in front of that desktop PC. That's very important, but that's just a piece of what we'll do. After all, the magic of the chip that brings intelligence and the magic of software are now spreading out to all different devices.

"Those devices are connecting up in very flexible ways. And so, small devices, whether they're pocket-sized, or wrist-sized, tablet-sized, wallet-sized, all of these things will come together. The TV experience will be a deeply changed digital experience. Even in the car, when you're interested in information, or being notified, that will be deeply digital. The way we think about phone conversations, how we set them up, find somebody, how we share information during that phone call, all of that will be completely reshaped during this Digital Decade. We can say that the idea of personal computing is far broader than ever before, broader in new experiences, broader in ways that systems connect automatically, and broader in greater productivity."

Gates was once again in his element, evangelizing the magical qualities of software, proudly making clear that Microsoft planned to recapture its rightful place in the sun. It would, however, take more than memos and speeches to convince others that the company had truly transformed itself into a responsible high-tech industry citizen and leader.

The problem was this: Microsoft was in the early 2000s a global institution, with more than fifty thousand employees, and yet, in many ways it still thought and acted like a start-up.

While the trial acted as the greatest catalyst in making Microsoft a mature enterprise, another event played a significant role as well. It was the dot-com revolution of the late 1990s. Suddenly, a whole new set of start-ups surfaced, anchored in the Internet, earning outrageously high stock valuations from Wall Street, and dishing out business models celebrating market share over earnings. Their arrival begged such questions as when would they make a profit and could they survive until then?

The whole dot-com experience made Bill Gates cringe—in part because he simply did not believe most of these enterprises deserved to be called businesses, and in part because he realized that the glow that was radiating from these bright, shining dot-coms had cast a giant shadow over that erstwhile start-up, Microsoft. It irked Gates that the dot-coms were not doing "deep technology" (his phrase) yet were promising financial rewards more quickly than Microsoft could.

Hiring great employees at Microsoft became tougher, and it became harder to convince people that Microsoft would bring better products to market. The dot-coms had all the brashness and hyperbole of start-ups and, quite frankly, Gates didn't like his thunder being stolen: He noted that "Banking was going to change overnight. Insurance was going to change overnight; the shopping mall would be empty overnight. It was all the land grab—if you had a Web site that did *X*, you were the future of *X*."

What offended Gates most was the nerve of these blips on the screen calling themselves start-ups. That implied they were real businesses. He recalled going to a meeting to discuss partnering with some companies that wanted to put advertising on Web sites. He brought an eight-member team with him. Across from the Microsoft team sat representatives of five companies each with a total valuation of over $500 million doing the same thing that Microsoft's small team had been doing. One of their leaders told Gates, "Well, gee, if the world is giving infinite capital to people doing this same thing, why don't you give us one hundred more head count?"

To which an irate Gates replied, "What you are doing isn't that hard. This is a feature. This isn't a company. It isn't even a product. It's just a feature."

Bothering him more than anything was the way the marketplace was rewarding these companies for gaining market share, not for making a profit; he had always understood that profit should be the key measure for rewarding shareholders. It was all very confusing to him.

Gates wanted to distance himself and Microsoft as much as possible from these tiny blips. It was already clear to him that Microsoft in the late 1990s had become much less of a start-up than these dot-coms. For the first time he began to realize that Microsoft in so many ways had already triumphed over these start-ups. If this was the look of start-ups in the late 1990s, perhaps Microsoft did not need to emulate start-ups quite as much as it had. The dot-com revolution made Gates think that it just might be acceptable to turn Microsoft into a more mature company.

Microsoft, in Craig Mundie's telling phrase, was growing up. It was trying to leave its past behind, the darker past, not the bright one. No one could rewrite history, not even Microsoft. But Bill Gates finally understood, not as quickly or as easily as Steve Ballmer had, but he was beginning to get it. Shedding the start-up mentality meant the shedding of some of the company's aggressiveness, and everyone knew how hard that was bound to be for Bill Gates. But that was precisely the kind of thing that a mature company did. "The company," said Craig Mundie, "is growing up. Microsoft is exiting adolescence. You see the maturation in the management team. The company is growing to accept its real role in society, to accept that it should have corporate social responsibility, and become more sophisticated, that we should deal with more finesse as we deal with global problems."

As the company sought to move into that new role, Bill Gates began to play a new role within Microsoft. It was a role he had wanted to play for years. Now he would get his chance.

PART III

How Bill Gates Reinvented Microsoft

5

Yes, Mom, I'm Thinking

If one character trait illustrates best what Gates is all about, it is his devotion to thinking. Even as a small child, he seemed to prefer the quiet solitude of introspection to almost anything else. For example, there is the legendary tale of sixth-grader Gates ignoring his mother's calls to dinner.

Finally, she asked him, "What are you doing?"

"I'm thinking," he shouted at her, making it clear that she was disturbing his own private world.

"You're thinking?" she asked, finding it hard to grasp that this was worth missing a meal for.

"Yes, Mom, I'm thinking," he repeated. "Have you ever tried thinking?"

As it turned out, thinking landed the sixth grader into trouble. His parents sent him to a psychologist for counseling for a year. Young Bill found the psychologist "a really cool guy," perhaps because he gave the youngster a book to read on psychological theory.

Young Bill Gates also performed feats that showed his mental acuity.

At age nine, he read the entire *World Book* encyclopedia from A to Z; at age eleven, he memorized all 107 verses of the Sermon on the Mount. A teacher estimated his IQ to be in the 160s or 170s. Asked in his childhood to describe his desired future occupation, he answered "scientist."

I Was Hooked

Even during infancy he had high energy. He rocked to and fro in the cradle and spent hours riding a coil-spring hobbyhorse. The rocking motion proved comforting and he continued it into adulthood; it became his most widely imitated personal trademark. He seemed to do it in one-on-ones or in small groups but not before large audiences, and certainly not on television.

Bill Gates, the thinker. It is a good image to cling to in recalling how he earned his fame. He was small and shy and loved to think on his own; it seemed only natural that he gravitated to computers as a young student.

He was growing up in a world that adults controlled—a world to which a youngster was largely denied. Computers gave him the chance to display his own personal talents—and, most important, to have power over something. He liked giving the machine orders; when it responded, it was almost as if it were obeying him. "I realized later," he wrote on the opening page of his book, *The Road Ahead*, "that part of the appeal must have been that here was an enormous, expensive, grown-up machine and we, the kids, could control it."

William H. Gates III, known as Trey to his parents and born in Seattle on October 28, 1955, had taken up computers in 1967 while a seventh grader. Acquaintances described young Bill as tenacious when confronting a computer problem. Though money hardly seemed a motive for his computer efforts, he once boasted that by age twenty he would make a million dollars. As he and a ninth grader named Paul Allen became spellbound by computers, young Bill created a class-scheduling program to ensure that he took courses with the most attractive girls. He had found a new value of computers: "It was hard to tear myself away from a machine at which I could so unambiguously demonstrate success. I was hooked."

He remained hooked throughout high school, helping companies use computers to uncover bugs in their computers; analyzing electrical power requirements around the Northwest and Canada; computerizing the electricity grid for the Bonneville Power Administration; and founding his own company with Allen to study traffic patterns for the small communities surrounding Seattle.

Young Gates wanted to show adults that he was just as smart if not smarter than they were. It was as if he felt an unrelenting need to compete—and compete successfully—against that adult world. The competitiveness was a Gates family trait; they loved to play games. Winning mattered; everyone, including young Bill, was expected to take the games seriously. During summers at their Hood Canal getaway, two hours from Seattle, the family organized competitive games—a tennis tournament on Saturdays, family-style Olympics on Sundays. Young Bill took more to individual sports such as waterskiing.

The Prelaw Student

Driven by the same competitive spirit but not, interestingly enough, by a desire to study computers, the young man enrolled at Harvard in the fall of 1973. He planned to major in economics but then switched to prelaw, hoping to follow in his attorney father's footsteps. While at Harvard, Bill befriended Steve Ballmer, who had impressed Gates with his sharpness. Meeting so many smart people such as Ballmer, Gates found college fun. At first he kept his distance from computers even as Paul Allen kept after him, urging Gates to become partners in a new software enterprise. Gates assumed, however, that he would attend Harvard Law School, clerk for a federal judge, and then join a prestigious law firm.

As a young man, he already was forming a set of core attitudes: being passionate about technology; needing to have control; being competitive; desiring to change the world. These attitudes eventually became the core elements of the Microsoft culture.

Determined to find a way to change the world, Gates decided the best way was to play a role in the dawning of the personal computer revolution. The new, powerful chip technology of the early 1970s made him and Allen increasingly confident that that a small, cheap, and flexible computer might soon be possible.

They were battling great odds. A software industry separate and independent from hardware did not yet exist. In those days, almost anyone who thought of computers focused on the hardware; software was considered an integral but less vital part of the machine. Bill Gates and Paul Allen, however, had their own vision of what software could become, the "crazy dreams," in Bill's phrase, of his youth. They wanted to develop software that would make personal computers all-purpose, a presumptuous notion because software for personal computers did not exist at the time; nor were there any personal computers. Of those days, Gates recalled, "Computers weren't personal. Computers were big, big, expensive machines that the government used and companies used . . . to print out bills or to keep track of databases. . . . But the idea that an individual could have their own computer and sit down, do their homework, play games, that was basically a crazy idea."

Gates and Allen did not give up. They wondered whether the new 8080 chip could support a version of BASIC, the programming language invented at Dartmouth in 1964. If it could, it would then be possible to get a personal computer to perform a whole array of tasks. Learning of the existence of what was arguably the first truly cheap personal computer, the Altair, Gates and Allen grew excited. Access to a time-shared computer using a Teletype cost $40 an hour for only part of the computer's offerings. A 250-pound, two-foot-square, six-foot-high minicomputer called a DEC PDP-8 cost $18,000! The Altair sold for $397.

Lacking software, the Altair could not be programmed, depriving it of practical value. To perform more complicated tasks, the Altair needed a user-friendly programming language. Gates and Allen decided to pursue the writing of such a language even though one minicomputer firm had argued that it was impossible to write a high-level language that would run on a personal computer. Gates grew paranoid that others might develop the language first and that the personal computer revolution might be launched without him at the forefront.

He and Allen, working out of Gates's small Harvard dorm room, spent February and March 1975 trying to write the language for MITS, the Albuquerque-based company that produced the Altair. Gates slept little, often falling asleep at his desk or on the floor. He could not tell day from night. At times he went an entire day without eating or meeting anyone else. For five weeks, the two men lived, without knowing it, the future Microsoft culture. Eventually successful in developing BASIC for the Altair, Gates and Allen created what became an industry standard that held the field for the next six years. They had in fact helped to create two new industries: the personal computer one and the complementary software one.

The two young men began to work in Albuquerque, Allen as software director at MITS and Gates as a software-writing freelancer. Ed Roberts (the head of MITS) and the two young men signed a nonexclusive royalty agreement for their BASIC. Although hardly a formal business strategy at the time, the nonexclusivity concept continued to work well for Microsoft.

Gates was getting only mixed support at home. His parents thought him talented but wondered how he would amount to anything in a field that did not even exist. Dropping out of Harvard at the end of his sophomore year in the spring of 1975 ended whatever hopes his father had of Bill's becoming a lawyer. The young man described his departure as a leave of absence, but once he formed Microsoft it seemed unlikely he would return to Cambridge. His rather exasperated parents wrote of him in their 1975 Christmas card:

Trey took time off this fall in old Albuquerque.
His own software business—we hope not a turkey
(The profits are murky.)

Just twenty years old, Bill Gates was so excited that he did not think that organizing a software company was so risky. But he knew he could always return to Harvard as a fallback position.

Certain parts of running a new business proved daunting to him. It was one thing to hire his friends, as he did. He forgot to take into account that they expected to be paid! Also, he naïvely assumed that anyone doing business with him would be around for a while, only to discover that customers sometimes went bankrupt, leaving him in the lurch. He quickly turned into a skinflint, declaring that he intended to keep enough money in the bank to pay a year's worth of payroll even if there was no money coming into the company. Such frugality became a hallmark of the Microsoft culture.

Deep down he knew how hard it would be to start a company at the beginning of his career, how raw and inexperienced he and Allen were at running a business. But he and Allen were deathly afraid that someone else might steal their thunder. Later, he guessed that he could have safely waited a year before starting Microsoft since others weren't entering the field that quickly.

Taking Taxis to Customers

At first his relative youth was a handicap. He had trouble leasing premises. He was too young to rent a car (the minimum age was twenty-five) so he was forced to take taxis to visit customers. At times, customers asked him to meet them at bars and he declined, since he was too young to drink! But at times he exploited his youth. Some assumed that, because he was so young, he was an innocent when it came to business—and to computers. They sensed it would be easy to gain the advantage over him in business deals. But he would start talking about Microsoft's first products and suddenly the playing field would become balanced.

The Gates–Allen partnership, at first 50–50, shifted to 64–36 when Gates persuaded his partner that he deserved the larger share because he was ending his college career.

The premise of Microsoft, considered preposterous to most back then, was that computing power would soon be nearly free. Only Gates and Allen believed optimistically that the cost of that computing power would drop enough to enable millions to own computers. It seemed bizarre for two young men to try to build a software-based firm when no software industry existed. And yet their seemingly bombastic vision was to help put a computer on every desk and in every home.

On the day that Gates was born in 1955, fewer than five hundred computers existed; the entire computer industry was valued at less than $200 million. The term *software* had not yet been coined. But by February 2003, there were 500 million computers in the world, one computer for every twelve people on the planet. While far short of the Microsoft vision, it was still an impressive leap forward after only twenty-eight years.

Even in falling short of that original vision, Gates built Microsoft into one of the most successful businesses of all time, largely by convincing people that they had to pay for software and by predicting correctly that computer power would largely be free. The Gates–Allen edition of BASIC became the first personal computer language.

By 1990, when the company was fifteen years old, Gates had become the undisputed leader of the software revolution. Software now determined what hardware was worth, no longer the other way around. The software industry had become an $18 billion business. Software was a spectacularly successful product because its profit margins were so huge and its costs other than the original research and development were almost nonexistent.

As the company whose software ran on nine out of every ten computers, Microsoft was valued at over $7 billion, grossing over $1 billion a year by 1990 with almost half a billion dollars in cash and no debt. Gates, with a 36 percent ownership of the company, was personally worth more than $2 billion. His influence was extraordinary. By deciding which computers to support with his software, he helped make or break companies.

A major turning point for Microsoft came that spring when it unleashed a new product, an operating system called Windows 3.0.

Earlier attempts to get Windows 1.0 and 2.0 off the ground had gone nowhere and most analysts had predicted an early burial for the new operating system, especially when IBM had refused to adopt it. But when Windows 3.0 seemed likely to catch on, numerous national magazines featured Gates and/or Windows on their covers. He and his new wonder product were touted in *Time, Newsweek,* and *Fortune* as well as on *Today.* The day that Windows 3.0 launched was, in Mary Gates's words, the happiest day of her son Bill's life.

By May 1991, a year after it hit the market, Windows 3.0 had sold more than four million units—more than all the Apple Macintosh computers sold since they had been introduced in January 1984. By the start of 1992, Microsoft was valued at more than $22 billion, making Gates, with more than $7 billion worth of stock, the richest person in America. A single share of Microsoft's first private stock issue worth roughly $1 in 1981 would have been worth more than $1,500 in early 1992; a $25 share from the 1986 initial public offering would have been worth more than $750 in early 1992.

The rest of the 1990s were glorious years for Microsoft financially. Through 1999, it had revenues of $19.75 billion and profits of $7.79 billion. Its work force had grown by the end of the 1990s to 31,575.

In the summer of 2003, Gates looked back at those nearly three decades and professed pride in what he had accomplished: "I've always felt it was the most interesting job in the world, taking what was a youthful interest in discovering the magic of software and being able to hire lots of smart people and figure out how far we can take software to create tools of empowerment. In the early days, that meant writing code, which I loved."

It did not mean, as far as Gates was concerned, presiding over a company that had grown as large as Microsoft had by 2003, with $28 billion in revenues and fifty-five thousand employees. The company's vision had been to create the kind of software that would lead computers to be installed everywhere, but not to create another General Electric or IBM. During that summer of 2003, Gates reflected on those early days and considered the paradox of the original vision, noting that he had also said that Microsoft would become the leader of the software business and that the software business would change the world by changing the way people worked and entertained themselves. "But we never allowed ourselves to then add on, 'Oh well, then that means Microsoft will be a very large company.'" During the early 1980s, no one would have bet that Microsoft would reach even $100 million in annual revenues, certainly not when hardware enterprises could simply give software away for free.

Gates let the long term work itself out. His idea of long-range planning was to worry about the next three or four years. He remembered the first *Forbes* list of four hundred billionaires in 1982; it contained a number of hardware company bosses such as Bill Millard of Computerland, An Wang of Wang Computers, and Gordon Moore of Intel. Noting that no software people had made the list, Gates told Steve Ballmer, "This thing will be full of software people some day." Ballmer laughed, replying, "That means you'll be on it." Gates found Ballmer's remark funny and realized that indeed if he were right about the potential for software, software company leaders might become very rich. But he gave the whole notion of Microsoft's growth and his own potential fortune no thought at all.

By 2003, Microsoft had become big business and Bill Gates had changed his own role in the company to take that growth into account, becoming chief software architect. It was sometimes hard for him to adjust to his new role. Once, at a meeting attended by Gates and Nathan Myhrvold, others kept referring to the "CSA." Finally, Gates turned to Myhrvold and asked, "Who is this CSA they keep talking about?" Myhrvold burst out laughing and said, "Bill, it's you!" But no matter how much his own personal role changed at Microsoft, he remained the key figure on the campus, the main attraction.

Despite the anguishing days of the Microsoft trial, employees still held him in near awe. He may have felt that, in his new chief software architect role, he would be quickly forgotten. But that was not the case.

One sign of the awe that still surrounded his persona was the exhibit at the Microsoft Museum on the Redmond campus, where Bill Gates's first business card was on display above the caption "Imagine what it would be like getting a business card from Bill Gates." That official awe of the cofounder trickled down to thousands of Microsoft employees.

We Trust His Instincts

Anywhere one went on the campus, people deferred to Bill Gates: What does he think? What's he in favor of? What's he against? Penetrating the inner mind of Bill Gates was a favorite game at Microsoft in 2003, as it always had been. Analysts who studied corporate life found such deference unusual. Normally, heads of companies did not fare so well with the rank and file, but then again corporate chiefs did not stick around at the helm for as long as Gates had, and few other corporate leaders attained Gates's accomplishments.

Sometimes the deference toward Gates turned into outright adulation. Employees talked repeatedly about how exciting it was to talk with Gates, how so many of his ideas were original, how his mind was photographic. "There is hardly a better way to spend an hour than talking with Bill," said Peter Rinearson, the man who helped him write the best-selling book *The Road Ahead,* and who in 2003 was corporate vice president for the Information Worker Business Unit at Microsoft. And employees talked constantly about the breadth of Gates's mind. Peter Haynes, Microsoft's director of strategic communications, once mentioned to Gates that he designed vacuum tube amplifiers as a hobby. To Haynes's surprise, Gates showed enough knowledge about the subject for the two men to discuss it for some time. Haynes was momentarily nervous, thinking, Oh my God, he knows about this.

The adulation reached such heights because Gates had been so successful. "We trusted the guy's instincts and knowledge," said Mike

Murray, the former Microsoft vice president for human resources and administration, "and he hasn't been wrong yet." Some found it disconcerting that Gates possessed so much knowledge. Once, Deborah Willingham, the one-time senior vice president for human resources, walked into a budget review meeting with Gates and began asking for more resources. But it was immediately obvious to her from his questions that "he knew exactly what drove everything in my business. He knew as well as I knew it, he knew probably better than I did."

Junior employees remembered vividly how many times they had met Bill Gates in a year and under what circumstances. Senior executives knew with the same precision how often they were scheduled to meet with the chairman. A senior executive acknowledged that one of his employees at the Microsoft research center in Beijing had been absolutely enthralled at the prospect of making a presentation to Bill Gates—enthralled and nervous as hell. Because Gates was so revered, it was automatically assumed that his time was worth a great deal. It of course was—and increasingly so as he spent less and less time within the confines of the Microsoft campus.

Back in His Technology Element

By 2003, most of the time that Bill Gates spent at Microsoft focused almost entirely on technology—"almost" because Gates has not completely abandoned the business aspects of Microsoft. While Steve Ballmer has the final decision on business issues, Gates provides input on many of those decisions. He also takes part in the hiring process of certain key executives.

But most of his time is now spent presiding over product review sessions with teams that are trying to design future Microsoft products. It is a labor of love for Gates. In the past he had struggled to find the time to monitor these teams effectively, distracted by the business side of Microsoft. Now he is back in his element.

Bill Gates's time is considered Microsoft's most precious asset. Executives call that time "Bill capital" and they won't let anyone, including Bill, squander it. "When you have a fantastic resource like that," explained Nathan Myhrvold, "you want to use that resource like crazy, but the more you overuse it, the more you will screw up the thing you need the most. It's a very interesting balancing act." Gates needed to perform that balancing act so that he could spend as much time on technology as possible.

Everyone at Microsoft agreed that by 2003 Gates had finally hit his stride, finally being able to devote the proper time to the company's product strategies and products. In the past, when there were many fewer products, his great talents had been put to the best use in sensing when a new market was emerging, in sensing when Microsoft should shift product strategies to exploit the emerging market. There was no great need to integrate products back then. Besides, the culture was so individualistic in orientation that no one imagined such integration was possible. As late as the mid-1980s, Microsoft employees tended to talk only to people in their own product units. They did not use anyone else's code. At that time, such individualistic behavior proved effective. But as the company grew, and many people were doing so many different things, the old, noncommunicative way would not work. Some overall monitoring system had to be put in place to exploit synergies and prevent overlap.

Hence it was that Microsoft developed the strategy of integrated innovation. Microsoft had come to realize in the 1990s that its core competency had become the synergy it created between its product lines. "That," said Craig Mundie, "made our products different from any other product. We were not seeking to be a conglomerate that might have process or talent synergies but not product synergies. We were moving toward a strategy that the businesses had to have a symbiosis between them."

All of this fit perfectly into Bill Gates's style of managing technology. With Microsoft producing so many products, Gates's talents could best be employed by sensing how to integrate the company's product line to make those products more useful to the consumer. By successfully integrating Microsoft's products, Gates was giving the company a great competitive advantage because no other company could offer such a wide array of software products; the more that Microsoft products interacted with one another, the better was Microsoft's total offering.

Helping Gates in that role as Mr. Integrator was his uncommon ability to remember with almost perfect detail facts dating back years and covering an enormous breadth of information. Mike Murray said it best: "My brain doesn't work that way. His spreadsheet has many more rows and columns. He can pick this cell here and that cell there. He remembers paragraphs from legal contracts from five years ago—not just the language but why we did it and 'How come you don't remember why we had to do this? Are you not paying attention?' I don't think he's trying any harder. I work as hard as I can. I can't do what he does. He's blessed with an analytic IQ. Something works different in his brain and he's chosen to exercise it in a constructive way."

Gates's unique talent in 2003 was in being the only one at Microsoft who knew what every single product group was doing, what features they were working on, what each groups' goals were. With that unique knowledge, he was in the special position of being able to guide product groups away from overlapping, away from wasting their time on activities that were better pursued by others, and toward efforts that utilized their time and knowledge most efficiently.

Anoop Gupta, who served as Gates's technical assistant from 2001 to 2003, noted, "Raw information is coming in to him and what flows out from that is the connected, synthesized information. Before, markets and products were simpler, fewer things were happening; now from Xbox to MSN to Office to Windows, to Business Solutions to Servers and the wireless, so much is happening. We are much bigger and so there is a much greater need for synthesis."

It was as if at any given time Bill Gates could download a photograph of the entire company into his brain and look over that photo when he needed to. Or, as Craig Mundie explained, "Bill's unique gift was always the way he does this complete and continuous synthesis. It's like he's a pipe, and all kinds of stuff goes in at this end and a continuous output of optimized strategy comes out the other end. What we are designing is critical infrastructure for everything digital going forward—business and government systems, communications, entertainment, you name it. The complexity of the challenge is unprecedented, but that just gets Bill's competitive juices flowing."

How does Gates run a product review? Nathan Myhrvold summed it up: "Bill is very good at taking those points of view that hadn't occurred to anyone in the project and looking at them. Often he isn't 100 percent correct. So it's not like whenever these impasses would be reached, the team had done the wrong thing. More often they had done the right thing, but they had not thought the thing through to realize the thing that Bill would pick up on. Bill wants groups to share code and strategies. Groups hate to do that. It takes time. You have to depend on someone else. Everyone wants to depend only on what they do. At one point, we figured there were eighteen word processor codes in the company. We asked ourselves, How do we go from eighteen to five? Bill is great at understanding all of those things."

Craig Mundie, who has spent hours with Bill in product reviews, found that Gates has an uncanny ability to absorb one thing at one meeting and then refer to that seemingly lost fact at another to make some point. "You never have to tell him anything twice. I can go into a meeting and we'll talk about something; then we'll go together to a product review. I realize he's now giving direction to this group that reflects the fact that I gave him in the meeting minutes before. It comes out completely woven into the fabric of the guidance he gives the group. That has been the integrating influence in Microsoft's product strategy. That has been this thread where Bill gives each of the product groups the guidance for their mission, and that guidance reflects how one group relates to the other in the business. That's a huge factor."

Don't Take It Personally

It was astonishing but at the same time not unsurprising that Gates was prepared to invest so much time and energy in the product review sessions. A company chairman or CEO who would take the time and who was qualified to preside over sessions involving technology was highly unusual. But for Gates, it was the thing he loved most at the company and the thing that he was uniquely qualified to do. For Gates, the product review sessions were marvelous illustrations of how Microsoft had retained its start-up qualities by remaining antihierarchical. After all, the teams were showing off their work not to some middle-level manager but to the man on top.

He preferred the product review sessions—indeed all meetings with Microsoft employees—to be with small, controllable groups. Five to seven people was much more preferable than twenty or thirty. He wanted everyone present to get a chance to talk. And he wanted to be able to interact with the group, not just be forced to listen to lots of presentations.

He listened far more than he spoke. He came to the product review sessions to learn, not to dictate. He was all too aware that anyone in his midst might be disinclined to differ with a Gates view once that view was aired. So he asked others to speak up first. If someone presented surprising data or some new logical approach to a problem, he was prepared to change his mind. He was always open to a good argument, a good debate.

Some members of product teams were understandably nervous at the prospect of a product review with Gates. His tongue lashings were legendary—and feared—around Microsoft!

Those who had endured such tirades offered advice to novices: When Gates starts to call you an idiot, don't take it personally. He doesn't really mean what he says. Even if he attacks you personally, don't try to defend yourself. Never say, "I'm not an idiot. I have an honors degree." Always keep your emotions in check. He'll be watching for how you handle a tirade. Before going into a product review, try to anticipate each and every question Gates will ask.

If Gates had his way, he would spend as much as 75 percent of his time at Microsoft in meetings with product development teams. He's getting close to that goal, but as long as he remains chairman of the board, he'll always want to keep his finger in every Microsoft pie, and he'll find it hard to allocate as much time as he would like to the monitoring of the teams.

Half of Gates's product review time in 2003 and early 2004 had been spent on Longhorn, the nickname for the project designed to turn out the next generation of Windows. Gates and the Longhorn team are taking a whole fresh look at what should go into a computer's operating system, including the way documents and other data are stored and the way users interact with the computer. In order to exploit Longhorn, other Microsoft software products and services were being overhauled, including MSN online service, the server applications, and Microsoft Office.

At one such Longhorn meeting, Gates got a report from Product Unit Manager Hillel Cooperman's ten-person team in charge of the "shell" or user interface. Gates's then technical assistant, Anoop Gupta, had already briefed Gates on what he could expect to see and hear and what questions he probably would have. The team walked in and said hello to Gates. Then, endlessly curious, he was pummeling team members with questions before they could even blink.

"That's interesting," Gates would say. "Why did you do it that way?" Or "I don't know that I would have thought to do it that way."

The team had brought a demo with them and they eagerly ran through it with him. Then Gates and the team locked in battle. Gates spent ninety minutes dealing with one issue after another, probing the team on what each component did, trying to figure out what issues still needed resolving.

In earlier days, when the company was much smaller, and when Gates felt much closer to the actual programming aspects of projects, a team spent much of the product review session discussing code with him. Although the last time Gates had done coding was 1983, he still knew programming inside and out. But the Cooperman product review and all of Gates's other product review sessions in 2003 were at a much higher conceptual plane. They were focused on what Microsoft executives like to call the "scenario," what the company was trying to enable the user to do, what experience it wanted the user to have.

Significantly, the Microsoft executive with senior responsibility for Longhorn, Jim Allchin, was not present at the product review. In most other cases, it would have been inappropriate for a boss to not sit in a meeting of one of the teams with a company leader. The boss would not want to be left out of such an important loop. "It wasn't that Bill was trying to exclude Allchin," said Corey duBrowa, the senior vice president at Microsoft's public relations firm, Waggener Edstrom. "It's that Allchin didn't feel he had any value to be in the meeting because he's not at the build-out level, but more at the stitchery level to get all those things to meld together." Later in the day, Gates and Allchin held a one-on-one during which Gates told him that he was pleased at how ambitious the team was. "I'm not looking to inject more ambition in what these guys are doing. I just want to make sure they are clear on the most important stuff."

Anyone meeting with Gates had to feel tension in the air after all the talk about how precious his time was, how much demand there was for a personal session with him. Everyone understood that a meeting with Bill Gates probably had the same weight as, in past times, a meeting with Thomas Edison or Henry Ford. "For the team," said Corey duBrowa, "it would have been the equivalent of doing a light bulb demonstration for Thomas Edison." Accordingly, product teams prepared thoroughly in advance, trying to think of every conceivable question Gates might throw their way.

During the Cooperman product review meeting, Anoop Gupta, a pretty calm fellow under any circumstances, sought to take the meeting down a notch whenever tensions cracked. As the meeting was winding down, he summarized what follow-up was required. He particularly reminded this team member or that of Gates's suggestion to contact someone else at Microsoft to check on a possible overlap or whatever (for product team members, the Bill Gates suggestion was, in fact, a marching order).

Gates still felt a need to get away from the day-to-day routines at Microsoft, and so in 2003, he continued his practice of going on what he calls a Think Week. During that five-day week, he broke away from the numerous tasks of the office by holing up in some isolated spot where he could do nothing but—think!

Gates had instituted Think Week in 1994 after realizing that he was spending 60 percent of each year on the operational side of the business when his goal at that time had been to spend 60 percent a year on technology issues. He felt overburdened by the day-to-day decision making required of overseeing the great Microsoft growth machine.

It's probably fair to say that Gates is unique among business leaders in going off for a week simply to ponder. To be sure, plenty of CEOs take a week off here and there, but their destination is often the golf course or the swimming pool—and they make sure to leave their work back at the office.

By 2003, Gates was actually taking two Think Weeks a year. The first that year was in mid-June. For five straight days, he left home and stayed at one of his other personal properties to do nothing but dwell in peace and quiet on what he thought should become Microsoft's new directions in technology. As he put it, he wanted "just to go off and take all the materials I or anyone in the company thought I should read, new research breakthroughs, new product advances, competitor activities."

During the June 2003 Think Week, Gates focused on improving the ways that support is given to Microsoft customers who feel that the company's software is slow or frustrating. Microsoft had been increasingly nervous that the company had somehow gotten away from the customer; that the customer felt frustrated by all the technology and frustrated even more by not getting the kind of support he or she expected and needed from the Microsoft.

Think Week Alert

In 1999 Gates doubled his Think Week time upon realizing that he was still not getting to all the reading required of the job. "If somebody mailed me a twenty-page article, I'd say, 'There is a 50 percent chance I'm going to mark this in red and try and read it this weekend, and six months from now it's still going to be in my in box.'" While most of the articles might not have been critical for him to read, he always worried that some point in an article could shape his thinking about where a market was heading, or about whether to partner with some company. He did not want to miss such an article.

For weeks, even months in advance, the entire company went on a kind of "Think Week Alert," deciding on which papers to shoot to Gates for his consideration during his time away from the campus. Memo after memo, article after article, arrived on the desk of Gates's technology assistant. When he was serving in that role, Anoop Gupta huddled with Gates just prior to the start of a Think Week and decided which of the many memos and articles Gates should take with him. When the Tablet PC was coming on the market in 2002 and concerns about its reliability still existed, Gupta made sure that, in addition to articles appearing on the Tablet, Gates had hard copies as well.

During these Think Weeks Gates tries to isolate himself from any sort of distractions. He won't say with great precision where he goes, only that it's "anyplace where there is zero distraction because all I'm doing is reading and sleeping and writing." He leaves his wife, Melinda, and three children behind at their home on Lake Washington near the Redmond headquarters. He has someone bring in food for the week. So no one is talking about Bill Gates showing up at a tiny grocery and ordering grub for a week. But how does Bill Gates go somewhere where no one recognizes him? "I'm where there are no people." He has stayed at Paul Allen's place on the Puget Sound's San Juan Islands a few times. He has a place at Hood Canal. "Other than somebody bringing the meal in, I don't see people."

There is minimal television watching. Gates suggested, "If I turn on the TV, that would be goofing off." He reads a small amount of e-mail, a big change from his usual office routine, where he spends as much as two-thirds of his time each day on e-mail. "E-mail is really my primary application, because that's where I'm getting notifications of new things, that's where I'm stirring up trouble by sending mail out to lots of different groups."

What about browsing on the Internet during Think Week? Yes, he browses, he admits. "I might goof off a total of two hours during Think Week and any browsing or turning on the TV would be in that two hour quota of goofing off. You really want to get your mind concentrated around [the issues]."

With so few distractions, he actually gets a lot done. And, as a result, some of the key milestones in the company can be attributed to Gates's efforts during a Think Week. He composed his "Internal Tidal Wave" memo on the Internet in May 1995 soon after a Think Week. After his January 2002 Think Week, he wrote his "Trustworthy Computing" memo. Sometimes he gets to the writing of the memo during Think Week, sometimes a week or two after his return. "In some cases I go into Think Week knowing, Hey, I have to pull together all this cacophony around, say, the Internet, [asking myself] does it change the rules of the game? I've got to pull together a memo that says, 'Of all this hype, what do *we* as a company think? What are *we* going to bet on? What are the things that we are going to do less of in order to do more of this?' "

Of course, apart from Think Weeks, Gates had sought to find free time to dwell on the large issues, but his life had now become so complicated, so filled with scheduled commitments, that finding time to reflect other than during Think Weeks was not easy. He may not know when he'll

Bill Gates talking at an internal Microsoft event.
Courtesy of Microsoft Corporation

Bill Gates at an internal Microsoft event in July 2003.
Courtesy of Microsoft Corporation

Steve Ballmer speaking at the Windows Server 2003 launch in April 2003.
Courtesy of Microsoft Corporation

Steve Ballmer at an internal Microsoft event.
Courtesy of Microsoft Corporation

Steve Ballmer at an N-Power meeting in October 2003.
Courtesy of Microsoft Corporation

Aerial view of Microsoft's headquarters in Redmond, Washington.
Courtesy of Microsoft Corporation

Bill Gates Sr. talks about community service with a young person involved in City Year, a foundation-supported program in the Pacific Northwest, in October 2000.

Jon Warren

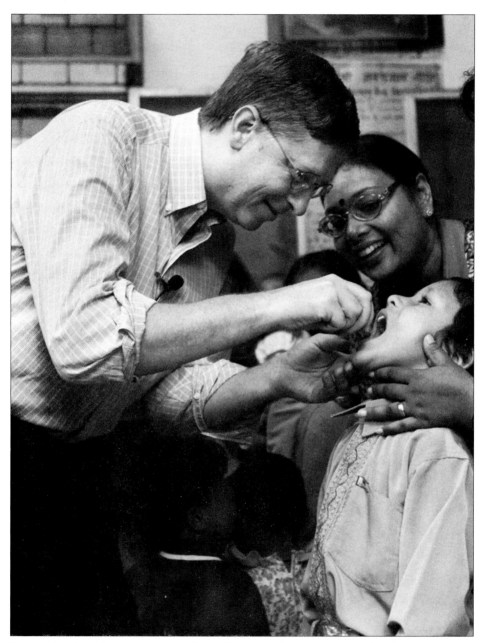

During his foundation visit to India, Bill Gates administers an oral polio vaccine in a New Delhi clinic, 2000.

Jeff Christensen

Mike Murray, former head of human resources at Microsoft.
Courtesy of Mike Murray

Nathan Myhrvold, the founder
of Microsoft's research arm
and a close associate of Bill Gates's.
Courtesy of Nathan Myhrvold

Deborah Willingham,
former head of Microsoft's
human resources.
Courtesy of Microsoft Corporation

Craig Mundie, Microsoft's chief technology officer.
Courtesy of Microsoft Corporation

find time to think; but he knows exactly how his year is divided. When we talked in mid-summer 2003, Gates said he was spending close to 75 percent of his time on technology over the course of a year. He also spent two weeks in Europe and two weeks in Asia (largely nontechnical trips), when he would meet with Microsoft customers. Most of his travel he put in the 25 percent nontechnical side, "when I'm introducing a product, going to Comdex, speaking at consumer electronics shows, going wherever in the U.S. to see customers." He also counted attending Microsoft board meetings, doing business reviews, and engaging in legal matters as part of the 25 percent.

He generally does about thirty-five hours of meetings at Microsoft in a week. He spends another thirty hours on reading and e-mail—part in the office, part at home.

A Real Break Is No E-mail

I asked him if he works seven days a week.

His answer came down to a yes. "Most weekends I do probably nine to ten hours of e-mail. Now there are weekends [when] I say, 'OK, this weekend we're off with these other people.' There are weekends that are zeros [in terms of work]. When I go on vacation, although I do long-term thinking about the company, I don't do e-mail. E-mail is the key to me. And it's just a stylistic thing. There are people who always want to be in touch with e-mail, but for me in terms of a real break it is when you're not doing e-mail. At Christmas and two other times a year, I will have a vacation where, unless there is some real problem, I stay off e-mail."

So, I asked, he defined a vacation as getting away from e-mail? He replied, "Well, there also better be a beach and the kids and some other things. But, yeah, that's a part of it."

When I mentioned that some people define a vacation as not taking their cell phone, he replied that he almost never used a cell phone.

As for his reading habits, in 2003, Gates was doing 60 percent of his reading online. He still read certain news media, such as *The Economist,* offline. But when it came to the daily newspapers (*The Seattle Times, The New York Times, The Wall Street Journal*), he perused them on screen, enjoying the immediacy. Only on Sundays—clearly his day to relax—did he wind up reading far more offline.

His favorite way to communicate remained memo writing. Since giving up the CEO post, he has been writing more memos than ever.

He reads a lot of fiction and, because bridge is such a huge hobby of his, a lot of bridge books. Reading an entire book once on the takeout double in bridge, he then confronted a bemused Melinda, who asked how anyone could spend 150 pages on such a topic. Gates later half-quipped, "And they don't even cover it nearly as well as they should. It needed to be a much longer book."

Because of his increasing interest in his own philanthropy, he spends half of each vacation reading books on world health. ("There are better detective stories there," he told Bill Moyers, "than there are in the area of crime.")

Bill Gates in 2003 was much more diverse than he had been before. In earlier years, he devoted virtually every minute to the nurturing of Microsoft and to the development of new technology. That was changing. In the next chapter, we examine how being a more diverse figure helped him to reinvent Microsoft.

6

Meeting with Former African Prostitutes

It all seemed to be coming together for Bill Gates that winter of 2003. He was spending a large chunk of time overseeing Microsoft's technology; he was pleased that so much of the technology he and his researchers at Microsoft had envisioned ten or fifteen years ago was finally gaining a foothold in the marketplace. The remarkable power and smallness of computer chips had enabled the transfer of personal computer technology to a whole new variety of digital devices from wrist watches to tablets, from cell phones to personal digital assistants. Gates had once dreamed of such things. Now they were reality. That gave him special pride.

The previous five years had been a period of highs and lows for Gates, for Microsoft, and indeed for the entire personal computer industry. As more and more computer technology was reaching the home and office, pundits were debating whether technology really mattered. A fierce debate ensued over the issue. Gates pointed to the technology advances of the past few years to buttress his argument that technology mattered very much. "For someone like Bill, who has religion about technology, yes it does matter," said Corey duBrowa, the Microsoft public relations man. "It's a sweet time for him. It's exciting for him because all of this is beginning to pay off."

It was a sweet time for him too in that he was enjoying the increasingly visible role he was playing in his philanthropy, studying what were the best uses for his vast wealth, and then applying it, often to save lives.

No wonder then that he seemed, as almost everyone who saw him in those days remarked, a different person, a more cheerful and relaxed figure, someone completely at ease about his life. His father noted that his son felt less overburdened. There was a softening in the son that was due, in his father's view, to Microsoft's maturing, to Steve Ballmer's taking on the CEO role, and, of course, to the formal end of the trial.

Bill Gates's main task, however, was to help Microsoft and himself turn over a new leaf, to portray himself and the company in a new, positive light. He never made that point in public because he understood, better than most, that it was in his and the company's interests to avoid airing controversy. He was quite aware that his critics and the public at large were still waiting and watching. They would continue to put him to a test and, for that reason, he wanted the public to see only Bill Gates the master technologist, the healer, the humble distributor of his wealth to the sick and uneducated. That was the image he hoped the media would help nurture. In that way, the image of him as a shrewd monopolist, trying to coerce companies to sell his products, could be erased forever from the public's mind.

And so he embarked on a personal campaign, cleverly choosing those moments when the public would have a chance to see him. He relied on his greatest assets—the facts that his was arguably the most widely recognized name on the planet and that he was the richest man alive.

A Malaria-Ridden Child

Clearly, Gates would have been pleased that one outcome of his philanthropy was a new, more benign image of himself. Not only would his image benefit, but Microsoft's would also. Nothing illustrated that better than a set of pictures that appeared across America one fall day in 2003. One was a photo of Bill Gates with a malaria-ridden child while on his journey to Africa on behalf of the Bill and Melinda Gates Foundation. Another was his appearance on the *Today* show that same day announcing that he was donating millions of dollars to inner-city New York City schools. Bill Gates was depicted as the benign, nice guy in action, saving lives abroad, helping poor kids at home.

The media could have reacted cynically to Gates's role in his own philanthropy. But, it was his good fortune that the media did not regard Gates's good deeds as so much froth; the media chose to treat his philanthropy with great respect, as if Gates was doing not only serious work but significant work as well. Buoyed by that warm, widespread coverage, Gates began to hope that such acts would help in his and his company's rehabilitation. Trying to project a new, softer, more positive image for himself was his way of saving the company he had cofounded; for he knew that the rehabilitation of Microsoft was very much wrapped up in the rehabilitation of Bill Gates.

The timing was just right for him. He was getting more and more comfortable with spending his time on non-Microsoft pursuits—on things that would project a positive image. Helping him, especially in his philanthropy, were his wife of seven years and his three children. There was certainly no more positive image than that of a man devoted to his wife and children.

Gates met Melinda French, his future wife, while she was working at Microsoft. She had grown up in a Dallas suburb and then enrolled at Duke University, majoring in computer science, graduating in 1986. A year later she received an MBA from the same school. That same year she joined Microsoft, helping to develop a number of Microsoft's multimedia efforts, including the Internet travel software, Expedia, and the encyclopedia product, Encarta.

On New Year's Day, 1994, Bill and Melinda were married on the golf course belonging to the Manele Bay Hotel in Lanai, Hawaii. To ensure privacy, Gates had taken all 250 rooms at the hotel— including his own $1,300-a-night suite. He also booked all helicopter services on Maui to prevent photographers from renting them. Willie Nelson provided the entertainment. Among the attendees were Warren Buffett, Paul Allen, and Gates's best man, Steve Ballmer.

Melinda retired from Microsoft in 1996 as general manager of information products to care for their first child, a daughter named Jennifer.

The addition of a wife and children had a profound effect on Gates. In earlier days, he had sanctioned carefree bachelorhood as the preferred lifestyle of the Microsoft culture. Now, with a family, he liked his new life; he became a proud father. He was, in his own phrase, more balanced.

Husbands are often reluctant to talk about their wives in public, but not Gates. He told the media that she had become a partner for him in his career. He talked to her every night, he said, about work-related issues. They talked a great deal about the way the dot-com era distorted values and how much that bothered the two of them. He credited Melinda as well with helping him through the transition with Steve Ballmer in the early 2000s.

Gates was a more balanced person at work as well. Some Microsoft employees recalled conversations with Gates revolving entirely around technology; but other employees who spoke to him after the birth of a Gates child found him eager to dwell on nontechnology subjects. There was the time in 1999 that Peter Haynes, Microsoft's director of strategic communications, sat down with Gates the day after Bill's second child, a son named Rory, was born. For twenty minutes before they got around to business, he and Gates talked kids. (The third Gates child, Phoebe, was born in 2002.)

Gates shelters his family from the glare of publicity as much as possible. Nearly everyone in Seattle knows where Bill Gates lived. The mansion he had built for an estimated $75 million on Lake Washington is visible to tour boats cruising by on the lake. But few have ever caught a glimpse of the family. That's how big the place is. Melinda remained largely anonymous, cherishing her privacy. Rarely did she appear in public. She gave the occasional speech. She rarely granted press interviews. (She did speak to journalists who accompanied Bill and her on their 2003 African journey.) She helped her husband salvage some privacy as well, making sure to sit on the outside of a restaurant table to keep autograph hounds as well as frustrated Windows customers at bay.

As his family grew, Bill Gates had to wrestle with the question of what to do with his growing fortune. He could give a small portion of it to charity and keep the rest. Or, he could donate most of it to others and keep a small amount for himself and his family. If his views toward philanthropy in earlier days had prevailed, he likely would have kept most of his wealth. He had shown little interest in creating a foundation, though he had much encouragement to do so. "He regarded it," his father, Bill Gates Sr., noted, "as another management problem which would intrude on his time, which was his most precious commodity and so he had uniformly repelled the idea of starting a foundation."

He always put the business first. When his mother mentioned that a company should be involved in civic affairs and suggested that Microsoft engage in a United Way campaign, her son resisted. "He thought the most important thing to do," his father said, "was to have the business succeed." The young entrepreneur told his mother that philanthropy was fine, but he had to pay his employees, to drum up enough business; after all, it was a very competitive environment out there. Eventually, young Gates came around, putting a United Way campaign in place at Microsoft. "So," his father said, "his instincts for philanthropy were there."

But those instincts led Gates to think of philanthropy as something he might do only in his sixties, after he had distanced himself from his day job at Microsoft. He had a few projects in mind that he would like to fund in the near future but large-scale philanthropy was, for him, many decades down the road.

A Visit to the Movies

In the meantime, organizations solicited Bill and Melinda Gates to give money or time to various causes. The Microsoft chairman and CEO was often too busy to give the careful answers required of the requests and so there were delays in responding. That led to complaints.

Then, late in 1994, Gates went to the movies with Melinda and his father. Bill Gates Sr. knew of the requests that had been streaming in to his son and that had gone unanswered. Some people were saying that his son was not generous. His father had an idea. While the three of them waited in line to buy tickets for the movie, Bill Gates Sr. volunteered to help them with those unanswered requests. "They thought that was a great idea," Bill Gates Sr. said. "My son decided maybe it was time to start a foundation." What had changed Bill's mind? "I think it was the revelation that maybe there was somebody available to take the responsibility for managing [the foundation]," his father said.

Other reasons existed for Bill Gates to become generous. By April 1999, his personal fortune had grown to $100 billion. He and Melinda had wanted children, but having those children raised the question of how much of his incredible wealth he would pass on to them. Gates came to believe that wealth of that magnitude was more of a handicap than a blessing. For his children to inherit a fortune of that size would not help society, nor would it help his children. It simply was not constructive, in his view, for his children to inherit billions of dollars. And so Bill and Melinda Gates decided that they would keep a small percentage for the children that would allow them to lead comfortable lives. The rest would be given back to society.

What was the best way to put the Gates's fortune to use? For Bill Gates the question was not trivial: He wanted to have a larger effect than other foundations had had. He was familiar with the work of the Rockefeller Foundation, one of the most prominent of the foundations, and he vowed to himself that his foundation would differ from Rockefeller's. It would do even more good work than the Rockefeller Foundation had. But upon delving more deeply into Rockefeller, he came to appreciate the attempts of Rockefeller University's medical research teams to prevent hookworm and yellow fever. What he liked most about Rockefeller was its global approach, its interest in devoting its resources to all of humanity, not just to American citizens. He decided to tailor his foundation after the best efforts of Rockefeller.

How Could This Happen?

As he looked at the work of other foundations, he began to focus his thinking on the hot spots of scientific research: information technology and medical technology. It was clear that in the coming two decades, significant advances would occur in these fields. But, he asked himself, who would benefit from these advances? Would only the wealthy be helped or would the world at large benefit? Gates feared that he knew the answer to these questions. He came around to the view that he must help the world's poor. He must direct his funds toward population-related issues, especially the field of reproductive health.

He came across *The World Development Report for 1993* that mentioned various diseases as well as infant mortality. The report told of a half million people dying a year, yet the media seemed oblivious to the fact. How could that be, he asked himself? Why wasn't the media focusing on the magnitude of that tragedy? It occurred to him that most people had difficulty relating to the deaths of so many people. Still, he was profoundly shocked. When Gates spoke to population experts, they mentioned how vaccinations would help; they also noted that such programs were very expensive.

Impressed that vaccinations were an important place for him to start, Gates made an initial grant for vaccine purchase and distribution. The grant included the establishment of an advisory group. At the time of the first meeting of that group, he invited the participants to have dinner with him and Melinda at his home. As the conversation progressed and the guests expressed such wholehearted enthusiasm for the vaccination program, Gates encouraged them to be expansive in their planning.

"Think big," he urged them as the dinner was winding up. The dinner guests were excited by the evening. As for Gates, he began to believe that his wealth just might do some good.

One thought bothered him: What if his wealth did improve global health, and then that improvement led to a reduction in population growth? "If you improve health, aren't you just dooming people to deal with such a lack of resources where they won't be educated or they won't have enough food? You know, sort of a Malthusian view of what would take place." But even such thoughts did not keep him from going forward with distributing his wealth. He had become far too sensitive to the plight of small children who were dying in such numbers from AIDS, tuberculosis, and malaria in the Third World. He was surprised to find what he called "such a systematic failure in world health programs. . . . Those lives were being treated as if they weren't valuable. Well, when you have the resources that could make a very big impact, you can't just say to yourself, 'Okay, when I'm sixty, I'll get around to that. Stand by.'"

By August 1999, Gates had given $6 billion to two foundations he had previously set up: the Gates Learning Foundation, which worked to expand access to technology through public libraries, and the William H. Gates Foundation, which concentrated on improving global health. Turning over another $17 billion in philanthropy, in January 2000 he merged these foundations and established the Bill and Melinda Gates Foundation. No one had expected Gates to give away so much so soon. Philanthropy specialists were staggered at the sums such a young donor was providing—while he was still alive. It could not escape anyone's notice, however, that the creation of the new foundation came in the midst of Microsoft's antitrust trial.

The foundation became the wealthiest charitable foundation in the world. As of November 2003, it had an endowment of $26 billion, which was ten times the size of the Rockefeller Foundation, three times the size of the Ford Foundation, and just a bit larger than the Wellcome Trust, a London charity that was once the world's largest such fund.

In its December 1, 2003, edition, *BusinessWeek* placed Bill and Melinda Gates at the top of its annual list of the fifty most generous philanthropists, noting that they had given or pledged $22.9 billion between 1999 and 2003. Second on the list was Intel cofounder Gordon Moore, having given or pledged $7 billion in that same four-year period; third, Wall Street investor George Soros, having given or pledged $2.4 billion.

Required to disperse 5 percent of its endowment annually, the Gates Foundation has been giving away over $1 billion for each of the last few years. In 2003, it gave $1.2 billion in grants.

In 2003, Gates seemed to be devoting the bulk of his time to Microsoft, but the truth was that the foundation was occupying more and more of his thoughts these days. Once, it would not have been possible to get him off the subject of technology. By 2003, all he wanted to talk about was conquering disease in the Third World. "If you get him talking about his philanthropy work," said one Microsoft executive, "you won't get him off that." He tried to separate his work at Microsoft from the foundation, but on occasion the two overlapped. Once he had on his desk ten issues of something called *The Morbidity & Mortality Weekly Report*. Microsoft employees curiously asked him what he was doing with such a report. Gates, noting that the issues were from the 1980s when AIDS had first appeared, said they were real collector's items.

No Weekend Philanthropists

Clearly, Bill Gates's philanthropy had added a whole new challenge for him, one that gave him a greater sense of contentment. His father, Bill Gates Sr., said it best: "He is comfortable in this role. . . . He believes he understands [the best way to distribute his funds] and he *does* understand it. . . . His time commitment has become less than 24/7 to the company. I don't mean to imply that he doesn't have a full commitment, but it isn't the extravagant commitment that he did earlier."

In 2002 and 2003, Gates deliberately increased his personal role in the foundation's work, made on-site visits to places where he donated his wealth, and granted interviews about his philanthropy, including a long one with Bill Moyers in May 2003. Gates could have chosen to stay at home and dole out his billions to all sorts of worthwhile charities; but he wanted to be personally involved in the foundation's work. "Both Bill and Melinda are not weekend philanthropists," said Joe Cerrell, director of public affairs for the foundation. "They spend an enormous amount of time understanding these issues."

Still, it would have been far easier to write a check and leave to others whether the money was spent usefully. Gates, however, knew that just cutting checks was not what he had in mind in creating the foundation. "Most people," said Cerrell, "can just cut checks and feel that they've done a good job supporting worthwhile causes; but if you're trying to have the impact on the scale at which Bill and Melinda are hoping, then it's an incredibly difficult process to understand how monies can be used."

If he was going to be personally involved, he did not want to hold back. When Gates met with foundation officials early on, he made it clear to them that he was prepared to visit any site, no matter how gut-wrenching or depressing the experience. He was undertaking such overseas visits for the foundation once a year.

He had gone to India in November 2002 to focus attention on India's increasing AIDS problem. (Some 25 million Indians were expected to contract the disease by 2010.) He pledged $100 million to government agencies and charity groups. At one clinic he personally immunized some children; afterwards he said he wasn't sure how good he had been at it.

While the visits abroad gave him the chance to see the problems up close, sometimes he became the main story, and that could be distracting. His visit to India was called the biggest event in that country since the Beatles had arrived there. He was worshipped, one Indian editor remarked, almost like a demigod. Wherever Gates went, he was the center of attention. One newspaper account noted that "hands were shaken, backs were slapped, and through it all, Gates wore the painful frozen grin of a Hollywood star at the Oscars. 'Mr. Gates, you are my idea of the ideal man,' purred one former Indian fashion model. 'You are rich, and you are powerful.'"

Grilled Prawns and Diet Coke

Gates paid his respects to Indian know-how, conscious that a significant portion of Microsoft employees come from that part of the world. Indeed, in 2003, 29 percent of the company's American-based technology-oriented employees (including developers, product managers, system development engineers, and test engineers) were of Asian origin. The Indians revered him enough to forgive a Gates remark from a previous trip, that South Indians were the "second smartest people in the world, after the Chinese." Had anyone else said this, one reporter noted, editorialists might have urged that he not be permitted back in India.

The Gates's visit to India was covered extensively in the local media. It was reported what he ate for dinner (roast lamb, grilled prawns, black lentils, vegetable kebabs), what he found in his minibar (Diet Coke), and what he did for relaxation (go online on his high-speed ISDN connection to check in with the office).

In September 2003, he traveled to Africa and announced a $168 million grant to accelerate research into malaria, a mosquito-borne disease that was killing over a million people every year, most of them young African children. Until then, malaria research had been seriously underfinanced, with only about $100 million a year spent on the field, far less than the amount earmarked for AIDS research. Gates went into hospital wards where patients were suffering from the final stages of HIV/AIDS where no treatment was available. In Mozambique, he visited two people with cerebral malaria, one of the most lethal forms of that disease.

He was willing to meet with anyone who could help save lives. In Botswana, he met with exprostitutes, who danced and sang for him and Melinda in a hospital. They were taking part in a program the Gateses were helping to fund aimed at eradicating AIDS in Africa.

Later, Bill and Melinda asked some sensitive questions of the women:

"Did the men of Botswana use condoms during sex to protect themselves or their partners from the AIDS virus?"

"Sometimes" came the answer.

"Were condoms easy to get?"

"Yes."

"Would men pay more for sex without a condom than with one?"

Again the reply was yes.

His session with the former prostitutes was undoubtedly the most bizarre scene of Bill Gates's travels, but it showed how immersed he had become in world health issues, how he had created another persona for himself in the early 2000s, and how at ease he was with his new life.

While he was on these journeys, he did not forget the public relations value such visits had back home. Accordingly, he wrote articles for such newspapers as the *Financial Times* and *The New York Times*, talking up his foundation's work, making sure the articles were timed to his visits.

Bill Gates was able to devote so much energy to philanthropy in 2003 because he was getting more and more comfortable with his wealth. It had taken him quite some time to adjust to having all that money. At the start, he had been uneasy and embarrassed about his wealth. Other people amassed great fortune, he had always believed; it could not have happened to him. Easily able to afford all consumer items, big or small, he became shy about such purchases. When Nathan Myhrvold tried to convince him to buy a jet plane for himself, Gates replied meekly, "Those are for big shots." Still, when Myhrvold bought his plane, Gates followed suit. When cell phones first appeared on the market at $1,500 a pop, Gates considered them far too expensive to purchase even though he possessed enough wealth to buy entire cell phone companies! Eventually, he saw a cell phone's practical value and obtained one.

It was certainly understandable for Gates to be ill at ease with his billions. In 1999, when he became the first person to amass over $100 billion in wealth, it was said that he possessed more wealth than all of the African countries put together. His personal fortune was greater as well than the economic output of all but eighteen of the world's richest nations. The media enjoyed calculating Gates's billions. For instance, Gates was earning $4.566 million an hour in April 1999 when he surpassed the $100 billion mark. If his wealth had continued to grow at the 61 percent compound annual rate it had enjoyed thus far, he was due to become the world's first trillionaire in 2004. That, of course, was not going to happen since Microsoft's stock, the source of Gates's wealth, had been reduced in value by nearly half after 1999.

There were all sorts of other oddball statistics related to Gates's fortune:

- In April 1999, his fortune was twice as much as all the $1 bills in circulation.
- On January 20, 1999, when Microsoft announced its quarterly profits, his riches grew by $3.5 billion in just three minutes.
- If he had stashed his cash in dollar bills under his mattress, he would have to parachute sixteen miles down to his bedroom floor every morning.
- Perhaps most spectacularly, with the United Kingdom's gross domestic product in 1997 at $1.22 trillion, if Gates's wealth were to continue to increase, it would have overtaken Britain's output by 2005.

In 2003, he was working hard not to let all that wealth corrupt what he believed to be the right kind of values for anyone to have. "I think your psyche about money is set by the time you're in your early twenties," he told a reporter. With a father who was a successful lawyer, he defined the Gates family as most likely upper middle class. Then he quipped, "At this point I'm clearly not by some definition 'middle class.' Hopefully my psyche hasn't been too warped in terms of the way I'll set my kids' allowance and the way I'll think about what they should be exposed to. It will be a lot like what my parents did." In time, so comfortable was he about his wealth that he could even joke in public about his fortune as he did at a Microsoft analysts meeting in July 2003 in Redmond. Showing some spam to the audience on a big screen, Gates congratulated the fellow who sent him an e-mail recently promising to get him out of debt. He obviously had the wrong person, Gates joked.

Gates had good reason to believe that stepping up his foundation efforts and becoming less visible at Microsoft would win him better media coverage. He had already been the focus of an extremely warm piece in *Fortune* magazine in July 2002 written by Brent Schlender. The writer suggested that the new Gates was "noticeably older, weirdly wiser, and maybe even a little humble." Schlender had spent a fair amount of time with Gates and found him now enjoying life in ways that he had not before. He attributed the upswing in Gates's mood to four people: first, his wife, Melinda ("There couldn't be anybody better for Bill"); second and third, the then two Gates children ("two of the nicest, happiest kids you ever saw"); and fourth, Steve Ballmer, presumably for freeing up so much time for Gates.

Saving Lives on a Vast Scale

Of Gates, *Fortune*'s Schlender wrote, "Now he is very happy. He has a smile on his face all the time." The writer found Gates's life not bad at all. "If you end up with a business you've created that's had incredible impact on the world, a foundation that is probably going to have more impact than any foundation in history, and a happy family life, then you're batting pretty damn good." Bill Gates or Waggener Edstrom, his PR firm, could not have written it better.

Buoyed by such favorable press, Gates had increasing confidence in 2003 that he could shape his image more positively. He might have won some favor in the press by permitting photographers to show his family in action; but he would not allow the media to focus on his family. Photographs of the Gates children never appeared in public. Melinda, as noted, was rarely seen as well. But he was perfectly willing to have extensive coverage of his work to save lives. It was easy to understand why after noting what *The New York Times* wrote of him on July 13, 2003: "Those who think of Mr. Gates as a ruthless billionaire monopolist, the man who was so testy and sarcastic with government prosecutors during the Microsoft anti-trust trial, may find it hard to reconcile that image with one of a humorously self-deprecating philanthropist." It was not that the *Times* had completely fallen in love with Mr. Gates. But a new tone was creeping into its coverage.

Astutely seeking to exploit this new tone, Gates invited three journalists along for his African journey in 2003 and the effort paid off handsomely.

Some people remained cynical and thought Gates was engaging in the philanthropy, making the visit to Africa, all because he secretly wanted to sell computers. Well, certainly in the beginning he might have thought some fringe benefit existed for Microsoft. But then he went to Soweto in South Africa, where someone wanted to power up a computer. To do so, they had to build a 200-yard extension cord that was plugged into a diesel-powered generator. It was then that Gates had a kind of epiphany and the journalists were there to record the moment.

Gates realized that these people needed other things first before computers. A time had existed when he had preached that everyone needed a computer, that he wanted all six billion people on the planet to own a computer; but now he considered the two billion people who lived in misery and poverty, and thought, They deserve to improve their lives—and computers won't do the trick, not at first at least. The only way was to improve their health conditions. When they got some food in their stomachs and got some education, then they would appreciate getting their hands on a computer; but not now, not yet. That was the moment he became a different Bill Gates. And the whole world had the chance to learn about the epiphany almost in real-time thanks to the presence of the media and their glowing reports back home.

One of the reporters on the tour of Mozambique, South Africa, and Botswana was *The New York Times*'s Nicholas D. Kristof, who wrote,

"[F]rankly, one of the best things to happen to Africa is their [Melinda and Bill Gates's] fervor to alleviate third world fevers. Maybe it's just a way of assuaging guilt for software sins, or a P.R. effort to burnish his image—whatever, he's saving lives on a vast scale."

It was the kind of image building Gates had been seeking and was now getting—and from no less an institution than *The New York Times*. Neither the *Times* nor any other newspaper still thought it necessary either to point out that Gates had until recently been one of the most vilified characters in the Western world or to explain why he had been! Instead, look at the kind of coverage he was getting from the *Times*'s Kristof, who wrote the following about the Gateses' African trip:

> The buzz among African aid workers is that Mr. Gates will be remembered more for his work fighting disease than for Windows. Certainly the wealth of the Bill and Melinda Gates Foundation is improving the prospect that vaccines will be found for malaria and AIDS. The foundation's most banal work is with vaccines, but those programs have already given out vaccines that will save 300,000 lives. Hey, that's better than most rapacious monopolists do.
>
> . . . AIDS, malaria and tuberculosis are all worsening in the third world and now kill a combined six million people per year. This slaughter is one of the central moral challenges we face today, yet Western governments have abdicated responsibility, and Western medical science is uninterested in diseases that kill only poor people. Many times more money addresses erectile dysfunction than malaria.
>
> So at least somebody is stepping up to the plate.

Among the journalists who accompanied Gates on his African visit, there was some quibbling with the fact that his philanthropy had not yet produced any new drugs or vaccines that it had paid to develop. The journalists noted that the foundation's greatest successes had been in helping Third World countries adopt vaccines that were developed before the involvement of the Gates. But the quibbling seemed secondary and injected, so it seemed, only to balance the incredibly positive treatment the journalists had been giving the Gateses' philanthropic efforts.

All in all, the coverage of Gates in 2003 had taken a remarkable turn. Only the year before, the federal government and Gates's company had been involved in one of the biggest legal battles of the modern era, and Gates's main image had been of that rapacious monopolist to which Kristof had referred. Now, in a complete turnabout, here was a reporter for *The New York Times* suggesting that since the same federal government had been exhibiting such neglect toward the world's poor, people ought to acknowledge Bill Gates for taking over and doing the job for it!

And, if positive treatment in *The New York Times* mattered, an appearance on national television was even more significant. Gates understood how important it was to create a positive image every time the public had a chance to see him on TV. That was why his appearance on the *Today* show on September 17, 2003, was so significant. It was on that day that his foundation announced it was giving $51 million to help increase graduation rates for inner-city high school students.

For Gates, the TV appearance was a chance to sit next to Caroline Kennedy Schlossberg and talk enthusiastically about giving these kids a second chance to break out of their problematic lives. But it was also a chance for him to be seen for five full minutes on national television projecting the most positive set of images possible. He was immensely aided by the softball questioning of Katie Couric, who moderated the discussion, largely skipping over Microsoft's recent dark past, only mentioning the irony that Gates later that day would hold a joint news conference with the new chancellor of New York City schools, Joel Klein, the same man who had prosecuted Microsoft in *United States v. Microsoft*. She asked Gates how it felt to be teaming up with Klein, and he responded tersely that he was glad to be on the same side with him.

What appeared on TV screens that morning throughout America was the kinder, gentler face of Bill Gates—and, indirectly, of Microsoft.

For Gates to have reconfigured his life and his career the way he did in 2003 was shrewd, even brilliant. As chief software architect, he was more valuable to Microsoft than ever. When he was at Redmond, he was supervising the company's product strategies in a far more focused way than ever before. He was not invisible, but he was less visible. He appeared at Microsoft's most important events, but he was as often as not sharing the stage with CEO Steve Ballmer. He saved most of his public appearances for the times when he appeared saintly, when the name Bill Gates and the phrase *saving lives* began to sound synonymous.

Though at times in 2003 he was wandering far afield from the company, Gates was playing his part in the reinventing of Microsoft, a part that was in many ways far more complicated and far more subtle than Steve Ballmer's. Both men put at the top of their minds the creation of a new Microsoft. We now turn to examine the major role that Steve Ballmer was playing in that effort.

PART IV

How Steve Ballmer Reinvented Microsoft

7

Open and Respectful

Until some time in the second half of the 1990s, Microsoft had been the undisputed king of software, the leading force of that industry. It had faced challenges in the past, sometimes gut-wrenching ones, but the company had always come through and figured out how to flourish. Now the challenges appeared not just greater; they seemed to test the company in a way that had not happened before.

It was all occurring at the same time—a whole set of changes and entanglements that dominated the second half of the 1990s for Microsoft and forced it into a defensive mode for much of that period. First it was the Internet that had come along to challenge its central place in the high-tech world; then it was the nearly lethal combination of its rivals and the U.S. government mounting a legal attack on the company; finally, the dot-com revolution suddenly appeared with its tantalizing offers to Microsoft employees of overnight stock option–induced riches.

One day Microsoft had an identity. The next, that identity was blurred. Was it still a start-up? How could it be two decades after its founding? Shouldn't it be a mature company, with none of the scrappiness but a good deal of discipline?

There were pulls and tugs on the company from all directions. Some people wanted it to remain a start-up, flexing its own muscles, thinking its products were the greatest, trivializing competitors, believing the worst of them, and always assuming that any problem was soluble given enough hard work and enthusiasm. But others hoped Microsoft would turn it into a more mature company.

One thing was clear: As the decade of the 1990s was ending, the company was suffering from a rather large identity crisis. Jeff Raikes, group vice president, business productivity services management, suggested that at a certain point Microsoft had to ask itself just who it was. "We are a company that focuses in on helping people realize their potential. But we are in an industry that has matured and our position in that industry had brought new responsibilities to us that we were not delivering on enough. We grew up working hard every day, in effect fighting to try and do the best job versus the competition in delivering value through software; but we had to learn that there were other things that were expected of us. We had to explain ourselves better and we had to do things differently."

As an example Raikes noted that as part of its sense of being an industry leader in the past, Microsoft had labored to integrate capabilities into the computer's operating environment. To Raikes—and to others at Microsoft—integrating those capabilities was an obvious thing to do. It was the company's way of helping the consumer to obtain better products. "Go back to 1990. You had to create a graphical environment to bring MS-DOS together. It was hard for the customer. So our responsibility was to advance each of those capabilities and integrate them in a way that provided a rich, simplified user experience." It was, in Raikes's view, great software and the integration of features into the operating system made eminent sense; so far so good. But Microsoft had failed to realize that it had to do more than simply come up with great software; it had to make sure that everyone in the outside world understood that the company had only the best of intentions. "We have to explain why [the integration of features into Windows is] not a bad thing and do more to explain what we have to integrate so people don't feel they are blind-sided. We have to work harder than other companies to be open as to what we are doing and what our plans are."

It would not be easy to be that open, he predicted. "This means sometimes we're sharing a lot of information and not getting a lot of information back. For most business relationships, that will seem strange, but that's part of the situation we're in today. Because we play a leading role in providing the components of software, others want to know where we're going. And this is a business where you can't always be perfectly clear. We have to say that sometimes our plans have had to change."

Who Should Lead the Fight?

Although the rebooting of Microsoft was about a number of things, it was especially about being more open and being more respectful of others in the outside world; and it was about communicating what the company was doing in a way that others would understand and appreciate what Microsoft was doing rather than condemn the company for its products.

But who was going to lead that initiative? Would it be Bill Gates or Steve Ballmer? Or should both men lead it together?

Certainly both men had been chastened by the legal battles and on the surface they both seemed ready to turn Microsoft in a new direction. But had they changed enough? Were they ready to forget the past, the nasty allegations, and get on with a whole new program of reform? Some at Microsoft were not at all sure.

One who thought both men had changed sufficiently to make the reforms work was Charles Simonyi, who began working for Microsoft in 1981. He became director of application development, chief architect, and, most recently, distinguished engineer. He hired and managed teams that developed Microsoft Multiplan, Microsoft Word, Microsoft Excel, and other best-selling software applications. More than two decades later, he spoke about how there were two ways for a company to be successful. One was to change the people at the top; the other was to hope that leaders change. "That's what Microsoft has done. If you look at the content of Steve's and to some extent Bill's communications, you will see that shift. You see more emphasis on the larger picture of the industry, the issues that are current with the customers; a greater variety in a customer base, the current initiative with trustworthy computing."

But even if Gates understood the need for a more customercentric Microsoft, he was still not automatically the best person to lead the fight for internal reform and to articulate what the company needed to do to improve its business practices. Gates *was* the right person to lead that part of the reform campaign that had to do with technology; and he was doing just that through his Trustworthy Computing initiative. In promoting that initiative, Gates had only to talk up the need to improve on the quality of Microsoft's products; he had no need—nor any desire, for that matter—to use the Trustworthy Computing program as an illustration of how Microsoft should adjust its ways of doing business. He still maintained that Microsoft was innocent of all legal charges. No, he was not the right one at all to call for Microsoft to set a new tone. That had to be left to Steve Ballmer. The timing was absolutely right. Ballmer was fast becoming the main spokesperson for the company. Gates remained a spokesperson, but Ballmer spent more time in front of Microsoft audiences, talking about business and product strategies; and he was talking to customers more than Gates.

Veteran Microsoft executives thought Steve Ballmer the ideal person to carry the ball because Ballmer had gone through a transformation, a positive one. "Steve is a totally different person from when I joined Microsoft in 1990," observed Jim Allchin. He did not present a complete list of Ballmer's previous alleged shortcomings, but he did spell out the way he had changed: "The way he treats people, the respect he shows, his controlled enthusiasm versus his being completely out of control in the earlier days. It's nothing but positive now. Steve is just amazing. One day he basically said, 'I'm not going to swear any more.' This is a man who has changed. He said, 'I'm going to lose weight.' It was done. 'I'm going to be respectful at meetings even if I disagree'; he's still working at that. The beatings [figurative, one assumes] that took place here when people didn't have their act together were significant.

Now he gets the same effect without the frontal assault. He's matured."

Softening some of his rougher edges, carrying less baggage, being less familiar to outsiders than Gates, Ballmer had gained a new authority, a new commanding presence, a new self-respect and respect—all of which made him the natural candidate to take the lead in putting the company on a new path.

A Need to Communicate

Ballmer seemed to understand that, if he were going to bring about reform within Microsoft, he had to manage that reform, he had to communicate the need for that reform, he had to articulate what that reform was all about in ways that had never been necessary in earlier days.

When the company was smaller, Bill Gates had no need to worry that everyone was on the same page, that everyone understood what company policies were and what their roles were in implementing those policies. He did not have to worry about employing methods to get across broad principles and the elements of the corporate culture, or to figure out how to keep people enthusiastic and aligned with the company's strategies. As long as Gates could meet with everyone in the company any time he wished, he knew that he had an easy channel of communication—and he was assured that every employee was within hearing distance.

Ballmer's challenge was far grander. He had to reach 55,000 people in seventy countries. He had to explain to them why it was necessary for the company to change direction when Gates had been saying for years that the company had been behaving properly and didn't need to change at all. He had to be willing to stand in front of Microsoft audiences and external audiences as well and say things that appeared to run counter to the company's once-vaunted culture.

To be sure, Gates understood how necessary it was to talk up the new reforms. It was not enough to say that there had to be reforms;

those reforms had to be sold to the rank and file. "Not only do Steve and I need to make really good decisions, we need to articulate why we are making those decisions. . . . They need to hear the criteria if they are going to really contribute." But he left most of the articulating to Steve Ballmer.

On November 13, 2003, Ballmer sat down for a question-and-answer session with *Business Week* editor-in-chief Stephen Shepard at the 92nd Street Y in New York City. Shepard asked him to talk about what he had learned from the whole antitrust trial.

The key takeaway, Ballmer suggested, was that people had "increased expectations" toward Microsoft and so the company had to step back and say, "It doesn't matter how we may have seen ourselves; we have to see ourselves as others see us."

Microsoft had learned, he went on, how to put processes in place that would put a stop to aberrant business practices. And, he hinted elliptically, it wasn't as hard as most at Microsoft had feared. "We know how hard it is and we're working super hard to make sure we absolutely comply with all of the responsibilities and obligations that we picked up in our consent decree, and it's harder probably than I guessed it would be, not to control errant behavior. You just want to make sure you absolutely have the right processes in place to make sure you're doing exactly what you committed to do to the U.S. government.

". . . We've educated our people with what it takes. We tell them that we're very focused on compliance; it's a hygiene thing, you could say. It's something we've got to do, we're going to do." Microsoft had a full-time compliance officer, Odell Guyton, as well as special training for officers and employees. It had an Office of Legal Compliance, a special committee of the Board of Directors. It had conducted hundreds of antitrust training sessions for employees around the world.

Ballmer was saying all the right words. He understood, in short, that Microsoft had to change. He had found a way diplomatically, without seeming as if he had lost his mind, to suggest that deep down he understood Microsoft's role in contributing to its legal entanglements.

To have even hinted at such a view within Microsoft prior to the trial's end would have bordered on the heretical, but once the trial was over, Ballmer felt he had an obligation to say these things as part of setting Microsoft on a new course.

Articulate a Vision

It was, of course, not enough to simply inform employees that they had to behave themselves. The world at large had to learn what Microsoft was doing. As Ballmer said, "We sort of have to make sure we're painting for our employees and for the world at large, repainting our vision of what's positive—I mean, let's get on with life now. Forget that you're a good company, bad company; what people really want to know is 'What's your vision for where you as a company will help take me as an individual user?' "

And then, Microsoft had to articulate a new vision.

Ballmer added, "What's your vision for eliminating the pain (the spam, the viruses, etc.) and what's your vision for sort of taking them to new grounds? So we've put a lot of time into this aspect. . . . Our people are working hard to make sure pain points get eliminated in every sense."

Making the process of reform more difficult was the challenging competitive environment that Microsoft faced.

Ballmer had gotten the mix of Microsoft products just right at a time when the personal computer field was dominated by the Internet and wireless technologies embedded in a new range of hand-held devices from cell phones to personal digital assistants to wristwatches.

Microsoft wanted to ride that new wave just as it was trying to ride a wave of business emanating from corporate enterprises. It was trying to evolve from selling software entirely for desktop personal computers to supplying software for the server computers that powered business networks, Web sites, and e-mail systems. By 2003, it was starting to make some important inroads in the highly important Server market as revenues had reached $7.14 billion. Its major offerings were Windows Server, SQL Server, and Exchange Server.

Microsoft hoped that getting a foothold in those corporate computing centers would leverage its business providing Web-based services; those services allowed users to transact business or exchange information online with whatever type of device they wished to use. Ballmer believed that in time Web services would become a major product for Microsoft.

But to move into all of these emerging fields posed a certain risk for Microsoft as it sought to advance growth and at the same time to be more open and respectful, to be more communicative to others, and to be a better partner and leader in the industry; for moving into those areas meant that Microsoft would be competing against companies that had been or were potential partners; and that had been a recipe for trouble in the past. One big question facing Steve Ballmer as 2003 got under way was where to start the reform process.

Wiping the legal slate clean seemed the best place. Microsoft's goal was to associate the company with its products, and not with its alleged improper business practices. If the legal cases could be settled quickly, fewer negative news stories would occur. "We're trying," said Steve Ballmer, "to the best of our ability, where we make reasonable accommodations, we're trying to put these things behind us so that it falls out of people's mindsets."

Ballmer had another good reason to get these cases settled. The torrent of litigation was taking up far too much of the company's time in meetings, e-mails, and memos. Meeting the demands of the discovery process was an increasing burden. By 2003, Microsoft's legal staff had mushroomed to three hundred to handle all of this. (Back in 1988, it had only five attorneys on staff.)

As part of putting the litigation behind it, Microsoft, in January 2003, agreed to pay up to $1.1 billion to California consumers, settling the largest class-action claim against it. Under the settlement, class members would be able to obtain vouchers with a total face value of up to $1.1 billion that could be redeemed for cash against the purchases of a wide variety of platform-neutral computer hardware and software. In 2003, Microsoft had also tentatively reached similar agreements to settle all claims in Montana, Florida, West Virginia, and North Carolina.

On May 29, 2003, Microsoft agreed to pay what was then AOL Time Warner $750 million as part of the settlement of a suit brought by the Netscape unit of AOL Time Warner in January 2002. The Netscape suit alleged violations of antitrust and unfair competition laws and other tort claims relating to Netscape and its Navigator browser. As part of the settlement, Microsoft provided AOL Time Warner with a royalty-free, seven-year license to use Microsoft Internet Explorer technologies with the AOL client. The companies entered into a separate agreement to collaborate on long-term digital media initiatives designed to accelerate the adoption of digital content.

In addition to resolving the AOL case, Microsoft resolved many of the state class-action cases against it.

On October 28, 2003, Microsoft announced that it would pay $200 million to settle consumer class-action lawsuits in five states along with Washington, D.C. There were similar suits pending in five other states. The suits all argued that Microsoft had exploited its monopoly position to overcharge customers for software.

Brad Smith, Microsoft's general counsel, said at the time that the October 2003 settlements meant that Microsoft was well over halfway toward resolving its consumer class-action lawsuits.

The company was still (as of early 2004) embroiled in a European Union investigation as well as a legal challenge from Sun Microsystems. The EU alleged that Microsoft had failed to disclose information that its competitors claimed they needed to interoperate fully with Windows 2000 clients and servers and that it had engaged in discriminatory licensing of that technology as well as improper bundling of multimedia playback technology in the Windows operating system. Sun had filed an antitrust suit against Microsoft early in 2002, but the trial was not expected before 2005.

. . .

Wiping the legal slate clean was the first step in the reform effort. The second was establishing the concepts that would serve as the new cultural underpinning of the company. Ballmer took steps to decide upon and articulate these concepts at the annual executive retreat held March 12–14, 2003, in Semiahmoo, Washington. Then, on June 4, he put the conclusions of Semiahmoo together in a memo that was distributed to Microsoft employees and called "The Microsoft Business Plan."

Throughout the memo, references were made to the way that Microsoft had to behave toward the outside world in order to improve its image. The underlying message was that Microsoft had to become more open and respectful to all those with whom it worked, but especially to customers and developers. Ballmer noted that, above all, customers and developers wanted Microsoft to be more responsive, flexible, and predictable. How to do that was the main issue.

Rethinking Business-as-Usual

Challenges were arising on the competitive front that were bound to test the new "open and respectful" culture that Ballmer was promoting. It seemed safe to say that the stronger the competition, the more difficult it would be for Ballmer to persuade his colleagues at Microsoft to be open and respectful toward outsiders. The biggest challenge was clearly coming from free or noncommercial software, especially Linux. "Without the threat of Linux," said a senior IT executive, "there is nothing that can stop them. I used to say the only thing that could stop them was the Government. But that didn't stop them."

Ballmer observed that "non-commercial software products in general and Linux in particular, present a competitive challenge for us and for our entire industry, and they require our concentrated focus and attention. We will rise to the challenge." He pointed to studies that credited Windows with providing customers with greater security and productivity as well as lower total cost than Linux.

Linux, which was still not that common in personal computers but was increasingly showing up on servers, seemed to have one big advantage, as the senior IT executive noted: "Microsoft is the standard in the world for the things they do, but on the other hand they're not free." Ballmer understood that Linux had that advantage. "We've always been able to go in, in any sales proposition . . . and say we have the best product and we have the cheapest product. We have a . . . weirdo competitor in a sense, because there's no company behind it, you don't exactly know who builds it, you can't call somebody up and find out exactly where it's going, so it's very unusual and it's free.

"For us it's just been new because we've never been at a price premium. We were cheaper than CP/M, our first big competitor. We were cheaper than Lotus, we were cheaper than WordPerfect, we were cheaper than Novell, we were cheaper than Sun, we were cheaper than Oracle, cheaper than IBM, and now you've got a guy basically you can't be cheaper than."

Nonetheless, Ballmer warned in that June 4 memo that Microsoft had to avoid complacency. It must, in short, overhaul all of its old habits. "We need to . . . seriously rethink business-as-usual. We must satisfy or exceed our customers' and partners' expectations for product reliability, security and engineering excellence. Our value proposition must continue to improve and must correspond, and respond, to customer needs. This will help re-energize enthusiasm around our products. We must be more open and consistent in our business interactions, and do a better job of communicating our vision and platform strategy to customers."

He noted that the company was starting to integrate the new "open and respectful" values into its performance review system and into its relationships with customers and partners; it was applying the tenets to all aspects of its business—from product planning to customer interaction to internal processes.

There were six areas in which Microsoft had to do well, he said, in order to take computing to a higher level for customers, to become more open and respectful:

1. Provide breakthrough, high-quality **integrated innovation.**
2. Deliver best-in-class **customer responsiveness.**
3. Make our platform **best for developers.**
4. Deliver **simple, high-value experiences** and services.
5. Reignite **customer enthusiasm** and **tell the Microsoft story.**
6. Build our **talent** pool and increase **productivity.**

The first area, integrated innovation, was a recent Microsoft initiative that Ballmer wanted to improve upon. The notion of integrated innovation was bound to prove antithetical to the normal way that a company scaled. Usually, the more a company grew, the more autonomous the parts farther down in the company became. But autonomy was antithetical to a coordinated execution of product strategy. In effect, Microsoft wanted to have it both ways—to pursue integrated innovation and to encourage autonomy within the lower managerial ranks.

"We have a strategy based on integrated innovation. But the structure," said Craig Mundie, "now allows us to have Steve Ballmer run the thing and add processes as if the businesses were decentralized.

"What we've got is unorthodox, it's hard to replicate, yet it is perfectly matched to the distinctive competencies and products of Microsoft. All of these are threads that are proceeding in parallel—it's the confluence of these things that catalyzes what you see. Before that, it was about features. In the past you bought the right to that product. We only made more money when we offered something that was interesting when you bought the new and abandoned the old. The annuity came only if we added compelling new features. That's how we succeeded in earlier years.

"Now we have to inculcate the company in trustworthy computing. Now with the question of trust, now people have a value associated with elements of our products in the aggregate that wasn't designed in the aggregate. Is it secure? Is it protecting my data? Is it there when I need it? When you hook them together, now the scale of failure is magnified dramatically compared with before. Our strategy was not to become a conglomerate so we didn't acquire other companies; our strategy was to grow in areas where we have our distinctive technology and strategy with integrated innovation."

Business Consistency

Improving what Ballmer called "business consistency" would improve Microsoft's behavior toward outsiders as well, he believed. Business consistently was required to attain customer responsiveness.

"Customers," wrote Steve Ballmer in his memo, "love predictability, and rightly so. . . . [B]usiness consistency means that you make sure customers understand what you're doing, why you're doing it, and the timeframe for whatever the transition is. For example, we shouldn't change from year to year which accounts have customer reps and which don't. We shouldn't randomly change which partners we're working with. We'll always need to be flexible and make changes, but there's a way to do this that appears predictable, rational and reasonable. In engineering, as we decrease support for some legacy technologies in favor of new approaches, we must provide appropriate notice, transition time and consistency for customers."

To improve its image, Microsoft was also trying to create more simplicity in its products. "We seek," said Ballmer, "to deliver software with great functionality that only involves learning a few fundamental concepts—whether you're an end-user, IT professional or developer. This is a great foundation on which to build simple and rich, yet affordable, value propositions for our customers. Our view on this differentiates us from IBM. They believe IT is fundamentally complex and confusing, and that customers should pay consultants for loads of services to help master that complexity."

He hoped to infuse in the high-tech community a new kind of enthusiasm for Microsoft. "We need to rekindle the kind of mass end-user, developer, and IT groundswell that were at the center of the Windows revolution. In recent years we've put a lot of focus on reaching out to CIOs, and we still have work to do to win in the enterprise. But we must also go back to our roots and reach out broadly—in person, online, wherever and whenever we can—to generate enthusiasm around the innovation we bring to market. We need to stimulate communities that support what these innovations can do, and create an emotional attachment to our products. We need to create many opportunities for customers to experience our innovations—demos, online trial, deployment and usage of the actual products."

To generate enthusiasm for Microsoft and its innovative products, Ballmer acknowledged that the company needed to communicate more broadly and in a more human and compelling voice. Accordingly, he promised to increase the company's advertising budget significantly for all audiences—developers, IT, information workers, consumers, small business, and business leaders. He wanted Microsoft to become one of the largest advertisers in its industry. In 2004, Microsoft planned to spend $600 million on advertising. While the amount earmarked for advertising has risen steadily over the years, the 2004 figure was still not a large sum given the company's size. In keeping with the goal of trying to get closer to customers, in 2003 Microsoft had shifted its advertising themes. Earlier advertising had been product-focused; now it was focused more on customer scenarios (looking at how the software helped a business) and on being aspirational (as in the 2003 advertising that spoke of "Your Potential, Our Passion").

The feeling existed within Microsoft, Ballmer said (based on conversations with customers and others), that people would appreciate its innovations and the value those innovations delivered more if they knew the company and its employees better. "This not only helps customers feel good but also helps them understand more of what we do and how to take advantage of what we do. We are putting effort into this by encouraging our developers to participate more in the communities around their products and by communicating broadly to the industry regarding important and often emotionally charged issues and trends such as security, privacy and rights management."

In general, telling the Microsoft story had to be given a new priority; communicating to outsiders had to be increased. Ballmer suggested that Microsoft had to step up its participation in community and online forums significantly. It had to try to communicate new product design to customers earlier through online design discussion. Headquarters staff had to spend time talking to customers—not just CIOs but users, schoolchildren, large groups of IT users, and developers. "All of this work should let people know us better and help them understand more about what we are doing and how to take advantage of it."

So much for the concepts. Now it was time to modify the company's business structure to reflect these new concepts. We turn to these efforts in the next chapter.

8

The Discipline Revolution

For quite some time, Bill Gates managed Microsoft with a few key business principles in mind. He understood the value of keeping head count low, of minimizing costs, and of centralizing as much of the operation as possible. He believed in the management notion of "stretch" before anyone had put a name to it. In time, the company accumulated cash, and spent money on research and development and big product launches, but he always wanted to keep the organization small, always wanted to get everyone to stretch beyond their seeming limits. These became the defining features of Microsoft as the classic start-up.

In Microsoft's early days, when the company was much smaller, Bill Gates's centralized management worked just fine. Scott Oki recalled just how fine: Soon after joining the company in 1982, he was asked to organize an international marketing operation. With only one hundred employees, the decision making at Microsoft was not complex. Oki wrote a business plan to begin an international division and simply showed it to Gates. No explanations were necessary. "I told Bill, 'This is what I want to do. I need $1 million.' He said, 'Go ahead. A million dollars is fine.'"

Even into the early 1990s, Microsoft was not a hard company to manage, at least not in Bill Gates's mind.

The company was essentially a two-product company: operating systems and software applications for personal computers. Most important, it avoided the kind of bureaucracy that plagued other growth-bound companies. Deborah Willingham had been at IBM for fifteen years before joining Microsoft in February 1993 in its product support organization, running its end user technological support. She was struck almost at once upon arriving at Redmond by the lack of red tape. At IBM she did at most one project a year, but at Microsoft she completed six to eight projects in the same amount of time. She saw her mission to be improving the quality of Microsoft's support, and for that she needed support from the top. She was pleasantly surprised to find how easy it was to get to Bill Gates or Steve Ballmer. "There was no bureaucracy. It was clear that decisions were going to be made by Bill and Steve, and that was it. It was simple. If you'd get them on e-mail, you could get a response the same day."

Bob Herbold showed up at Microsoft after twenty-six years at Procter & Gamble. He was also impressed with the quickness of decision making at Microsoft. His previous employer did not let anyone shift on a dime. It was countercultural to do things quickly. "At P&G," Herbold recalled, "there was a ritual way of informing people with fancy memos, but by the time you got the message, four cover notes had been written by other vice presidents. There wasn't the clarity that you had at Microsoft."

Back then, Microsoft executives referred to the way Gates ran the company as hub-and-spoke. Others would say it was simply highly centralized. Through the 1980s and well into the early 1990s, the hub-and-spoke system worked well. But by 1994, with over fifteen thousand employees and nearly $5 billion in revenues, Microsoft's size was causing strains, particularly on Bill Gates. To ease the burden on him, in November 1994 he hired a new executive vice president and chief operating officer, Bob Herbold, luring him away from Procter & Gamble; during Herbold's last six years there, he had been senior vice president for advertising and information services.

Gates, hoping that Herbold would institute some of P&G's big-company efficiencies in budget and management, put the new man in charge of finance, manufacturing and distribution, information systems, human resources, corporate marketing, market research, and public relations—in other words, everything but technology.

Gates had given his all to the technology side, created great products, and built the company into a multibillion-dollar growth machine. But he had cared little about management techniques and had simply let things slip into chaos.

What Herbold found upon arriving was just that: The centralized system of management was shipwrecked. Business units had too many information systems, too many human resources employees, and too many unguided marketing directions. The units defined financial terms differently, complicating Redmond's task of closing the books each quarter. Without adequate performance standards, employees were shifted around willy-nilly. The procurement process was in shambles. No one even had a list of Microsoft's vendors.

Herbold's repair job plugged important gaps. He instituted new business processes, brought headcount down, and got costs under control. He could take partial credit for the fact that over the next six years, profits rose from $1.16 billion to $9.4 billion.

Feeling Burdensome

But, even with someone such as Herbold imposing order, the company remained in its increasingly outmoded hub-and-spoke phase. It was simply growing too large for any one person to manage. And grow it did. Head count was going up. The company was launching numerous products that put new burdens on the sales force. The good news was the spectacular record of growth. In 1996, 1997, and 1998, revenues grew 49, 32, and 28 percent per year, respectively, reaching $15.2 billion in 1998. The company that year employed more than twenty-seven thousand people.

Executives were finding that they too had a hard time corralling the growth that was all around them. "It was like a bucking bronco," recalled Deborah Willingham, of the go-go growth days of

Microsoft in the 1990s. "You were just trying to hold on. We were trying to get all these strategies implemented and hire people to execute them. It was a very challenging and fun time because of the pace of growth. We didn't have to get promoted for our jobs to get bigger." Before she knew it, she was in charge of one unit with 2,500 people.

Whether the decision was big or small, it had to flow through Gates or Ballmer. "Just to get approval of resources," Kevin Johnson remembered, "or an incremental head count, or decisions on pricing, it had to go to Bill and Steve. As a result it would start to slow things down. Also, it probably wasn't always clear whether something should go to Bill as opposed to Steve." Executives tried to lessen the burden on the two leaders. Deborah Willingham recalled, "We began to feel like, Wow, it is feeling burdensome to always have to go back to Bill and Steve for head count. . . . I felt sometimes, Wow, these guys must be so busy. Do I really want to take their time on my business?"

The company's business processes were simply not in tune with the growing complexity of the high-tech world. As profits from Windows and Office were plowed back into the company's new ventures, that created new complexity; the company had to worry about how development groups worked with each other and that required more sophisticated management techniques. Microsoft's customer base was changing as well, as the company provided many more products and services to the largest corporations.

In time the hub-and-spoke system simply "ran out of gas," in Steve Ballmer's phrase. "Things were too complicated: the number of people, number of projects, number of a lot of things. It probably ran out of gas a year or two before we started making changes."

Why did it take so long for the company to deal once and for all with the question of Microsoft's business organization?

The plain truth was that Bill Gates enjoyed the way the company was organized, top down, with him in charge; he liked keeping his hand in every aspect of the company. He created hub and spoke for a reason. He liked the power it gave him over everyone else. Decentralizing meant less power for him. Over the years he assigned others, such as Jon Shirley and Bob Herbold, to handle the business processes, but he was always careful not to cede basic power to them.

He also saw no reason to tamper with the company, given its great success record. Much of its success, Gates believed, had to do with Microsoft's remaining in start-up mode, keeping its informality, its aggressiveness. Why change any of that?

A Few Can Run the Place

The company's growth put him in a quandary. To handle growth, the company needed more personnel. But he was determined not to become overly bureaucratic. He believed that, even with a small head count, the job would get done, one way or another. He viewed his programmers, but never the financial people, as the stars of the company. Retaining the crucial financial numbers in his head, he shared them with no more than one or two others. Having that information helped him stave off pressures from down below to expand the payroll.

Convinced that imposing business processes on the company only complicated matters, he saw no reason why the company could not be run by just a few people. "You don't need a lot of process," Gates told me. "We didn't need a lot of formal process because, believe me, it's better to have three guys who really know what's going on than to have all of the processes that allow twelve to fifteen people to all sort of think they are part of that decision process.

"And our decision process was very clear. There were things that Steve and Jon [Shirley] would help decide: the things of significance like head count. There would be meetings I would be in and we would make those decisions. And so there was no confusion, there was no politicking, there was no overly long memo trying to explain something or posturing. That's how we would make those decisions."

To him, decision making was simply not that complicated that it had to be shared. "You don't need a whole bunch of P&L owners or structure." He was referring to the 1980s and 1990s.

Gates, however, saw the handwriting on the wall. By the early 2000s, he grudgingly conceded that the company's growth required those processes. "We were always making the system somewhat more formalized. To be clear we always had budgets and we always controlled our head count extremely well. . . . [A]t some point you can't discuss every head in France and [have] the one guy at the top saying, 'No, no, no. You want fifteen . . . you need eleven.' You can't . . . you just can't . . . so eventually you have to delegate that."

By the late 1990s, even if Gates and Ballmer were prepared to impose new discipline at Microsoft, they were too distracted to expend the time or energy on such a large project. Microsoft's legal entanglements had become a key distraction; so had the company's growth.

Indeed, the legal difficulties and growth were related. During the trial it had been critical for Microsoft to demonstrate that it was operating routinely and that meant showing solid growth figures. The fear always lingered that introducing business processes would slow down the growth. Few wanted to do that, and for one very good reason. Growth was intoxicating. It made people at Microsoft feel good. It reinforced their conviction that they were doing something right. Though it looked hard to achieve—and in many ways was hard—because it had its own momentum, growth was the easy path to take. Like a roller coaster gathering steam, it was impossible to get off in the middle even if for good reason. To impose constraints on the company in the midst of growth seemed to make no sense at all.

Some did believe, however, that there was no better time to impose discipline in a company than during its best growth days. After all, without that discipline, no way existed to monitor and control that growth. But even with highly successful managers, noted Jim Cash, the Harvard Business School professor who has been on the Microsoft board of directors since June 2001, "Their instinct is to err on the side of growth; they want to insure they are as close to the marketplace and product develop evolution as possible; and so at a certain size you don't have the capacity to do everything. What gives is the attention to management control structures."

To be fair, this intoxication with growth seemed to be a trait found in most of the Microsoft crowd but not its chairman and CEO. He did not let himself get carried away with the mind-numbing effects of growth. It was part of his DNA to be very skeptical about his company's long-term prospects. And because he was so skeptical about those prospects, he failed to see any strong reason for curbing that growth—such as imposing new business processes on the company. Gates liked to ask what Microsoft needed to do over the next few years but not for a longer term. "We were always very one-step-at-a-time," he told me, "not thinking ahead."

He resisted bigness, greatly concerned that Microsoft might one day resemble an unwieldy conglomerate more than a start-up. His antibureaucratic attitude filtered down into the company, hardening the company's resistance to new efforts at discipline. Mike Murray, who had become the company's first vice president for human resources in 1992, recalled that Microsoft was always highly suspicious of initiatives that might transform the company into a mighty corporate power. Accordingly, on the hit list of barred practices were new levels of management, training programs, job titles, and long vacations. Introducing such initiatives, many feared, would only encourage employees to be less aggressive.

For years, observed Murray, the company was antimanagement, but proleadership. "Historically, they believed that strong people with clear vision could lead the company. You didn't need management dealing with people issues, or processes, or worrying about budgets or paper work. It was as if they had said, 'We're a bunch of twenty-year-olds who back in 1974 took a few basic ideas of how to run the company. It seems to have worked. So who are you to question us?'"

At the time, it seemed like a very fair question. "They wanted it to stay Microsoft for as long as they could before it became GE," explained Murray. When he was selected to run human resources, he tried unsuccessfully to create various development and leadership programs to identify and nurture future company leaders. His efforts were shot down and he was accused of padding expenses and creating needless layers of bureaucracy.

Why Are You Doing This?

Maybe the company should have realized during the heady growth days of the 1990s that the time had come to put in controls on all that growth, but no one really felt scared enough to do it. No institutional memory of failure existed, no memory of what might happen to a company if it did not impose those controls. There had been, after all, no job layoffs, no cuts in salaries. Indeed, it had been just the opposite. When Jim Allchin, the group vice president for platforms, arrived at Microsoft in 1990, he found the place something of a mystery. He remembered sleeping on floors, sweeping the coffee room, and being around for dismissals at previous places of work. But Microsoft, in his view, for a long, long time, "never really understood that things could get worse quickly; or that discipline even in good times is a great thing—hard-line discipline."

Allchin tried to introduce stricter ways of handling personnel: flat head counts, forcing a harder stack ranking of people so the company would always encourage the most successful people, and so on. But all he heard back was "Why are you doing this?" When Allchin tried to do some belt tightening during the good times, he got strange looks from superiors who argued that, with competition growing fiercer, Microsoft had to spend what it took to compete. Start-ups, he was told bluntly, do not cut expenses; they build for the long-term future; they seek growth.

Without the discipline, Microsoft's growth got more and more out of hand. For those at the helm the task of managing the growth grew overwhelming. "There were only so many hours in a day that you can spend deeply in any one business," asserted John Connors, the company's chief financial officer in 2003, "and the complexity, whether people, sales, or strategies, was getting too much." One example that he noted was that no one was making sure that the R&D wing was being aligned with sales and with resource allocations. And there were numerous other examples, said Connors, "where we came out with a new technology but didn't have marketing and a field plan to exploit it." The company was conducting surveys to gauge customer satisfaction, asking questions as if all of the problems with customer satisfaction lay in the field:

> *What do you like about our account management in the field?*
> *What do you think of our partnership management structure?*
> *What do you think about our licensing programs?*

But no one was polling about the real problem: the lack of business processes in Redmond.

By the early 2000s, the time had come for a change in Microsoft's business organization. First and foremost, the company's torrid growth years appeared to be over. In 2000, growth was up 16 percent; 10 percent in 2001; and 12 percent in 2002. Those were good figures for most other companies, but not for Microsoft, where annual growth earlier in the decade had been more than twice that percentage. No less important, with the trial over, Microsoft's leadership could devote the necessary time and energy to a revamping of its businesses.

The question no longer was whether to undertake these changes, but what changes to make.

The basic issue confronting the company was an inability to move beyond the personal computer desktop in any significant manner. Searching for the Next Big Thing, Microsoft was getting into such product categories as its Web site MSN, mobile and embedded devices, and home and entertainment systems.

But these investments had not yet yielded profits. The company still revolved around Windows, Office, and, to a lesser degree, its server products. What was of concern: No one could even guarantee Microsoft that the company would retain its hold on the operating system and software applications market, especially as the Linux open-source operating system was gaining increasing acceptance. For that reason Microsoft was delving into other product segments with great zeal.

This search for new markets created a different environment at Microsoft. When all was going well, when there was growth in the core products, Microsoft could afford to take risks in its secondary businesses. But growth had slowed. The company was eager to find a way to return to the heavy-growth days so that it could pay for its expensive moves into those secondary markets. One way to make a dent in those secondary markets was to make the company more efficient. By becoming more efficient, the company would have greater staying power in the new markets; for that it needed to revamp its business structure. That was the theory, at any rate.

For Steve Ballmer, all these ideas were coming together in 2002 and 2003, as he was gaining more confidence in his new role as CEO. He wanted to shore up those secondary markets and he wanted to place his own personal stamp on the company. "I don't know what it's like in a lot of companies," he commented, "but you've got to have something you really just totally know, you're expert on, or people start losing respect for you." To become expert in that one area, he decided, upon becoming CEO, he had to take on a very centralized role for himself, not delegating too much responsibility to subordinate managers.

But he eventually understood that the company was too large and complex for him to micromanage every aspect of the place. He still looked to place his stamp on the job, asking himself what it was that he understood the best. In the past he had acquired special expertise in marketing and sales and applied that knowledge for much of his career.

But in 2003, he wanted to paint on a broader canvas; he wanted the whole company to be his specialty. Then it came to him: What he understood best and was perfectly willing to micromanage was "the process that we use to run the business." As the CEO, that process was in his power to control and organize. And so he set for himself the mission of putting a new process, a new discipline, into Microsoft.

A Larger Mission

He had of course, a larger mission and that was to show a new, more positive face of Microsoft to the outside world, a more open and respectful one; to get personnel to communicate more fully and earlier what the company was up to. Instituting these new business processes would help toward that goal, he was sure, for it would help Microsoft get closer to its customers. And getting closer to its customers became nearly synonymous with becoming more open and respectful as well as with communicating more openly.

Ballmer's creation of the new process became a large part of the rebooting of Microsoft.

As Ballmer studied the way Microsoft had organized itself over the years, he became conscious that the company had during its first few decades geared its business segments strictly around its products. Its earliest clients—through much of the 1980s—had been individual clients who were the early adapters of the technology, and what mattered to them exclusively were the product's features. They did not want or expect Microsoft to develop products to help them run their businesses or entertain them in their homes. They were simply enthusiasts who wanted to get their hands on the newest cutting-edge products in software, for at the time software was new; it was not clear at all whether large numbers of people would want to buy and use computers and the attendant software. All that mattered to Microsoft back then was to give these enthusiast clients the highest-quality products imaginable, and that meant giving them the best software features available. Because its clients didn't care about the larger issues revolving around business productivity, Microsoft did not either—at that stage.

But then in the late 1980s and early 1990s, the company's client base began to look different. Early adapters still looked to Microsoft for great new software products, but in time Microsoft acquired large-sized corporate customers who saw the software not as a hobby for their employees, but as a productivity tool that could make their companies run better. And so the driving force for Microsoft was how to help these larger-sized customers assimilate the company's software into their workplace.

With early adapters, it was easy for Microsoft to know what the value proposition for its products was: It had to come up with the best possible product features. But with the newer customers, the value proposition for software might differ from case to case. In some markets, the value proposition might be one thing, in other markets, another. To address these diverse value propositions, Microsoft needed to develop business processes that focused on markets and segments, no longer on individual products. With the requirements of each market different from the other, Microsoft had to put managers in place who could manage these markets as if they were running stand-alone businesses. These new managers required new skill sets and new metrics to judge performance.

Eager to get started after becoming CEO, Steve Ballmer went through several reorganizations, but he later admitted that he had been too quick off the mark. The initiatives failed. One failed, he acknowledged, because "I didn't recognize the importance of integrated technology and integrated innovations. We sell the same technology to a bunch of different customers. You try to cleave too much by customer and split up the things that should logically be integrated for a variety of good reasons, and so I kind of blew that. And I tried it with just marketing and I tried it with technology, but it didn't work."

Disappointed, Ballmer figured he had better take his time before making any further sweeping changes. And he ought to do some research on how other companies were handling similar issues.

The one business leader who had always impressed him was General Electric's chairman and CEO, Jack Welch. Through Jeff Immelt, who was moving up the ranks at GE, he was able to learn almost firsthand how Welch was reshaping his company. He also read Welch's memoirs. Though he was reluctant to adopt directly the style or tactics of other business leaders, Ballmer admitted to borrowing parts of Welch's business style, including the GE leader's yearly calendar. Ballmer, like Welch, aimed for consistency in all aspects of his work, and so the new Microsoft CEO devised a schedule that contained its constants year after year:

Management sync weeks—Week-long meetings each quarter aimed at developing new leaders at Microsoft. The first was held in June 2002.

May 29—Seven days of business-plan reviews began.

October—The company's senior vice presidents met for two weeks with their staffs, analyzing organizational structure and development needs.

November—Leaders of the company's seven businesses gathered for a week of brainstorming aimed at identifying new market opportunities.

January—Soon after the results of Microsoft's yearly customer-satisfaction survey were available, the same executives met for four days to analyze them.

Jim Cash found the calendar so closely tied to Welch's that he, as a member of both the GE and Microsoft boards, had to ask Steve Ballmer to make some changes so he could attend both GE and Microsoft board meetings. Cash told Ballmer, "I'm willing to catch the 'red eye,' but I can't be at two meetings at the same time." Ballmer accommodated him.

Continuing with his research, Ballmer sought out companies with business processes that Microsoft might employ. But, as he studied other companies, he found most of them to be too different from Microsoft to make borrowing worthwhile. However, if he was going to create a more mature Microsoft, he had to understand how other companies had become mature. Here is what he learned: Most companies had created a management system that had monitoring mechanisms at the top. But most of these companies had given a good deal of autonomy to their operating segments.

How Do We Divisionalize?

The main thing for Microsoft, in Ballmer's judgment, was to decentralize. "At the end of the day the key for us is really finding businesses that know how to manage themselves but also have the same challenge to meet, which is managing a large integrated R&D effort."

He began by asking, How could he "divisionalize this stuff? We have more people we've got to get involved, more scenarios, more complexity, and more things to track. I had to have smaller chunks to think about, because I wasn't thinking about the broad set of things quite as easily and I was trying to get our business divisions more aligned toward customers."

Even as Microsoft needed to decentralize, Ballmer understood that he had organized the company so that it could deal with that new complexity, so that he could get his arms around that "broad set of things"—all in order to get closer to customers. He realized that the solution lay in an emerging theme that Bill Gates had been drumming up—something Gates was calling innovative integration. Ballmer decided to align the new business processes with the new Gates theme.

Trying to think through the best way to organize the company for this new theme, Ballmer offered an example of how the company's business segments had to make sure that all of their various products could interact with one another. He chose as his example reading on the screen. "If it's going to be a good experience for you to read on-screen and annotate, Windows has got to do it right. The security system has to do it right. The browser needs to do it right. The Office application needs to do it right. So there are a bunch of different products that have to do it right."

What was needed, Ballmer thought, was a management process that lets those various Microsoft products integrate, "but still gives each of those groups the chance to be close to their customers, to respond to customer issues, and have some financial authority and control, and autonomy. Whatever the answer, you want to make sure there's enough feedback so that the specific market requirements of different kinds of customers get into the core technology, but you don't want to start cleaving up the individual technologies in some senses by customer."

A Type of Customer

So decentralizing was crucial. Only in that way could the business segments get closer to customers. Ballmer was not talking about total autonomy but some autonomy. Redmond still had to be in charge of certain aspects of the business simply to ensure that Microsoft did not seem to be speaking with more than one voice. "We've got to have synergy in some of our messaging and marketing. We don't really want to talk about the same products in six different ways to six different customer types. So things still need to be grounded in the products that we ship, but each of the product groups has to have responsibility for a type of customer. It's a recognition that we need to decentralize some things while we highly centralize other things."

Customer scenario planning—how Microsoft's leadership thought about and planned those scenarios—had to stay centralized. "Strategically, we try to think very holistically about scenarios in terms of how customers use computers and, if there's some very popular scenario we're not investing in, we're probably letting our customers down because they'll want those new scenarios to tie in well with other things that they're already doing with us, with Windows, with Office, with servers, with business applications, et cetera.

"We're looking at all the big scenarios to say how this stuff can be applied. That's our job. Part of our job is to push ourselves to do that.

We've pushed ourselves in some areas that were only sort of software based and then we got out of them. Take Expedia [the Internet travel product]. When it was clear that that wasn't primarily a software business, we spun it. So you could say we're looking for the next big thing, but if the next big thing is really tangential to what we do, we're willing to divest ourselves of that."

Once the scenarios that Microsoft wanted to invest in were identified, Ballmer suggested, the question became who at the company had responsibility for them. "Even if the ownership spans multiple groups, everybody's got to understand who the owner is. That's got to be very centrally managed, and some of those scenarios need the extra wisdom of Bill Gates applied to them or Rick Rashid [head of Microsoft research] or Jim Allchin. That's got to stay very central, as does some kind of über-marketing about those scenarios that we want to make to our customers."

What Microsoft needed to do, in addition, was to decentralize a wide variety of responsibilities related to implementing those customer scenarios and these included the creation of products, the decisions about how to take products to market (whether the markets were developers or IT pros or large companies or small companies), and resource allocation.

Ballmer wanted the external world (Wall Street, the media, and so on) to understand that Microsoft was preparing itself to tackle a whole new set of emerging markets head on. That in part was what the new reorganization was about. The company could not afford to miss opportunities in a new, potentially lucrative market. "If there is a business that emerges over the next ten years that's got a billion dollars of profit in the software area and we choose not to participate, that's crazy."

In the early part of 2002, Ballmer had made his mind up. He began the deliberations on transforming the business process in talks with senior executives that January.

He wanted to move fast. But other executives, who had watched his previous attempts at reorganization go up in flames, cautioned him to go slow. Still, he wanted the new reorganization to begin in the next fiscal year that started in July. Ballmer was adamant. When other executives seemed less enthusiastic, he stormed after them, insisting they get on board. Inevitably, egos were bruised in the new setup: According to one news report, Jeff Raikes found out that under the Ballmer reorganization, $2 billion of revenue would fall within the server segment; Raikes wanted the revenue in his Office applications segment. Ballmer took the Solomonic decision to split the revenue between the two segments.

The Reorganization Begins

On July 1, 2002, the new Microsoft reorganization plan went into effect. Ballmer regrouped the company into seven separate business segments, with products assigned to one of seven different segments:

1. Client
2. Server and Tools
3. Information Worker
4. Microsoft Business Solutions
5. MSN
6. Mobile and Embedded Devices
7. Home and Entertainment

Each segment contained many of the functions of a stand-alone company, with its own general manager who had responsibility for managing the segment's profit-and-loss statement; each had its own product development, sales, marketing, and finance arms. Granted a great deal of autonomy, managers of the new segments faced a whole new era of accountability as well. Breaking the company into these seven new segments and making each manager responsible for the segment's profit-and-loss results in a very visible way put a good deal of pressure on those managers to perform.

Under the new reorganization of the seven new segments:

The **Client** segment included Windows XP, Windows 2000, and other standard Windows operating systems.

The **Server and Tools** segment included server software licenses and client access licenses (CALs) for Windows Server, SQL Server, Exchange Server, and other servers. It also included developer tools, training, certification, Microsoft Press, Premier product support services, and Microsoft consulting services.

The **Information Worker** segment included Microsoft Office, Microsoft Project, Visio, other information worker products, SharePoint Portal Server CALs, an allocation for CALs, and professional product support services.

Microsoft Business Solutions included Microsoft Great Plains, Navision, and bCentral.

MSN included MSN Subscription and MSN Network services.

Mobile and Embedded Devices included Windows Mobile software, Windows Embedded device operating systems, MapPoint, and Windows Automotive.

Home and Entertainment included the Xbox video game system, PC games, consumer software and hardware, and TV platform.

By 2003, the new reorganization was one year old. The general managers and the newly appointed chief financial officers of each of those segments were setting financial targets and deciding on their own how to spend money in order to reach those targets. They were now able to spend as much or as little money as they wanted—within the confines of their budgets—on head count, marketing, acquisitions, and so on. Ballmer, as CEO, had been making those decisions in the past few years. Before Ballmer, Bill Gates did. Consequently, when Robbie Bach, the senior vice president for Home and Entertainment Division, got together with Steve Ballmer, they discussed head count for no more than a minute. In the past, when Ballmer made those decisions, all the junior executives could do was lash out at the fledgling CEO in disagreement. Ballmer had the final word. Things were different now.

The managers of these seven business segments no longer had to wait for a company leader to make a decision while they remained in the dark about all the various considerations that went into the decision. In previous times, managers knew the costs of developing a product but had no idea what the costs of selling it were. Now, they saw those costs from start to finish, giving them the kind of data they needed to figure out how many resources to allocate.

Quickly, Microsoft found whole new efficiencies in the reorganization. John Connors, the company's CFO, noted, "It allowed us to talk about the company internally and externally in a consistent way. It allowed us to show shareholders how we were performing in each group. It also allowed us to scale our business processes and management processes into more manageable chunks. Finally, it's allowed the organization development, the business management, and the long-term strategy to be organized and compartmentalized [in a way] that reflects how large and diverse we are today."

In granting more autonomy to the segments, the idea was, more specifically, to strengthen people lower in the ranks to feel more emboldened—to speak out, to make decisions, to advance their causes. One of those feeling more emboldened was Elijah Hurwitz, a young financial analyst in the Information Worker business segment. "This company is big. Before, we had a dotted line between finance and business on the work chart. Now it's a solid line. We in finance have a larger influence on the business. We're expected to give a lot more guidance to the business on where to invest its money, how to manage its resources, and head count, etc. And we're listened to more."

All of this autonomy, this emboldening, was meant to give the people in the business segments a greater opportunity to get closer to customers, to improve the customer experience with Microsoft.

In the past many of these people had neither the decision-making power nor the resources to take the initiative in trying to help customers. Now they did.

In July 2003, a year into the reorganization, Ballmer announced the appointment of chief financial officers for each of the seven business segments. It had always been Ballmer's contention that Microsoft, though strong in product development and sales, had been traditionally weak in financial management. As a result, as the company expanded, it never seemed possible to tell how the business segments within the overall enterprise were truly performing. The faulty financial management had to be laid at the doorstep of Bill Gates. Not only had he not thought it important to elevate financial people at Microsoft into roles of importance within the company; he rather enjoyed handling the financial end himself as a way of preserving his power. Historically, one of the classic traits of start-ups was a weak financial base. Keeping that base weak was yet another way in which Gates prolonged Microsoft as a start-up for too long.

That was now changing with this beefing up of the company's financial leadership. As part of granting more autonomy to the new segments, Ballmer wanted to segment Microsoft into seven separate financial reporting and financial planning operations. The new CFOs were added to the seven business segments to do just that. Each CFO was to report to the segment's manager and to be responsible for developing financial targets, developing a budget, and measuring the segment's performance.

Over the years, Microsoft had became a much more complex, more diversified company with many more segments, making it increasingly more difficult to track its various components. The reorganization was in part designed to remedy that by making it easier for investors and company employees to track performance. By way of comparison, here are excerpts from the first-quarter results for 2002 (showing revenue by business division), and from the first quarter results for 2004:

First Quarter 2002 (in millions)
Desktop and Enterprise Software and Services: $5,402
Consumer Software, Services, and Devices: $501
Consumer Commerce Investments: $94
Other: $129

First Quarter 2004 (in millions)
Client: $2,809

Server and Tools: $1,866
Information Worker: $2,287
Microsoft Business Solutions: $128
MSN: $491
Mobile and Embedded Devices: $53
Home and Entertainment: $581

The 2002 first quarter results show a far more generalized set of categories than the same comparable categories for 2004.

It was now possible to say, for example, that during the initial three quarters of Microsoft's fiscal 2003, the most profitable business parts of the company were the desktop Windows division, with operating income of $6.4 billion, and the Microsoft Office division, with $5.7 billion in operating income; and that four of the company's divisions had losses for the same period, among which were MSN, with an operating loss of $346 million, and Home and Entertainment, with $715 million.

In one more sign that Microsoft was attempting to become a more mature company, it decided in 2003 to get rid of one of the trappings of a start-up, its long-standing policy against declaring dividends. In the past, though shareholders had obviously been keen for Microsoft to declare a dividend, Gates had insisted on keeping the cash for various contingencies, including adverse legal ones, and for major investments in company projects. Finally, on January 16, 2003, the board decided to pay an eight-cent-per-share annual dividend.

It did not escape anyone's attention that Bill Gates, as the company's largest shareholder, benefited the most. His first dividend check came to nearly $100 million.

Shareholders were to receive a relatively small amount in what Microsoft called a starter dividend, just 0.3 percent of the stock price (Intel's dividend, in contrast, was 0.5 percent; IBM's, 0.7 percent). The annual cost to Microsoft would come to only $870 million, less cash than it was able to store each month.

The no-dividend policy had been etched in stone, but never articulated in public. The truth was that Gates had wanted to keep Microsoft a start-up for as long as possible, and start-ups did not issue dividends. And so Microsoft had taken the cash that would have gone to shareholders and reinvested it back in the company.

While it was certainly true that Microsoft's cash on hand had grown almost too large (Windows and Office were kicking off $1 billion a month in free cash), perhaps the real reason for the dividend reversal was the company's confidence that it would not need to hoard so much cash to pay for unfavorable legal cases.

Not only had Microsoft concluded its long-running trial with the U.S. government the previous November, but in January 2003, it had reached a settlement with California consumers in an antitrust case and was on the path toward settlements with other states as well.

With Microsoft deciding to settle outstanding legal cases as quickly and frequently as possible, it became clear to its financial experts that there was enough cash to distribute its first-ever dividend.

In November 2003, Microsoft paid its second dividend, sixteen cents a share. Microsoft was going through a whole series of changes, the declaration of a dividend being one of those changes. But the real test of the reshaping of Microsoft would come down in no small measure to whether the company would be able to recruit the kinds of employees who would know how to drive those changes.

9

Great People with Great Values

The rebooting of Microsoft meant an overhaul not only of the company's organization chart, but also of the kind of personnel it wanted to attract.

In the software industry, what mattered most to a company was the gray matter inside an employee's head. This meant that people, not buildings, not equipment, were the most important component in a software enterprise. Bill Gates certainly thought so. He cited as two of his best business decisions picking Paul Allen to help him cofound Microsoft and selecting Steve Ballmer as his business partner. Finding the right talent was crucial, he believed, and he once said that if the twenty best people were ever taken away from Microsoft, it would become an unimportant company.

People were so important to Microsoft that the company took a far more serious attitude toward recruiting than most other enterprises. Its recruiting staff was far larger than most other companies. In 2003, it had more than two hundred recruiters worldwide. It insisted that not only human resources executives interview job candidates, but senior executives play a role in the process as well. When trying to lure major business figures to Microsoft, Bill Gates and Steve Ballmer were brought into the interviewing process.

In earlier years, when the company revolved entirely around programmers and everyone wrote code, choosing the right kind of people meant picking people who could write great code. Gates saw programming as Microsoft's core competency; hiring people to build hardware or to sell the company's products simply diverted the company from its true path. Programmers were expected to sell products and deal with customer service issues.

All of this was fine when the company had no more than thirty employees; but as it grew, Gates had to modify his stance. He broadened his view of the kind of people Microsoft should hire. He still wanted to hire people who were the best and the brightest programmers, but now he wanted people with general intelligence, who could then be molded into the Microsoft way. Alan Levy, who went through the Microsoft interview process recalled, "They wanted someone who could complete a job, but they were also looking for people who could do strategic thinking and who could analyze and solve problems. Other companies hired for the job. Microsoft was hiring for the big picture."

During the early years, Gates wanted someone with no previous business experience. The fear always existed that the overexperienced person had done his or her best work already or had already been indoctrinated in the ways of previous employers. "I used to tell the HR people that we don't want to get so focused on experience that we wouldn't hire the next young Bill Gates," Nathan Myhrvold commented. That explained why Microsoft liked to recruit from college campuses, especially from those considered the best in the country: Harvard, Yale, MIT, Carnegie-Mellon, and Stanford. In time, the company was recruiting from as many as fifteen American, four Canadian, and six Japanese colleges.

Eventually, Microsoft cast a much wider net, seeking the best and the brightest from around the world, turning the Redmond campus into a mini–United Nations.

Weird Is OK

Microsoft defined the best and the brightest as those with a high analytical IQ—that is, possessing analytical problem-solving abilities, especially in mathematics and computer science. Only the cream needed to apply: the top 10 percent of the top 10 percent, as the expression went within Microsoft. Job candidates did not require a high social IQ. They did not have to dress in a certain way, nor did they have to be great public speakers. They just needed to know how to code—and how to solve problems. "The list stopped there," recalled Bob Herbold, the company's executive vice president in 2003. "You could be very weird, you could dress funny. You could look strange, you could have all sorts of other issues, but if you were smart and excited about information technology and what your role would be at the company, you were a strong candidate." At Procter & Gamble, where Herbold had spent more than a quarter century, the hiring standards were different— someone who seemed strange did not get hired. At Microsoft, that person could become a star.

If a person's physical appearance and wardrobe mattered little, a passion for technology counted a great deal. So did high energy and, perhaps most important, a willingness not to shirk from dealing with intricate problems.

From the company's earliest days, Gates and his colleagues knew the odds were heavily against building any kind of successful start-up, and the odds were even greater against creating a successful software enterprise. The only way to shorten the odds was to attract the best possible employees. During the 1980s, Charles Simonyi joined Gates in visiting college campuses in search of prospective employees. Simonyi noted, "We could not afford then to make wild bets. The people we were looking for had to have energy and be comfortable with the software industry."

When Microsoft's recruiters scoured college campuses, they were not seeking people with great moral values. They wanted someone with a passion to change the world, who would give up sleep to get the job done—a person, in short, who liked to win. Jeff Raikes said he learned recruiting in the early 1980s "from the school of Steve Ballmer. The person we hired had to have high energy. We wanted people who were passionate, whose eyes lit up when they talked about what they did." As part of his interviewing of candidates, Raikes asked them to look back upon what they had done and to say what they had been most proud of and where they felt they had had the most positive impact. "Frankly, I was looking for body language. If you ask that question, and somebody doesn't have an answer, that means they're not likely to be passionate about what they do."

Always the emphasis was on the individual, what the individual could accomplish, how much passion he or she could bring to the job. Though Microsoft talked about the need for collaboration in the workplace, when it explained to employees how they could get ahead it was always predicated on what the individual needed to do working alone.

Cleverness was critical. Raikes noted, "We were doing things that weren't done before. You had to have people who learned quickly. We weren't after just street smarts or raw IQ. We wanted someone who saw the essence of mistakes and learned how to do things better, who figured out opportunities." But, as Raikes learned, learning quickly and discovering opportunities was not enough. "I found I could hire those people who had both, but they didn't get things done. Sometimes the person was smart and worked hard, but he didn't seem to get things done. So you look for a track record of success; for someone who can focus, who has a persona of making things happen."

It Goes with the Job

Hard work then was the sine qua non of programming. The story is told admiringly of a bunch of Microsoft programmers who, back in the 1980s, had been up most of the night working and then showed up for work the next day at 12:00 noon, spending the next eight hours putting code together, breaking for Coke and pizza at a nearby restaurant; then returning to work into the early-morning hours. When a waitress, looking at the bloodshot eyes of some Microsoft employees, asked if they were on speed, they replied politely, "No, we're programmers."

During the company's early years, Gates paid his programmers $20,000 a year, somewhat above the industry average. He paid himself

$16,000 annually. Hard work, he believed firmly, was part of the job and was not to be rewarded with a bonus. "Microsoft," he wrote in one memo in the early days, "expects a level of dedication from its employees higher than most companies. Therefore, if some deadline or discussion or interesting piece of work causes you to work extra time some week it just goes with the job."

The model for the typical Microsoft employee was Bill Gates. He set the tone for the culture and if a Microsoft employee wanted a quick checklist of what that culture was all about, it was only necessary to find out what Bill Gates had done that day, or any other day for that matter, and then emulate him. By emulating him, people became models for the ideal Microsoft employee—the kind of person who should be hired.

At first, Gates hired mostly his friends, who, it just so happened, were among the brightest people around. College was fun, he had thought, because he could sit around and talk with so many smart people his age. CEOs at other companies often were uncomfortable in the presence of the high-IQ crowd, but not Gates. "Bill," said Nathan Myhrvold, "is not threatened by smart people, only stupid ones."

Those whom he hired at first were all in their twenties, dressed casually, and were prepared to work around the clock if necessary. They had no home lives to speak of, no wives, no children, no reason to leave the office—except for pizza, Coke, and the movies. If there was a single phrase that summed up those early Microsoft employees, it was *hard core*. To be hard core in the Microsoft context was to be intensely focused, supremely aggressive, verging on the lunatic when it came to technology.

At first, with the company still relatively unknown, few people applied for jobs. But then, as word spread about this tiny start-up near Seattle, with its wondrous products and supersmart people, more and more people with an interest in software wanted to work for the premier software company in the world. "The opportunity to challenge the world gets them to come," said Jim Allchin. "Where else could you come and have these kinds of resources to change society?" In 2003, Microsoft was receiving 1,500 resumes a day.

Winning the loyalty of employees was not a huge problem in the early years. It became a feather in someone's cap to work at Microsoft. To start with, being employed there offered the unique experience of working closely with the man who pretty much created the software revolution as well as working closely with other very smart people. But the greatest lure for these youngsters in their twenties was the positive way Bill Gates treated them, giving them good salaries, fun jobs, and a sense of self-worth. They were made to feel as if they were making significant contributions to society while many of their own friends were cast aside or denigrated by the adult world. Here was Bill Gates treating employees as if they mattered, giving them their own offices (for entry-level programmers that was no small perk), their own computers (no small perk either), and free Coke (a very big perk!). This was all heady stuff for the young employees at Microsoft.

As Microsoft expanded, as it still sought the best and the brightest, it became more challenging to find the best candidates; but it continued to enjoy a luxury that few other companies did: thousands of people wanted to work for the company. That meant that among those thousands, some exceptionally bright people might surface. But not refusing to lower its standards, the company hired only one of every one hundred candidates.

Even with so many candidates, Microsoft still felt it had to be very careful. "We'd rather have ten people who might end up being great," said Peter Rinearson, the corporate vice president for the Information Worker Business Unit, "than have one person who isn't good."

To keep from making such mistakes, the interview process at Microsoft was no routine procedure. In most businesses, a job applicant normally had only one interview and that was with the applicant's potential future boss. With far higher hiring standards than elsewhere, Microsoft made a prospective hire go through the hoops. Four to six interviews on a single day were standard; and if anyone had the slightest doubt about the person, the candidate was scrubbed. "It's a rigorous environment," said Deborah Willingham, the former head of human resources. She went through the interview process herself when she came to Microsoft. "But it's also energizing. They want to see how you think."

Because it was so rigorous, the Microsoft job search became famous throughout corporate America. It was studied and emulated, and other companies were convinced that they too could, if they followed the Microsoft Recruiting Way, find the best and brightest.

Confronting the Brainteasers

In painstaking fashion, Microsoft interviewers probed candidates to check their problem-solving abilities. There was no right answer, nor was there a wrong answer. Interviewers were searching for something else: whether the person was comfortable dealing with the problem-solving process.

The most famous part of the interviews was what Microsoft insiders called the "brainteasers," the trick questions that were designed to test the candidate's mental dexterity. The idea was not necessarily to solve the problem, but to demonstrate some creative and imaginative mental skills in *trying* to get the right answer.

Sometimes job candidates came up with the "wrong" answers for a brainteaser only to be hired! Few employees forgot their brainteasers. Some had been astounded that they had been hired, considering how poorly (in their own view) they had done on them. At times, the interviewer intentionally left out key information, waiting to find out if the candidate asked for more data (which was considered a mark of intelligence).

The best way to flunk an interview was to treat a question as trivial or uninteresting. If the recruiter asked how often does someone use the word *and* in a twenty-four-hour period, the candidate had better show some deductive reasoning or some creative response and not dismiss the question as irrelevant for a future Microsoft programmer.

When an interview ended, the interviewer e-mailed the interviewers due to meet the job candidate later in the day. At the top of the e-mail the interviewer typed "hire" or "no hire." Candidates could not just scrape by. If only marginally satisfactory, they were scrubbed. As the interviewing process wore on during the day, the other interviewers sought to probe the candidate for weaknesses, and that was when the process became really tough.

If the candidate was still considered a potential hire by the end of the day, the person's prospective manager then met the person. To guard against that manager yielding to the temptation to hire an un- qualified person simply to fill a specific job opening, an interview was also scheduled with someone who would not be working with the can- didate and who had immediate veto power.

The bar had to be kept very high. Steve Ballmer insisted that inter- viewers think of the default position for any candidate as "no hire." A very strong reason had to exist to hire the person. Ballmer and Gates wanted to keep the head count low and Microsoft began calling this attitude "n minus 1," where n was the number of employees actually needed. Gates always feared mediocre hires. The bad hires could easily be weeded out, but the mediocre ones were more difficult to detect once at Microsoft, occupying the place of some other brilliant prospect. In the spring of 2003, Peter Rinearson was engaged in hiring one hun- dred new employees. His boss, Jeff Raikes, warned him to be careful, not to rush into things, advising him to interview not only his own future direct reports but also those who would report to his direct reports. Only the best for Microsoft—that was the watchword.

One way to get hired by the company was to enter Microsoft's sum- mer intern program, but even that was no easy trick. At the least, the intern got a barbecue at Bill Gates's home at the end of the eight-week program; at the best, the intern was given a job. Of the eight hundred summer interns each year, five hundred were asked to join Microsoft as full-timers. For Microsoft, the summer intern program had the advantage of being low cost. It did not have to pull recruits out of industry and pay them $200,000 a year plus a signing bonus. "It was," said Mike Murray, the former human resources head, "the ultimate blind date. We got to watch them, and they watched us."

Inside the Fishbowl

Elijah Hurwitz was one of those interns who joined Microsoft full-time. He had managed to get on the short list of those people interviewed for the internship program after one of his professors at Indiana University contacted an acquaintance who worked at Microsoft's human resources unit. Hurwitz went through several challenging interviews in Redmond. Aware that he would be thrown some brainteasers, he prepared for the interview as if he were studying for a college exam. Three years later, long after the interview was over, he still remembered the brainteaser. "It was quite unnerving."

The recruiter took a simple piece of paper, drew a fishbowl, and said, "You've got a bowl full of fish. There are two hundred fish in the bowl; 99 percent of the fish are guppies. How many fish do you have to remove from the bowl so 98 percent of the fish are guppies?"

Hurwitz thought the brainteaser was "seemingly simple. I fumbled around with it a little bit. I think I actually got it wrong. The idea is that you get your thought process out there and you're talking about the question and you're thinking out loud so that they can see that you're going through a logical process even if you don't get to the right answer."

He wasn't quite sure whether he gave as his answer two or four guppies. The right answer was to take one hundred fish out of the bowl. "I was trying to do a ratio, but it was a trick question."

Trick question or not, he was hired in 2002, and a year later was working in the Information Worker Finance and Business Development Group. He was convinced he was hired because he had completed three internships at other companies in finance and accounting. "That separated me from others." That and the way he thought about those two hundred fish in the bowl.

. . .

Another way to get hired at Microsoft was for someone inside the company to recommend an acquaintance. Great faith was placed in Microsoft employees recognizing other Microsoft types among their acquaintances. When Deborah Willingham ran the human resources department from 1999 until early 2003, one-third of Microsoft's hires came through referrals from Microsoft employees. "It's hard to figure out if a person will fit into our culture," she observed, "but if an employee refers that person, the cultural fit is usually there."

As the company grew in the 1990s, the company began hiring some people not just for their intelligence, but also for their management leadership experience. It still favored the young person who had no deep experience but was very smart. But more and more, as the company required people who could manage large groups and who could talk with business leaders elsewhere, it became very important to recruit people with experience, albeit a certain kind of experience. "It was scary," Mike Murray recalled, "that we would be hiring people who were middle-aged and not in their twenties, people who had a point of view about how to do business, who were trained by other companies, and who had different expectations of what a work ethic should be."

The kind of person Microsoft was searching for was changing by the early 2000s.

The very fact that Microsoft was still searching for new employees was remarkable in and of itself. When many companies had imposed job freezes due to the weakened economy of the early 2000s, Microsoft was still hiring. As of January 2004, it had a work force of fifty-five thousand with plans to hire five thousand more.

While Microsoft needed employees with job skills in addition to what it required earlier, it was, to be sure, still on the lookout for the best and the brightest. In his June 6, 2003, memo outlining Microsoft's business plan for that year, Steve Ballmer noted, "In a world where competition like Linux and other non-commercial software has essentially no cost structure, we must focus on talent and constantly improve our efficacy and efficiency. We cannot afford to have anything but the best people at Microsoft."

But under Steve Ballmer, talent management took on a new twist. It was no longer enough for new hires to be smart and passionate about technology. They had to appreciate and be willing to internalize the new corporate values that Microsoft had introduced: They had to work collaboratively; they had to be open and respectful and be willing to communicate frankly and thoroughly to outsiders. Above all, they had to focus on meeting customers' needs. They would have to show a whole new face to the external world. Mary Snapp, the corporate vice president and deputy general counsel, understood that Ballmer wanted Microsoft interviewers to look for a new kind of hire. "Being open and respectful is now a theme when I interview people for a job," she noted. "I say, 'This is how we work in the company. This is how we are changing as a company.' The candidate is either excited about it or not. We want to hire the ones who are excited about it."

Steve Ballmer dared not say that Microsoft had ceased to look for job candidates who were as passionate about technology as they were about winning. But something subtle had definitely happened in the recruiting process. It was not enough to put existing employees through training courses in what business practices were acceptable and what were not. There had to be a new effort to hire employees who had competitive zeal, but who knew the limits of that zeal. "It's not that Microsoft is not looking for people who have that [competitiveness] now," said Corey duBrowa, the senior public relations man from Microsoft. "It's not that they say, 'We don't want overly competitive people, people who want to win.' There has to be some balance with the idea that back in the day what was important was to win. Now the thing that's important is probably to win but also to win trust which is a different thing. I don't know that trust was a huge part of anybody's responsibility."

Minimum Characteristic

The new hire had to have the right set of values. In the past, "the right set of values" was being competitive and aggressive. But in the early 2000s, as Ballmer said in his memo of June 5, 2002, Microsoft needed "people who have their own strong personal values, as well as those necessary to be successful at Microsoft. These are the kind of people who, with their passion for helping others realize their potential, will push themselves to ask: What does the customer need? How do you build it? How do you make it successful? How do you support it?"

The values that job candidates had to be scrutinized for were, he added, "the importance and value of people being open—with their ideas, thoughts and in receiving input—and demonstrating respect for others. These values must shine through in all our interactions—in our workgroups, across teams, with partners, within our industry, and most of all with customers.

"Great people . . . share the following values:

- Integrity and honesty
- Passion for customers, partners, and technology
- Open and respectful with others and dedicated to making them better
- Willingness to take on big challenges and see them through
- Self-critical, questioning and committed to personal excellence and self-improvement
- Accountable for commitments, results, and quality to customers, shareholders, partners and employees"

In our interview in September 2003, Ballmer explained that Microsoft was now looking for employees "who are open and respectful and dedicated to making others better. If you went back probably twenty years, we'd say we were looking for just the flat-out smartest, most passionate people we could find; and some of them were open and respectful and dedicated to making others better, and some weren't. And I would tell you now that [with] all of our people we're saying, 'Look, there's a minimum threshold that you've got to have of this characteristic.'

"At the entry level we're mostly looking for people who sort of fit with our values—passionate, bright, but also people who have good integrity, open, respectful, people who are going to take on big challenges. It's hard to tell with a kid coming right out of school really how much of a manager they are or aren't [going to be], but let's get in the people who sort of meet the value test and the capability test and give them some opportunities to prove themselves.

"We're trying to be more open. Some are going to work and some aren't going to work out, but let's not let the fact that some don't work out scare us off."

What was remarkable—and new—was the emphasis that Ballmer put in finding and nurturing employees who had value systems that led them to be open and respectful and to have integrity. None of these things had been important to the Microsoft recruiting teams of the 1980s and 1990s. They should have been. But they were not.

The new recruits whom Ballmer had in mind would find a more congenial atmosphere within Microsoft, one that had a little less of the fierce competitive drive of earlier years. To be sure, the people at Microsoft still got fired up about technology, still longed for the day when they personally would change the world. And the strain of individualism still resided in the Microsoft employee even as the company stressed teamwork and collaboration. In the past, the individualist strain had been the great spark that had ignited Microsoft. But now the place was so much larger and there were so many more projects going on that it seemed less likely that any single person was going to produce the Next Big Thing all by himself or herself. Most important, Microsoft was not interested in finding the great individualist any more. It had been the stress on the individual that had produced an overzealous atmosphere.

Rallying Teams

For Ken DiPietro, who became the new corporate vice president for human resources in early 2003, Microsoft was after a new breed—the team player. "We will never back off on the need for candle power [intelligence]. It will always be central. So will passion and energy. So will conviction and a love of technology. But, whereas before we turned you loose on a big job and we didn't care, now it's different. Going forward, what we will look more and more to are people who can rally teams, build great organizations, and do it on behalf of customer requirements."

Rick Rashid, Microsoft's head of research, has picked up on the need for collaboration in a big way. "I tend to go for people who have a lot of energy and are very entrepreneurial. They really want to make something happen. I like to build teams, not just single individual research topics. I want synergy. I want my people to accomplish something." Elsewhere in corporate America, he noted, research groups comprise smart people, but they are too small to take advantage of synergies among them. "I wanted each area at Microsoft Research to have critical mass and to have an impact. And we've built that." And so a typical work group may have as many as twenty to thirty people. "It's all about hiring the right person. There aren't that many of them. They aren't that mobile. You have to find the right person at the right time of their career and at the right time in their lives."

New Microsoft employees also had to have backgrounds that were far richer than their counterparts of earlier years. Life had so many more choices and opportunities for consumers. In past days, a programmer could get away with being just a programmer. Now, programmers had to know what was going on in the outside world. John O'Rourke, senior director for consumer strategy, noted that when he began at Microsoft in the early 1990s and the company had six thousand employees, the place was filled with incredibly smart people who loved customers and loved products. But many of them were unfamiliar with the latest cultural and social trends that impacted what people bought. "Now," he said, "as the market broadens, you need expertise not only in technology but in branding and retail marketing. And for that, you need various categories of people. The customer is broader. So we need to find employees with expertise who can put us in touch with younger customers . . . who know music and photography, digital photography."

In the early 1990s, he noted, much of what Microsoft did was research around attitudes—how people used their product. The company thought of customers simply as users. Now Microsoft has to develop its products and bring them to market with the behavior of those customers in mind, not just the way they will use the product. "You have to be much more sophisticated about the consuming audience. Microsoft has evolved. We have had to attract a different kind of best and brightest. We don't just hire technologists now, but people with a passion for games. We want marketing expertise combined with passion. They don't have to be technologists. We need employees who can explain the visceral experience of the game. Very little of that has to do with technology. So we want people who can think outside of the technology box. It's a product-driven company in many ways, but for a consuming audience we need people who are not technologists. That's a big change."

With the company so large, with so many products groups—large and small—leadership skills have become important, and Microsoft came to need a new kind of executive. "The future leaders of this organization," suggested Ken DiPietro, "will really know the technology well but will be able to bring people with them and do it on behalf of customer requirements; that's the Holy Grail—what the future hire will be. It's happening already, but it's not perfect.

"Very few people here both get the technology and happen to be great on the business side. We are hiring for technology first and foremost: Do you have credentials; do you know how to do what we need you to do? We'll hire him. But if we have two equal technology people but one is a better leader, gets it, is better at general management, the latter will get the hire for sure."

Executives with that combination of technology and leadership skills were more likely to come from the world beyond Microsoft. The typical Microsoft employee had little time to accumulate the requisite academic degrees and leadership experience that the company needed now. During the heady high-growth days of the 1990s, those employees were filling orders, not asking for leaves of absence to get MBAs.

But now Microsoft wanted to help its own employees become better managers. "In the past," noted Microsoft board member Jim Cash, "if you were hired by Microsoft, we were on such a growth trajectory that you learned on the job, you didn't go back to programs or MBAs. Microsoft managers didn't have MBAs; they got responsibility for a product and it was growing underneath them. They either grew with it or were replaced."

Now, as Microsoft moved into a new maturity, as growth was slowing down, an effort to fashion future leaders from within was both feasible and advisable. With the advent of the seven new market-oriented business segments, Microsoft managers needed a whole new set of skills to be effective. Again, Jim Cash: "If you're running a profit-and-loss center, you will need skills in areas of market research, customer interaction; you will need skills for dealing with vendors, supply systems, human resources. These are different skills from being focused primarily on what are the product and its features. Before, you had a half dozen general managers and a whole lot of gifted product unit managers that were running product units. Now what you need for the profit-and-loss units are general managers."

The company's business processes had been restructured. Talent management had taken a new twist. These were important steps in the rebooting process. But nothing was as vital to the reforms that Microsoft was undertaking as the tweaking of the company's original culture. We turn next to a look at how that culture was changing in the early 2000s.

10

The New Culture of Being Friendly and Humble

Aggressiveness, a key Microsoft cultural trait, seemed embedded in the company's DNA. Bill Gates felt himself the underdog and set the bar very high. Other Microsoft employees sang the same tune.

The results were visible for all to see. Because it had enjoyed such dominance in the operating system and software application markets, it was simply assumed that Microsoft had achieved this monopoly by employing nasty and brutish tactics. Accordingly, the company acquired a reputation for using brute force and unabashed threats to get its way. The reputation, whether true or not, was enough to scare off many a would-be rival. "I think of Microsoft's persistence," said Robert S. Rosenschein, a consultant to Microsoft in the 1990s, "like the Roman army. It just went in and besieged its target. It didn't matter if it took a month or three years. When they set their mind to it, they stayed with their goal. If Microsoft was going to go into your market, you held an emergency meeting of your board of directors. Sometimes Microsoft didn't even have to do anything, and people ran."

Dancing on Graves

Mike Murray, the former head of human resources, always found the public perception of Microsoft's aggressiveness off the mark. "The perception was that Microsoft was king of the hill and we had every-one in a stranglehold and we were up here in Redmond dancing on our competitors' graves."

But he was familiar with a far different, more nervous, more inse-cure Microsoft. He had a favorite example: For each of his ten years (1989 to 1999) at the company, Microsoft's stock went up enormously. "But we were certain every year that this was the highest the stock could possibly be. We thought it would go down. We were nervous that the Internet would kill us. This wasn't paranoia. These were cred-ible threats and we knew that we had vulnerabilities in our technology and product lines."

To combat the competition, Gates's great weapon was a willing-ness to reinvent the company over and over again. Most companies had neither the will nor the knowledge to change their fundamental business strategies even once. Many tried. Most failed. Gates shifted product strategies, sometimes overnight. It seemed to him the only way to survive. The most famous example was his decision in the mid-1990s to take the Internet into account and make sure that all Microsoft products interacted with it. Microsoft's Robbie Bach vividly recalled the Windows 95 launch and how, a month later, all the talk was on how Microsoft had to reinvent itself to take advan-tage of the Internet. "That was symbolic. We had just done the biggest and most important thing in the company's history—and people moved on to the Internet. That speaks volumes about how we think about our business."

Fostering a culture that embraced such sudden change forced Gates to create an environment at Microsoft that was not for the faint of heart. Pleasing Bill Gates became the main goal for employees. Incur-ring his wrath was the worst sin. He purposely chose to make life tough for his programmers. "That's the stupidest thing I have ever heard," was his classic comeback to employees who had not pleased him. Product reviews could be a brutal experience. "Do you want me to write this code for you?" he might bark. "I could do it over the weekend." The truth was that not since 1983 had Gates written any code; but no one doubted that if he had to, he could indeed write the code over a weekend.

His temper was legendary. So was the meek praise he sometimes offered—it was usually brief and unemotional. He championed tough love as a business strategy. Time was too precious, he felt, to waste on laudatory speeches. If Microsoft was going to change the world—its most grandiose cultural tenet—his employees had to work hard and excel, and only in a confrontational environment would that happen. So he believed. "It wasn't a place to come to relax," admitted Deborah Willingham. It was a place where people were direct, where there was a good deal of debate. "You couldn't be a shrinking violet and be happy here. People were in your face. We wanted to be good; we wanted to be the best. So questioning one another was part of the culture."

Gates encouraged contentiousness. He viewed it as a positive work style. Gentle civility was out. He got a kick out of junior employees who challenged him (as long as they made a valid point). Steve Ballmer claimed that Gates was showing a sign of respect when he shouted back at someone; but it was unlikely that the recipient of a Gates outcry agreed.

Working hard was not simply a cultural imperative in the early Microsoft days. It was, for the young (average age: twenty-six), unmarried programmers a way of life. Stories that might seem apocryphal were all too true: the programmer who never left the office during six weeks to complete a project; sightings of employees fast asleep with their hands still on the keyboard. When a Microsoft executive scolded employees for not having enough fun, some asked seriously what they might do for fun! They thought sitting in front of computers day in and day out was sufficient amusement. "When we had ship parties [honoring a product launch] that were scheduled between 1:00 and 4:00 P.M.," recalled Mike Murray, "we wanted to finish at 2:30 P.M. so we could get back to work."

Intellectual Pissing Contest

As previously noted, the early Microsoft culture was very individualist in its orientation. It was up to employees to sink or swim in the tough, take-no-prisoners environment. A kind of Darwinian only-the-best-will-survive atmosphere prevailed, an "intellectual pissing contest" in the colorful phrase of Harvard Business School Professor of Business Administration Chris Bartlett. It was up to each employee to fight for a place in the Microsoft sun. And fight they did—because they were used to succeeding and they did not want to get left behind. "We were hiring straight-A students," recalled Mike Murray. "People were used to getting A's, but now you might be told you were only an average student, and you didn't want to be average. You liked getting attention from Bill or from his right-hand guy."

How well employees performed as individuals counted, not how much they contributed to a team effort. Thinking on one's feet was valued. Consulting others was frowned upon. The company did not financially reward teamwork. The performance management system focused on individual results. Employees were left to their own devices to work out problems. "If you grew up in a family where people didn't raise their voices and didn't interrupt you," said Mike Murray, "you'd be a fish out of water. If you couldn't adapt to that, it wouldn't be your kind of company."

The individual performance culture discouraged intimacy. "It wasn't a collegial environment," remembered Mike Murray. "You worked hard with your team, but you were not buddy-buddy with them. It wasn't a company that inspired or valued close friendships because everyone was so driven." Six-month performance reviews were held for everyone. The numerical rating an employee received influenced his or her pay raise, annual bonus, and the number of stock options.

Microsoft executives took special pride in those individual performance evaluations. "Many other companies dream about having a culture that would numerically score people's performance," said Craig Mundie. That analysis of performance created a culture of meritocracy that simply was not found in other companies. "We were never very title conscious, never very age conscious, never very hierarchical," said Mundie. Microsoft was, however, individual conscious.

For as long as the company's entire work force was in one building, Microsoft encouraged a form of behavior known as "lapping." The first person who arrived at work parked his or her car closest to the door. The next person parked next to the first car and so on. The culture was such that people were primed to work long hours and it was a badge of honor to stay in the building and work around the clock so that your car would still be there when the other cars came to work on the second day—hence, "lapping" the other cars. Lapping was a kind of moral victory for the workaholic.

By the early 2000s, the Microsoft culture was going through a powerful seismic shift. Few within the company liked to talk about just how powerful a shift it actually was. To make such statements was a kind of slap in the face of Bill Gates for he had created and nurtured the original culture; and no one had any doubts that he wanted it preserved in its entirety. Still, the shift was occurring.

To be sure, much of the old culture would remain, as Steve Ballmer made clear at an early stage. In a memo that he had written on June 8, 2001, he talked about those parts of the culture that would remain in place:

A passion for technology would not change. "This takes different forms," wrote Ballmer, "depending on whether you're writing code, conducting research, or working in sales, services, or operations. At the core, though, it's a passion for innovation, exploration and creativity, and a belief in the value of software and the difference it can make in people's lives. Most importantly it is reflected in people's ability to think analytically, react quickly, pick up trends and instigate or adapt to change as needed."

The "never give up" attitude would remain a cultural norm as well.

"Our product history is full of examples where if at first we didn't succeed, we'd try and try (and try) again! This kind of *never give up* attitude has meant that we get things done that other companies most likely would have given up on. Windows, Office, our Enterprise products, MSN and, most recently, .NET, underscore the kind of persistence that has—and will—return great benefits.

A third cultural feature that would not be abandoned was the company's policy of self-examination. "However tough our competitors and customers are on us, I think most of us are even tougher on ourselves. Our capacity to be *honest and self critical* is one of the greatest and most unique things about our company, and has enabled us to self-correct when we get off course or make mistakes."

Later in the memo, Ballmer acknowledged that Microsoft seemed unrelenting in its pursuit of winning. "No one doubts that Microsoft has a strong *competitive* gene. It gives us intense focus and motivation, and has enabled us to survive and prosper in a highly competitive industry."

And he concluded by asserting that "the combination of these assets results in a focus on *individual achievement*. This has enabled us to achieve some remarkable breakthroughs, and is a quality we have celebrated through recognition and compensation."

Certainly in the case of the first three of these cultural values—a passion for technology, persistence, and self-examination—Ballmer meant what he said. He wanted Microsoft to retain these cultural values. But in the case of the last two—being competitive and focusing on individual achievement—other statements and other actions he would make later on suggested that Microsoft hoped to jettison these in favor of other cultural values.

The fact was that the old culture had focused on the twin traits of being aggressive and competitive. The new one was going to revolve around a single key phrase, *open and respectful*. In everything the company did, it was now supposed to be open and respectful toward anyone and everyone in the outside world. Microsoft was supposed to find ways to communicate what it was doing to outsiders early and often.

The company was supposed to go after their hearts and minds, not just their pocketbooks. By not doing so, it had landed into trouble. That had to change.

It was no accident that Bill Gates said very little about the need to change the culture. At times he grudgingly acknowledged that Microsoft was making changes in the wake of the trial. And he certainly was making a big effort to give Microsoft a new "open and respectful feel" through his Trustworthy Computing initiative. But he never spoke directly in either his speeches or his interviews of the changes that had come to be more associated with Steve Ballmer. One was hard put to cite an example of his encouraging people at Microsoft to be more open and respectful. To him, the company's policy had *always* been to be open and respectful to others. He gave the impression that he wasn't sure why the company had so many changes in the culture.

A Rock and a Hard Place

When he did make a rare allusion to the changes the company was making, he seemed mostly concerned that too much of the old culture was being stripped away; after all, it was his view, it had been that original culture that had propelled Microsoft to greatness. Some of it, he seemed to be saying pleadingly, had to be good. He almost certainly had in mind the need to be passionate about technology and to be fiercely competitive. Gates seemed uncomfortable with any tinkering of the culture. Looking back, he knew how easy it had been for him to infuse the original culture into every employee. When the company was small, when every employee could fit in a room (later, an auditorium), all it took to transmit the culture was for him to get up in front of the crowd and talk. Mostly he talked about the cool technology Microsoft was creating and how important it was to be competitive. He had no need to issue marching orders for employees to become more aggressive or to work harder. They got the message simply by hanging around the office.

But none of that was possible for a company that had grown to 55,000 employees in 2003. Of that total, fully 18,500 worked overseas. No longer was it possible for someone to show up and address the entire work force. Thus, in 2003, it was much more difficult for Microsoft employees to learn what the culture was all about. To get those messages across now, someone had to take the time to communicate systematically to the whole Microsoft community through in-person speeches, Web casts, and e-mailed memos. As we noted earlier, Bill Gates was in no position to be the bearer of a new culture. So the task fell to Steve Ballmer. It would not be easy for him to carry out the task since Ballmer was stuck between a rock and a hard place.

His close friendship with Gates made him reluctant to play around too much with the culture that the cofounder had created and nurtured. But Ballmer sensed the urgent need for Microsoft to show a new, more benign persona to the outside. Ballmer's dilemma explains why, after he became CEO, he thought long and hard before attempting to redefine Microsoft's culture.

The push and pull that emerged from his dilemma was evident when we talked in September 2003. "I love our culture in many, many ways and certainly I feel as a partial creator of the culture. But given what we need to do in the marketplace, given what we need to do internally, there are some things where I think we're going to need to improve. . . . We've got to be . . . more responsive to our customers. . . . We've got to work better with our industry and we've got to work better internally with one another."

Often when he spoke in 2003, Ballmer reflected the dilemma of having to decide which parts of the culture to keep and which to discard. When asked that summer to describe the new Microsoft culture, he suggested that it still contained the traditional element of intensity. But today there had to be intensity not just about the product line, but toward the people with whom Microsoft was dealing. "I'd still say hard core works pretty well—but I'll put one little difference on there. Hard core means passionate. Hard core means intense. And hard core also needs to encompass this value we call open and respectful, which [means] you can be hard core, sometimes so passionate, so excited, so over the edge that you're not as respectful as you need to be to other people."

But getting people to change overnight was not easy. After all, an almost inherent conflict had emerged in asking employees to be kinder and gentler, yet at the same time to continue to be aggressive in their sales and marketing behavior. The balance Microsoft had to achieve, Ballmer said in November 2003, was "How do you really behave as responsible leader for the industry, and yet at the same time let the company know, the employees know, we're still going to be innovative, we're going to still try to provide great value, that means our innovation at low prices, we're going to compete?

"If we lose a customer, we're going to feel bad, we're going to want to know what we need to do better next time so we don't lose that customer the next time. So how do you hit that balance between being forceful, and aggressive, and still being a great participant, talking to your industry partners, even if you compete with them sometimes, right level of cooperation, right level of cooperation with government?"

Making Others Great

The kind-versus-aggressive dilemma also explained why it took Ballmer eighteen months (until June 8, 2001) as CEO before he issued an e-mailed internal memo to employees on the need to change the Microsoft culture.

Ballmer decided that the place to start was with the old Microsoft emphasis on the individual. Encouraging and rewarding employees for their collaborative efforts should become a new cultural norm.

"[W]hile individual achievement will always be recognized, we need to put more effort and priority into *making others great*. This includes our colleagues and our partners. For those of you who follow sports, think of players like American basketball star Larry Bird or Brazilian soccer legend Pele—the truly great players don't just demonstrate individual excellence; they also make every individual on their team play better.

"As our business becomes more complex, and groups become increasingly interdependent on one another . . . it is critical that we foster an environment where people place as much emphasis on helping other people, other groups and our partners succeed as they do on individual achievement. At the end of every day, I'd like people to go home asking: 'Did I make the people around me more productive? Did I help them get more done? Did I offer insights that will enable them to do their job better?'

"This means problem-solving and collaboration at the individual level, and focusing on being good managers and leaders through strong hiring, management, communication, and motivation of teams. It means looking for win–win situations with partners—understanding that our success as a company depends on the success of many other companies and partners."

In so many words, Ballmer was saying that the new stress on teamwork was necessary, to help Microsoft pursue a diverse array of new markets. Teamwork created more discipline, more efficiency, less waste. And, only by being open and respectful—toward outside partners, toward one another—would collaboration truly succeed. But the way had to be cleared for the new push toward teamwork. The company had to soften the long-time competitive urges. No longer did Microsoft talk of changing the world; the goals in 2003 became more modest—enabling people and businesses throughout the world to realize their full potential. No longer did Microsoft give the impression that employees had to be competitive at all costs. Now employees were simply asked to strive for excellence.

In his June 6, 2002, memo, Steve Ballmer made it clear that excellence was the company's new goal, not being competitive or winning. "Excellence must be at the core of everything we do and is central to everything we value. There are several pillars of excellence to which we must all aspire:

- Excellence in people
- Excellence in every part of our relationship with customers and partners
- Excellence in product quality
- Excellence in how we make decisions and orchestrate our work internally to be efficient and predictable
- Excellence in shareholder value"

Steve Ballmer did not have to issue a decree requiring Microsoft employees to become less aggressive. That part of the culture had begun to change on its own. For instance, the practice of lapping eventually died out when Microsoft became too big and could not contain all of its personnel in one building, and when a lot of those young men in their twenties married and had children, and no longer thought it was cool to lap a fellow employee.

On average, the company was older. As many as 23 percent of the company's fifty-five thousand employees were over forty years old; another 50.1 percent were in their thirties, and only 26.8 percent were in their twenties. No one was under twenty years old. Fully two-thirds were married.

No more poignant moment depicting the changes in the Microsoft culture existed than one morning in the summer of 2003 when a Microsoft employee and his wife pulled up in their sports car to the front of Building 34, the headquarters building on the Redmond campus. The wife got out of the car with her husband, kissed him good-bye, and, as he was walking away, asked him when he would be able to get away that afternoon for some family activity. She drove off and he began his day's work. In the old culture, such scenes could hardly have taken place—or at least certainly not in the quantity that they did now. Then the typical scene was of twenty-something youngsters, huddled over a computer in a small office, with pizza boxes and empty Coke cans strewn around.

Now the importance of balancing work at Microsoft with family life was fast becoming a new cultural normal. Both Gates and Ballmer set the tone. Both had wives and children. Both made sure to spend quality time with the children. Gates made sure to spread the word in news interviews that he was a doting father, making sure to get home in time to play with his children before they went to bed. In the old Microsoft, Gates often replied to e-mails from colleagues on the spot. Now those colleagues had to wait for Gates's children to go to bed!

End of the 24/7 Era

Sometimes it was hard getting used to the fact that the 24/7 start-up days were over. On one occasion Jeff Raikes had skipped a senior management meeting to attend an art show at his daughter's elementary school. During the show he spotted a familiar face. It was Bill Gates, whose daughter Jennifer attended the same school. Poking fun at Gates, Raikes knew he was poking fun at himself when he asked the chairman, "Hey, aren't you supposed to be at that meeting?" Gates's reply went unrecorded, but he probably gave Raikes a "Hey, this-is-the-new-Microsoft" smile. None of this meant that people at Microsoft were loafing. After one nonstop two-day session at Microsoft in January 2003, Steve Ballmer seemed embarrassed at how hard they had all worked. He was certainly not going to brag about it, he said meekly, and then quickly added in a comment that could have been made only in the new Microsoft, "I'm probably apologizing for it."

That attitude filtered down to the rank and file, who—while insisting that they were working just as hard as ever and did not shrink from working fourteen hour days—also noted that such workaholism was no loner the norm—and for good reason. Their managers worried that they might burn out. Their managers actually ordered them to take weekends off! "It takes so much effort to find, interview, recruit, hire, train, and get our employees productive," said Mark Zbikowski, an architect in the Personal and Business Systems Division. "It takes so much time, it's a shame to burn them out after a couple of years. I've told my people, 'Go home. This is Friday night. Don't come back until Monday. Do something else; because I want you to be here in five years.'" When Zbikowski started with Microsoft in 1980, only two or three employees were married. Today most are married. "That changes how people work," said Zbikowski. "If you're married and you have kids, you can't put in fourteen-hour days. It just doesn't work." So, few of today's employees have to be pushed out the door to go home to their families.

If it had been a badge of honor to "lap" others or to fall asleep at one's desk, the new badge of honor was staying home with the family on weekends. Robbie Bach, the senior vice president for the Games Division, was happy to wear that badge. "I don't work on weekends," he proudly declared, a statement that, if said two decades earlier at Microsoft, might have branded him a traitor. "I haven't worked on weekends for the last three or four years."

That did not mean he worked less or that his commitment to the company had weakened. "Everybody works hard. But people are smarter and we use technology to have flexibility to get work done when we want to do it." He came in to work at 8:30 A.M. the morning of our interview "because I wanted to help my wife get the kids to school. I get home by 6:30 P.M. I can do something from home in the evening; no one asks a question. Before it was a badge of honor to see how late you stayed at work. That badge doesn't exist anymore."

Robbie Bach knew that saying such things in public was nothing to worry about. He knew that Microsoft's CEO devoted his weekends to the family as well. Indeed, after noting that Bill Gates typically sent him ten to fifteen e-mails each weekend, Ballmer proudly noted that he did not respond to them until Sunday night because "That's my deal with my wife."

A central theme was emerging for Steve Ballmer as he took the culture through some major changes. He was less and less interested in the individual Microsoft employee as a central focus of the culture; he was much more concerned with perceptions of Microsoft within the external world. This would be evident in his attitude toward the sensitive subject of stock options; and it would be equally apparent in the way he handled the issue of employee incentives.

The discarding of stock options in the summer of 2003 in favor of stock awards was an apt illustration of Ballmer's emerging theme—the need to make significant changes in the way Microsoft presented itself to the external word. When Ballmer took the decision to scrap stock options, it may have seemed odd to some who remembered the stock option program as the goose that laid the golden egg.

But Ballmer had his reasons. He knew that once Microsoft's stock had plummeted, stock options no longer held much glamour. Microsoft had always wanted to pay its employees for their achievements, and, with stock options losing value, another way had to be found. Stock awards had the distinct advantage of rewarding employees even when the stock was falling. Someone was not going to get fantastically rich from the stock awards, but neither would that person watch a fortune disappear overnight. Stock awards were unquestionably more valuable if the stock was worth more and less valuable if the stock was worth less. This was a much more level-headed approach for rewarding employees than the once highly appealing stock options.

Winning the Lottery

By 1999, Microsoft's stock option program had turned an estimated ten thousand Microsoft employees into millionaires. "No one," said CFO John Connors, "could have foreseen the unnatural phenomenon that stock options became an incredible short-term lottery win. No one could have foreseen how well we would do. What was designed as a long-term program became a short-term payout program. Instead of giving people long-term compensation, they were making enough money to send three thousand kids to college; instead of buying one home, they could build thirty vacation homes. It became almost a lottery system, and lots of people won the lottery."

But, just as many won the lottery, many eventually lost it too. It was simply assumed that the goose would go on laying golden eggs forever.

That was not to be the case. No one could have foreseen that stock options would one day lose their appeal. But that's what happened when the company's shares fell sharply in value from 52.6 in March 2000 to 27.1 in March 2001.

John Eng, a group product manager for the SQL Server Product Management Group, arrived at Microsoft with the expectation that he would do very well from his stock options. That was in 1999, when the stock was doubling every eighteen months. "It shot from 75 to 120 in my first six months." But he could only exercise his options in small portions over the next four and a half years. And so he watched with mounting disappointment as the stock dropped.

In April 2000, to provide some compensation for the diminishing stock price, as well as to sweeten the pot in the wake of rumors that the company was about to be broken up, Steve Ballmer granted employees new stock options priced near the company's fifty-two-week low. News reports suggested that morale had hit a new bottom at the time. Employees were to receive a one-time stock option grant equal to options received with their July 1999 review. New employees were also eligible for the grant. Options were priced at $66.63, the closing price on April 24, 2000, the day that the stock fell 15 percent following a series of analyst downgrades. "He didn't have to do that," said John Eng. "There was no contract between Microsoft employees that said, 'Yes the stock will double every eighteen months,' but yet he did that. So I'm in a situation where it's a good mix of options and stock awards. Either way it seems like I could win."

The ending of the stock options was one more visible sign that Microsoft's start-up days were ending, the days when an employee combined hard work and aggressiveness and watched his or her bank account grow and grow. The options had come to symbolize the Microsoft focus on the individual, rewarding an employee for boosting company performance. But the options remained a symbol as well to the outside world of a Microsoft that had become excessively greedy. And that was one big reason why Ballmer wanted to kick them out the door. In the past, if the outside world thought Microsoft employees excessively greedy for making millions on the stock options, the company could not have cared less. But now, as part of the emerging cultural tenet to be concerned about what outsiders thought, it cared a great deal. And so in place of the stock option program, Microsoft erected a more straightforward stock award program.

Ironically, the company had not designed the stock option program at the outset to make employees superrich. But, with the company's supergrowth in the 1990s, that is exactly what had happened. Originally, Microsoft's stock options were meant to give employees an extra financial incentive to stick around. Though generous, a Microsoft salary did not provide that incentive nearly as much as the options did.

Bouncing Up and Down

Eager to keep the cultural emphasis on the individual, the company used the stock option program along with bonuses to create incentives for one's performance. An employee had an incentive to work hard, to boost productivity, to help the company grow—and ultimately to keep the stock price getting higher and higher. In addition to a salary, employees received a 15 percent bonus that was based on their hard work and productivity, and they also received stock options.

In their time, stock options were a great way to compensate employees, but as a means of rewarding individual achievement, ultimately they backfired. As options became more valuable, employees were rewarded whether or not they had achieved anything in their work. In the past someone could get 100,000 stock options, be vested after seven years, and then leave. While very few people stayed the seven years and then quit (many who became incredibly rich continued to work for Microsoft), the point was that someone *could* get fabulously wealthy regardless of the quality of that person's work, which was clearly not what the system had been intended to do.

With the new stock award system, this could not happen. "You can't rest and vest," said CFO John Connors. "You have to perform. The longer you stay and perform, the more income you will receive."

But what the new stock award program really did was to make Microsoft employees think less about the chance to get rich quick and more about the other nonmonetary elements of job satisfaction. It put the emphasis back on such job goals as having an impact on other peoples' lives and on rising within the company to new levels of responsibility.

In the old Microsoft, no one publicly admitted that he or she had joined the company to become a multimillionaire; but once an employee learned that others had done so, such thoughts were hard to put out of one's mind. For the current crop of Microsoft employees, such as John Eng, it was simply not possible to dream about riches. So other parts of the job began to matter more. "Most who come here," he said, "come here to do some pretty interesting work, so the work content is as important as the compensation, if not more." He liked hanging around smart people, being with a company that made big bets, and impacting many people's lives. "It's as good as being a doctor in that sense." Most of all he liked the company's efforts to help employees grow. "Not many other companies that I've worked for have a goal to make you a successful individual today and next year. It's not just training. When you sit down with your Microsoft manager, you have a growth plan, where you want to be, what you're good at, where you need some help, how we help you build those skills so you can get there. That's very different from other places."

These were all ways that Microsoft was trying to keep its employees from leaving. The stock options system had backfired by providing an exit strategy to still-young, highly talented Microsoft executives who suddenly had little incentive to stay at the company. Once a big fan of stock options as the driving force behind the New Economy, Bill Gates grew disenchanted with the approach for serving up that exit strategy to some of his most talented executives.

When the options lost so much value, it provided one more reason for employees to reconsider their loyalty to Microsoft. It was ironic. For so long, retaining the loyalty of its employees had never been a problem at Microsoft. Few employees at any company had it so good.

By designing exciting new software, they got to do the work they loved, they knew they were having a strong impact on how millions worked and played, and they were getting staggeringly rich.

But that was changing. Within the short space of two years, Microsoft employees had their loyalty tested on three fronts:

First, there had been the advent of the dot-coms, those get-rich-quick start-ups perched on the Internet, promising to change the way America and the world did business and the way it entertained itself. In the process, Microsoft employees found themselves easily seduced into leaving for these greener pastures. While it was true that Microsoft's attrition rates were consistently 50 percent of those of the rest of the industry, it was losing to the dot-com world too many top-flight executives, and that was hurting. "In terms of our reputation," said Ken DiPietro, the new corporate vice president for human resources at Microsoft, "we had become the monopoly and start-ups were the cool places to go. People played Russian roulette with their careers."

Second, there was the Microsoft trial, proving an embarrassment and an open wound to employees who suddenly questioned whether they wanted to work for a company in which they felt less and less pride.

And finally, there was the dismal tale of the stock options, never the only reason to work at Microsoft, but certainly the icing on the cake; and now they were gone.

A Different Life

Andrew Wilson, when he joined Microsoft in February 2002, had no expectations that he would become incredibly rich from stock options. Still, for recent arrivals such as Wilson, the company's ups and downs have caused some odd moments. Wilson, a researcher with Microsoft Research, joined MSR after finishing his doctorate at the MIT Media Lab, where his work explored gesture recognition from video and other sensors in a machine learning framework.

"Some of the lunch-time conversations can be kind of interesting," Wilson observed. "You have sitting next to you some guy who has several sports cars and a couple of boats and so he tends to have a somewhat different life; some of those guys are here because they enjoy the work, not because they need the money. It's great to have them. So there is a bit of a funny thing going on with that.

"It's not a real problem. When I took the job here, I did not go into it with the expectations that the stock options would pan out." He tried to convince his recruiter to reduce his stock options in favor of hard currency "because I just didn't think it was going to pan out. I was right." He did not get his way, but the human resources unit came up with ways to improve his overall package.

Viewing the problems together—the dot-coms, the trial, the sagging stock options—people who left Microsoft complained that its reputation among its own employees as a top-flight company was slipping to an all-time low. Microsoft's leadership knew it had to reverse the trend. And so, part of the new culture centered on retaining the loyalty of its employees.

Microsoft's human resources managers and others as well began to ask a question that had never been asked before: How do we make sure that we have the right kind of workplace environment? In the past, the company had not had to be too concerned with retaining the loyalty of its employees. Most of them loved the environment, loved the chance to impact the world, and loved the vast wealth that came their way. In the past, the company had never boasted that such an environment included the likelihood of getting fabulously wealthy. Certainly, many people at Microsoft acquired great riches, but that had never been a company commitment. In the new Microsoft, there would be an equal soft-pedaling of wealth as one of the perks of working at Microsoft. The reason: No longer was personal wealth probable or even possible.

In 2003, Microsoft's HR executives, in trying to build loyalty within the company, were talking up the excitement that came from working at the company: the chance to be around so many smart people, to be able to collaborate with them, to work under great leadership. It was considered a feather in Microsoft's cap that employees number one and number eleven were still running the place and that both had become high-tech icons. And Microsoft talked up employees' great opportunities to move from one team to another within the company.

Just as Microsoft was shifting away from a focus on the individual with its new spin on its stock program, it would make the same shift in carving out a whole new approach to the issue of employee incentives. As with the stocks, the individual no longer held center stage; Microsoft's relations with the outside world did. And no group figured more importantly to Microsoft in that outside world than its customers.

The whole customer issue was a hard one for Microsoft executives. Deep down they had long believed that they were doing right by the customer or at least trying their best. But despite their efforts, customers were more and more upset with the company. One didn't have to go beyond the day's headlines to see Microsoft branded as a monopolist, and a greedy one at that. Whether it was true or not, its customers were reading those headlines, digesting them day in and day out. Microsoft had the feeling that it was in the midst of a losing battle.

Something had to be done.

As part of the tweaking of the culture, Steve Ballmer decided that the time had come to get Microsoft's personnel much closer to the customers. It was part and parcel of creating a more open and respectful Microsoft. But this whole new effort to improve relations with customers seemed strange to many at the company who asked, Hadn't it always been part of the company's culture to cozy up to customers?

Of course, it had. But no one would deny that, for years, the customer had not been a very important priority for Microsoft. No one thought it very important to measure just how satisfied customers were or at least to pay much attention when customer satisfaction was actually measured.

In the early days, Microsoft did not deal with consumers directly. This suited Bill Gates and his colleagues quite nicely. An historic tradition existed within Microsoft to keep a certain distance from end users, the people who actually used the software. Gates, it was said, explained to employees, "We do not talk to any end users." Gates was not fond of them as a group. They kept phoning the company with silly questions; they stole software. He wanted to deal only with customers at the OEM level and let the OEMs stay in touch with the end users.

Coupled with this distancing from customers was a feeling within the burgeoning company that it knew best what customers wanted—or should want. That was fine when customers had very little computer savvy, when few could tell the difference between this feature or that, and when Microsoft was only in a few markets. If customers had complaints—and of course they did—it wasn't as if they had a lot of choice of what software products to buy. With so many people using Microsoft products, it became impractical for anyone *not* to use them.

But as the company moved into more and more markets, and as customers grew more and more sophisticated about computer software, they grew tired of being told by Microsoft what to buy, when to upgrade, generally what to do about computer software.

Betting the Farm

Furthermore, once large corporations began acquiring Microsoft products, the software was so crucial to the daily operations of those corporations that Microsoft began to understand just how important customers were to its own survival. "A Daimler Chrysler," said Bob Herbold, Microsoft's executive vice president, "is betting the farm on our software to produce cars every second of every day. So customer satisfaction is of the utmost importance." As recently as the late 1990s, most big companies had not been so dependent on the reliable functioning of their software. "If the software didn't work for six hours back then," said Herbold, "maybe secretaries wouldn't have been able to type their Word documents, but at least the factory was still running. If our software crashes today, the factory will not be running.

That's a huge difference for us. We become almost a part owner of the company."

Being so involved in the daily operations of its customers, Microsoft could not afford to turn those customers off. But that was precisely what had been happening. If Microsoft needed a fresh lesson in how important customer satisfaction was becoming, it learned it the hard way when in the summer of 2001 it offered a new licensing arrangement designed to make Microsoft's sales less dependent on new product releases. Historically, companies had purchased an initial single license for a single user and a discounted upgrade license whenever upgrades became available. The new arrangement forced users to purchase a license and then pay a maintenance fee on both client and server software. Once the fee was paid, upgrades were available for no further cost; but if the maintenance package was not bought, upgrades had to be purchased at full cost.

The problem for Microsoft was that it really could make money only by putting out one upgrade after another. With that kind of pressure, it did not have adequate time to come up with the needed features nor could it test those features adequately. So it searched for a new way to lock its customers in to sales.

Microsoft used a carrot-and-stick approach in the new licensing arrangement. Promised were regular product upgrades. But customers saw the deal as benefiting Microsoft, not them. They argued that they were going to have to pay more than they did under the old arrangement, and were concerned that future upgrades might not be equal in value to the price they were being forced to pay up-front.

The new licensing arrangement simply did not offer the customer enough value, and Microsoft paid a very heavy price in its customer relationships. "In the transition," admitted Kevin Johnson, senior vice president for Microsoft Americas, "we created customer dissatisfaction."

Incidents such as the licensing fee problem led Ballmer to take a very close look at customer relations. By the fall of 2002, Ballmer was focusing his thoughts more and more on how to make Microsoft more customercentric. In a memo he distributed October 2, he explained why it was so hard to satisfy customers when selling software products. Not only was information technology more complex and interdependent than consumer products, but, "The challenge has more to do with the flexibility of technology and its continual, rapid advance. To take advantage of this and expand what people can do with hardware and software, computer products must constantly evolve. As a result, products are seldom around long enough in one form to be fully time-tested, let alone perfected. And customers continually come up with new uses for their technology, new combinations and configurations that further complicate technology companies' efforts to ensure a satisfying experience, free of hiccups and glitches."

What Microsoft had to do to approach the level of customer satisfaction with other consumer products, he argued, was to obtain a "more detailed knowledge of customers' experiences with our products. We must do a better job of connecting with customers. For a company such as Microsoft, with many millions of customers around the world, the connections must be very broad. While we are working to deepen our relationships with enterprise and other business customers, we also need to make innumerable, daily connections with the very wide array of people who use our products—consumers, information workers, software developers, and information technology professionals."

There was, he acknowledged, no way to prevent a piece of software, often with millions of lines of code in it, from having bugs. This was a huge admission, but it was meant to respond to the widely held belief among customers that Microsoft could and should get rid of every bug in its software—before the company shipped the product!

Microsoft had made a lot of progress, he said, in eliminating past flaws, but more work had to be done. A key problem was that customers did not report bugs. They simply closed down the program. Even when customers reported a problem, they did not provide enough detail to help Microsoft solve it. A small team in the Office group had devised a new system that helped Microsoft gather real-world data about customer problems, specifically crashes. This error reporting software existed in more and more Microsoft programs. One stunning discovery was that a relatively small proportion of bugs—20 percent—caused most (80 percent) of the errors. Even more stunning was the discovery that only one percent of the bugs caused half of all errors. Learning all of that has helped Microsoft focus on solutions to the remaining bugs.

E-mails and Speeches Won't Cut It

The question of customer relations was of such importance, Ballmer believed, that he could not rely on e-mails and speeches to convince Microsoft personnel to get closer to customers. He had to do more. He had to create incentives. The incentives would reward employees for adding customers and properly servicing existing ones. Rather than spread the incentives around the whole company, he thought it only necessary at first to apply the incentive program to the most senior executives. Once the senior executives got the message, the new attitude toward customers would hopefully pervade the company.

The whole issue came to a head in February 2002 during a meeting of senior Microsoft managers at a four-day retreat at a ski resort in Bend, Oregon. It was there that Orlando Ayala, at the time Microsoft's senior man in sales, spoke with great emotion about the company's need to improve much of the way it was doing business. He urged other executives to start to put the customer first, acknowledging that customers frequently thought that Microsoft simply did not care about producing great products and that, as a monopoly, it believed it could get away with inferior workmanship. Ayala said that some at the meeting deserved to lose their jobs and that all of them there were accountable for what had happened. The executives' reaction was remarkable: Ayala received a standing ovation.

Echoing Ayala's sentiments, a large number of managers expressed worry that Microsoft had acquired a reputation as an arrogant monopoly that had become obsessed with its own profits and that had been frequently insensitive to customer needs. That kind of reputation would, they argued, hurt the company in the long term. That reputation was clearly at odds with the image these managers had of the company, but most of them recognized that Microsoft had a problem.

While everyone at the retreat was in accord on the need to improve Microsoft's customer relations, rancor erupted over how to get that improvement. Much of the contentiousness had to do with Steve Ballmer's proposed plan to link the future compensation of these managers to customer satisfaction. Under the plan, a significant portion of the stock awards of the six hundred most senior Microsoft executives would now depend on the growth in the number and satisfaction of Microsoft customers. Some openly resisted the idea, arguing that it was much more difficult to measure customer satisfaction fairly than sales and profits. But with Steve Ballmer's encouragement, those who favored the plan prevailed.

Ballmer might have sympathized with the vagueness of the customer satisfaction incentive program, but he had to get the entire company thinking about how to improve customer satisfaction, especially with Bill Gates's new theme of integrated innovation. What Microsoft wanted of customers increasingly—under the integrated innovation theme—was to gain an appreciation for Microsoft's uniqueness, that it had product offerings in most software fields and that those product offerings were cleverly integrated with each other. Historically, a member of the Office team, for instance, knew that the number of his or her stock options was based exclusively on the shipping of the Office product. What mattered to that person therefore was getting the product out the door—nothing more. Certainly the Outlook employee wanted to satisfy customers, but only his or her customers. The successes and failures of others around the company had no real relevance to any particular employee.

But now it would no longer be possible for a Microsoft employee to worry only about his or her product areas; the notion of integrated innovation forced employees to think more broadly of how to improve customer satisfaction across the widest possible span of product segments.

The Bend, Oregon, retreat proved a turning point for Microsoft. Ballmer understood that the company had to put the customer at the center of its thoughts and strategies. "We changed in that meeting," said Orlando Ayala. "We changed our mission as a company."

As the retreat was ending, Ballmer announced that he was making the issue of customer trust the main issue of his weeklong sync week meetings for September. That announcement brought down the house as well.

In just two years—2002 and 2003—Microsoft had embarked on wide-ranging reforms in many areas of the company. Its leadership was new; it had new business processes and structure; it was looking for a different kind of new employee. It was making important changes in its culture.

All of this had been designed to help repair its sliding reputation. But after all these changes were in place, was there a change in its reputation? Was it too soon to even make such an evaluation? Or was the world starting to take notice of a new Microsoft?

We try to answer these questions in the next and final chapter.

PART V

The Rebooting of Microsoft

11

Has the Revolution Begun?

As 2003 came to a close, some in the media were writing that Microsoft was carrying out one of business history's boldest experiments. Within the company such talk seemed hyperbolic, not to mention premature. For one thing, the people at Microsoft were always experimenting, always reinventing, always reorganizing. The reshaping of Microsoft certainly was bold. But whether it was their boldest ever undertaking remained to be seen. Whether it would even work constituted a much more burning question for the Microsoft community.

Unquestionably, the exercise of transforming the company in 2002 and 2003 had gotten off to a good start. The mere fact that coleaders Bill Gates and Steve Ballmer had permitted the reforms to go forward was progress in and of itself. Both had much to overcome to even begin the journey; both knew that the journey would be long and the results were not guaranteed; but the two men knew that they had to try.

As the experiment moved through its early paces, it appeared that the different roles Gates and Ballmer had carved out for themselves in the recasting of the company were paying off. It seemed in retrospect just as wise to have Gates play the much less active role as it was to have Ballmer play the lead role in the reforms.

By taking a less visible role in the company, Gates had permitted Steve Ballmer to gain authority and respectability as the new person in charge of Microsoft. It had not been an easy transition for Gates. He had held power at Microsoft for so long that yielding it to Ballmer in the early 2000s had proven far more difficult than he had imagined. Yet it had been the right thing to do, and he appeared to understand that. He knew that he had no choice. He was also doing the company a big favor by stepping beyond Microsoft and engaging in a host of activities—some involving industrywide efforts, some his philanthropy—allowing the company to go forward without him at its forefront. Again, he understood that he had no choice.

Gates remained active at Microsoft. At other companies, in other circumstances, the departing CEO understands that he or she would be doing a disservice to the incoming chief executive by hanging around the company. Some departing CEOs still take an office down the corridor from the new leader; but those situations are far from perfect. They simply add to the burdens of the new leader. Yet, even if someone had suggested to Bill Gates that he would have done Steve Ballmer a big favor by retiring from Microsoft entirely, Gates would have resisted such an idea.

For Gates was not ready to leave Microsoft. He was as of October 28, 2003, all of forty-eight years old. He believed that he had plenty more time and energy to give to Microsoft and to the software industry. Unlike some other innovators and founders of companies, Gates did not lose his passion for the work he had done in his career; he seemed just as energized about building magical software (a phrase he used a lot those days) as he was back in the founding days of Microsoft. Although he had discovered a whole new career through his philanthropy, and although it made him passionate about saving people's lives, it did not require his presence or his talents on a full-time basis. He had knowledgeable people running his foundation and he could easily do his part by paying periodic visits to the place. He could accomplish a great deal for the foundation's work through his overseas visits, but he had decided to make just one a year. He clearly wanted to leave the bulk of his time to Microsoft.

In his view, and he was right about this, Microsoft still could benefit from his being on hand, devoting himself nearly full-time to the technology side of the company. Indeed, by stepping down as CEO, he was in an even better position to help the company with its technology program, and in 2003 he seemed especially delighted that the extra time he was putting into the company's product strategies was yielding positive results.

One more point to keep in mind: Had he suddenly retired soon after the Microsoft trial had ended, his critics would have counted his departure as one more victory in their campaign to weaken Gates and Microsoft. The blemish from the trial that Gates had so assiduously worked to avoid might have become a permanent stain on his record. By continuing to play a role at Microsoft, Gates showed that he was not being cowed into a hasty retreat. He showed that he was prepared to take those steps that hopefully would help Microsoft recover from the agonies of the trial.

So Gates stuck around Microsoft, and Steve Ballmer had to manage the company with the former leader in his nearby office.

It seemed fair to say that Gates never really contemplated retiring from Microsoft once the trial was over; nor does he dwell seriously on taking such a step in the near future. He's simply too happy as chief software architect. When a reporter asked him in November 2003 if he would like to take a year off to travel or spend time with his family, he responded predictably, "Hey, if I didn't love my job so much, yeah, that would be a lot of fun. I'll probably find some time this decade to take some months away, but I want to contribute to Longhorn and make sure that's great; I want to help solve security problems; make sure we're driving all the other breakthroughs. With the rest of the world not being so optimistic, I like this thing where I'm going to be able to prove that there are more neat things coming."

Gates appeared to have yet one more reason for sticking around Microsoft, but he had a hard time articulating it. The reason: without saying it precisely, Gates seemed genuinely concerned that, as time went on, people would forget the company's accomplishments under his sole leadership. That concern may have been the most important reason he was not fleeing Microsoft so quickly. It was not hard to pick up the concern he felt, during our interview in the summer of 2003, that in the emerging Steve Ballmer era people would start to draw comparisons unfavorable to Gates. "It's very easy," he told me, "for somebody to write a book that says, 'New CEO. Everything had to change [from the way] everything was done before.' I'm the most biased person on that because I was the previous CEO, but I don't think that would really tell the story."

He seemed to understand that one could not tell the whole Microsoft story by concentrating solely on the software it had produced. "If the story was 'Hey, they have always been good at software and that's worth a lot,' that alone wouldn't have seen us through all the problems and success and a few other [things] that got thrown in with bad luck and a few other [things] that we just made mistakes and imposed on ourselves." To tell the story of Microsoft properly in 2003, and Gates appeared to understand this, one had to portray the company's turmoil during the trial, its emergence from that turmoil, and its efforts to reform itself.

Gates's frustration in trying to decide just how much to associate himself with the revamping process comes through clearly in this next part of the interview: "[There is] this willingness to change a lot of things and try and make things work for this scale that we've got today by drawing in all of this talent that we've got. Anyway, that's the thing that is fascinating that Steve is absorbed in. Now I'm secondarily absorbed in that. I'm primarily absorbed in magical software products. The more magical they are, the more latitude for error there is in some of these other issues that are certainly superimportant."

By the end of 2003, the rebooting of Microsoft was in full force. It had been slow in coming, as we have explained on earlier pages, though the urge for reform had been bubbling underneath the surface for some time.

In earlier years, when the would-be reformists put forth their case, they were rebuffed in every instance by those who wanted Microsoft to cling to a start-up mentality, and who thought that reform would dampen that mentality. But then the trial had occurred. It was the great turning point in the modern-day Microsoft. It started to make people at Microsoft think that changes had to take place. Those changes could no longer be put off.

Over the space of only two years—2002 and 2003—Gates and Ballmer set in motion the most important changes the company had ever experienced, and that was saying a lot for a company that had generated change time and time again, a company that had reinvented product strategies and products sometimes at the drop of a hat.

Gates took part in the reform effort in a minimalist sort of way. He took personal charge of the Trustworthy Computing initiative, but never identified or promoted it as part of the reform package. He did little else to promote the reform effort, leaving that "thing" (as he referred to the reforms in our interview) to Steve Ballmer. Meanwhile, Ballmer was ordering changes in just about every sphere of the company with the one exception of product strategies and product development. That had always been and still remained the exclusive area of responsibility of Bill Gates. Ballmer's was the rest of the company, and within that environment he began the rebooting.

On the leadership front, by the end of 2003, Ballmer and Gates were finally getting comfortable with their new comanagement arrangement. It was comanagement only in the sense that Gates managed the technology and Ballmer managed everything else. Gates was in fact no longer managing important aspects of the company. He was more and more playing a secondary role. Meanwhile, Ballmer was pushing himself to the forefront without seeming ambitious or aggressive.

On the cultural front, Ballmer increasingly acted like the leader of a mature company, much less like the leader of a start-up. In 2003 alone, he had scrubbed stock options, issued the company's first and second dividends, resisted pressures to deplete its huge cash position, and solidified the seven new business segments by adding a chief financial officer to each segment. These were, by Microsoft standards, significant steps in the maturing of the company.

The tweaking of earlier parts of the culture were underway as well during 2003, but Ballmer was discovering that putting an end to the classic traits that had fueled the company in earlier days was hard to accomplish in so short a time.

Still, he had performed a remarkable cultural shift in putting forward new themes stressing that personnel had to be more open and respectful, more communicative, and more forthright in their dealing with outsiders. He understood how such phrases would sound to the cynical, but he felt that he had to pound home the message in the hope that farther down the road, the message would take hold.

Intimidated by Microsoft

He tried to anticipate the cynics by acknowledging that some companies would continue to be intimidated when Microsoft moved into new markets, that some would be distraught at finding their market opportunities diminished. In the old Microsoft, no company leader would have ever been so blunt. No leader would have professed any regret at the company's attempts to vanquish its opponents.

But here was Ballmer addressing the issue frontally; and the media covered his remarks in a very straightforward way with none of the attendant suspicion and scorn that had characterized its earlier coverage. "I think there are probably plenty of people in the industry who wish we wouldn't do anything new," he told one interviewer early in 2003. "We could stop R&D spending and do nothing, and that creates plenty of opportunity for others, I suppose. But I don't think it's in the best interest of customers. So we have to let everybody know this is in our customers' best interest.

"Are we going to have to be aggressive in telling our story and convincing people we have new things? Yeah, we are. That does not go away, it cannot go away. The day we're not . . . being vigorous in terms of pursuing new ideas at low prices with sort of incredible persuasiveness, that's the day you ought to write us right off."

Ballmer was saying, in effect, We're going to try to be more open and respectful, more communicative, more up-front with others; but we're not going to curb any of our traditional aggressiveness. That aggressiveness had its positive aspects and it was what had propelled the early Microsoft forward. Ballmer and others within Microsoft seemed to fear that the more the company embraced the notion of being kinder and gentler, the weaker it appeared, the less aggressive it seemed. And no one at Microsoft wanted to see that.

And yet, becoming kinder and gentler was definitely part of the new Microsoft. How far along in that effort was the company? The question was put to Steve Ballmer in November 2003.

It was hard to quantify the answer, he said, but "We're farther than 20 [percent] and less far than 80 [percent]." What was significant, he said, was that more and more people within the company were starting to understand how to be more cooperative, more open and respectful toward the industry and toward government.

"Take spam, where we've had a big initiative, where we've been trying to work with our industry, and with government on antispam initiatives. Take the work we've been trying to do to reach out to our competitors. We're really partnering now on a set of important interoperability standards with IBM, despite the fact that IBM is in every sense our biggest competitor, a very different place for us to be. I think we've made appreciable progress, and yet I'd be the first to say, I know our customers, our industry wants us to still do better."

He said yes, there was a kinder and gentler Microsoft afoot. "Of course, there is. You know, I've worked hard on it. . . . I can bring all the excitement, and all the enthusiasm, and all the passion, and all of the desire to do the very best job we can for our customers, I can bring all of that, but I have to bring it in a different way."

He was reaching out to long-time Microsoft rivals, to people like Scott McNealy and Larry Ellison. There had been, he said sorrowfully, more public feuding in the software industry than in others. But now he at least was trying to repair some of that damage. "Certainly we've reached out. We've reached out with IBM." He went to see Larry Ellison soon after becoming CEO and talked about how to work cooperatively with him. After not seeing Scott McNealy of Sun for years, Ballmer played in a golf tournament with him in June 2003. Ballmer found it "tough" to play since Microsoft was in the midst of an antitrust suit that Sun had filed against it in early 2002.

Competitive but Fair

Beyond Ballmer, others at Microsoft insisted that the new cultural imperative to be competitive, but fair, was taking hold. "The vast, vast majority of our people," said Robbie Bach, the senior vice president for Home & Entertainment Division, "do what's right for the business. But there are things in the [antitrust] settlement that we have to think about differently." He seemed to suggest that all of Microsoft's new rhetoric was nice, but that was not the real test. "Our actions speak louder than anything else. When people see us competing hard but fairly, that will impact their perception. We're going to try to win in a way we can be proud of. People will either see that or they won't. There's not much I can do about that [the perception]."

It was, of course, Microsoft's group of senior executives who had to become more open and respectful. They were the ones who dealt with the outside world far more than the company's rank and file. Mary Snapp, one of the company's senior legal staff, felt very comfortable trying to be more cooperative with external factors. She had a very precise sense of how to be more open and respectful. "We do it in our negotiation styles and with words on paper and in other small things. In working with the Government, I purposely don't use the word *negotiate*. We should assume that we will get on a plane and travel to them [the Government] as opposed to a give-and-take, where we say, 'You come to us next time.'"

She thought there was still room for improvement. "There are lots of nuances in how we deal with various third parties that we need to be much more sensitive to than in the past. We have to avoid being Redmondcentric. We are worldwide. If we're negotiating with a Cannon or a Nokia, we need to understand cultural sensitivities that they bring to the table. It won't work to negotiate with them the same way as with an American enterprise."

The company's new proactive role especially appealed to Craig Mundie, the senior vice president and chief technical officer for advanced strategies and policy. He liked it that the company had stopped simply reacting to complaints from outsiders. "For many of us," explained Mundie, "the dialogue [with outsiders] has gone from nonexistent to confrontational, then it was remedial, and now it's proactive." Indeed, part of his own role, Mundie suggested, was to develop standing for the company with policy people "on a prospective set of issues as opposed to dealing remedially only with angst that was created later."

Microsoft's early aim was to have industry and government people get to know the company and its people better. "It's harder to hate us when you know us," said Mundie. Microsoft had suffered in earlier days, he argued, because "we had a set of adolescent managers in the business sense, big, strong, strapping people growing quickly. They had lots of energy, but they didn't know what they didn't know and partly what we didn't know was how to be engaged with a lot of people. The company was vilified in the abstract and the only thing people knew was this abstract representation."

Why had it taken so long for the company to act proactively with all of those who defined Microsoft's image? "It wasn't configured to do it," said Mundie. "If you don't know what you don't know, you aren't focused on fixing it. There were a set of broken things that were broken, but we didn't know they were broken so we didn't make an attempt to fix them."

It was Ballmer's hope that as the public began to sense that a new Microsoft was in the works, the continuous attacks and allegations against Microsoft would abate. Without Bill Gates running the business, the theory was that the critics and the media would have less reason to vilify him day in and day out.

The theory bore fruit as the media showed an increasing willingness to treat the company's recent dark past as old news—and treat Gates's hands-on philanthropy as new grist for the mill. Though news stories of Microsoft's legal battles appeared from time to time, they were more about the company's willingness to settle long-standing legal cases than about allegations of antitrust violations. An interesting thing was happening. Articles still appeared about the involvement of Microsoft in this legal case or that. But, in contrast with the front-page treatment of the Department of Justice trial, these newer articles were given less play within newspapers. At the same time, Gates's philanthropic efforts, especially his visits overseas, were getting widespread media coverage, projecting a benign image of Gates that helped the company immeasurably.

To be sure, Microsoft remained under the microscope, but with the trial over, with Bill Gates focusing on the company's technology and on his personal philanthropy, and with Microsoft doing its best to wipe the legal slate clean by settling cases expeditiously, the media's coverage of Microsoft seemed less stinging.

The mere absence of front-page headlines depicting Microsoft as an alleged monopolistic predator improved its image. Moreover, Gates's high-profile forays into the world of philanthropy were reaping important public relations dividends for him even at this early stage.

But it was not simply the absence of those nasty headlines that was helping Microsoft. By addressing the issue of its reputation head on, by going public in a very demonstrable way, the company was causing the media to focus on a new Microsoft. It was not that reporters or editors had suddenly become more sympathetic to Microsoft. More than likely, they still clung to the notion that Gates had done and may well still be doing some unsavory things. But the new Microsoft was getting a much more evenhanded treatment in the media.

It was not that the media had stopped getting on Microsoft's case for alleged strong-arm tactics. One of the more strident pieces of writing, "Microsoft Sticks with Tough Tactics," appeared in the *International Herald Tribune* on May 14, 2003. The reporter, Thomas Fuller, noted that during the summer of 2002, Orlando Ayala, at the time the head of worldwide sales at Microsoft, had sent an e-mail message marked "Microsoft Confidential" to senior managers in which he laid out a company strategy to dissuade governments around the world from selecting less expensive alternatives to Windows.

Under No Circumstances

Fuller wrote that "Ayala's message told executives that if a deal involving governments or large institutions looked doomed, they were authorized to draw from a special fund to offer the software at a steep discount or even free if necessary. Steven A. Ballmer, Microsoft's chief executive, was sent a copy of the e-mail message." The memo on protecting sales of Windows and other desktop software mentioned Linux. "Under NO circumstances lose against Linux," Ayala wrote.

The reporter then suggested that the memo reaffirmed, for anyone who had doubts, that Microsoft remained a very large culprit. "This memo, as well as other e-mail messages and internal Microsoft documents obtained from a recipient of the Microsoft e-mail, offers a rare glimpse these days into the inner workings of Microsoft. . . . They spell out a program of tactics that were carried out in recent years, ranging from steep price discounts to Microsoft employees lying about their identities at trade shows.

"The Microsoft campaign against Linux raises questions about how much its aggressive, take-no-prisoners corporate culture has changed, despite having gone through a lengthy, reputation-tarnishing court battle in the United States that resulted in Microsoft's being found to have repeatedly violated antitrust laws."

Microsoft's response at the time skipped any reference to the allegations of tough tactics: "We have programs to address technology access and availability, and programs that help us deliver a compelling value proposition for customers. As an industry leader these programs address important long-term priorities. Our primary objective is to make technology available to customers at low prices. In competing with Linux and commercial companies, like IBM, that deliver solutions and services on top of the Linux OS, we must offer customers the best long-term value for their IT investment. Equally, making technology available to government and education customers in low-income countries is an important long-term priority."

The article was indeed stinging and not a small setback to Microsoft's reform effort. The point the story was making was this: No matter how much Microsoft tried to recast itself as a more benign, lovable enterprise, the same old Microsoft lay just under the surface and every once in a while popped up for all to see.

Accordingly, Steve Ballmer had a very hard assignment. The *International Herald Tribune* article demonstrated that it was not going to be easy to convince a cynical public that Microsoft had changed its ways.

To try to gauge how Microsoft's reform program was doing, I spoke with a number of leading figures in the computer industry, some of whom spoke on the record, some insisting on anonymity. The majority of them remained skeptical that Microsoft had turned a corner and had become genuinely committed to behaving with integrity in every single instance. Most offered personal examples of alleged Microsoft improprieties of which they claimed to have personal knowledge. No one put forward specific evidence of the alleged misdeed, but all who made the claims insisted that the events had taken place as they described them.

One who spoke on the record was Eric Benhamou, the information technology pioneer, who adamantly insisted that, for all of the new Ballmer rhetoric, Microsoft had not changed much since the Department of Justice trial.

Benhamou is chairman of 3Com, where he served as CEO for ten years. Prior to that, he cofounded Bridge Communications, an early pioneer in network computing. He now advises numerous technology enterprises, serving on the boards of technology companies palmOne, PalmSource, and Cypress Semiconductor.

"All that I see from Microsoft suggests that they believe the trial was unjustified to begin with; and they never really understood, let alone admitted, that they had done anything wrong. Bill was extremely clumsy and self-revealing about his inner motivation and showed utter contempt for the entire process.

"Their behavior has not changed; it's more polished and less egregious. It's almost like long-time criminals who get caught. They need to figure out ways to function in society without being too noticeable."

Asked what Microsoft would have to do to repair its reputation, Benhamou contended that "it's very hard for people to change and certainly for companies that are molded around strong personalities like Gates and Ballmer to change. It's hard to mandate that they change. It's like mandating that people should lose weight. It's against human nature to perform these changes."

Benhamou offered a "small window" into Microsoft. In 2002, Palm, which competes directly with Microsoft's mobile software, decided to open an office in China. Soon after signing a licensing agreement with a major PC manufacturer in China, Microsoft, according to Benhamou, "attempted to get the deal undone using the usual combination of promises, bribes, and threats, the same ones that came out during the Department of Justice trial. This is the sort of behavior that is engrained in the organization that you cannot change." In the end, the Chinese PC firm, while a little nervous at first, stood up to Microsoft, and the deal with Palm was made.

None of this appeared in the media nor did Palm consider legal action against Microsoft, Benhamou said, because in the end no harm was done to Palm. For Palm to have litigated against the much larger Microsoft would have cost it money, energy, and time. "Microsoft knows this," said Benhamou, "and this is why they get away with this bullylike behavior. This leads me to believe that nothing has changed. They tone it down one or two degrees—just enough to fly below the radar of the court systems.

"This is a small, small story. Not a lot of dollars are involved. But you can be assured that countless other similar Microsoft actions are happening every day. They may be trying and some policies may have changed, and I believe they have, but the behavior and natural instincts have not changed.

"The behavior is a reflection of culture; I don't put the blame just on Bill Gates. He has many other redeeming qualities; but this organization is not just Bill; it has its own culture; its own way of thinking about itself and just because it works hard and spends a lot of money on research and development doesn't exonerate it from all of these misbehaviors."

Not everyone with whom I spoke was as harsh toward Microsoft as Eric Benhamou.

Lew Platt, the former CEO of Hewlett-Packard, believes Microsoft has changed. "They are a kinder and gentler Microsoft. I'm not sure they are any less competitive, but I don't think they throw their weight around as much as they used to. They have changed enough that the world doesn't see them as they were before." In Platt's eyes, they no longer boast about being so competitive nor do they tout their strength. "That's a kind of reinventing. They saw they were being taken to task for certain things; they are much more careful."

Even for those who are prepared to say that Microsoft is trying to improve its reputation, it is difficult to imagine that the company can really change. To industry analyst Dwight Davis, the vice president and practice director at Boston-based Summit Strategies, the main change in Microsoft, since the trial, is an awareness that appearances matter. "Ballmer has set the tone that the company has to be a better corporate citizen. It has to understand how its actions play in the world of industry perceptions. But I don't think fundamentally Microsoft has changed because of this. Internally it's not any less arrogant. It does not show any signs of being any less competitive and fighting any less tooth and nail for any market it wants to play in and dominate.

"But it's been a superficial change. They're more aware of the importance of masking some of that aggression and putting forth a kinder face, while behind that face there's still a pretty hard company that will do what it takes and not really pull punches when it goes after a business."

It is that awareness at Microsoft that has prompted Bill Gates to seek fresh ways to appear friendly and benign to the outside world.

As part of that effort, in the latter part of 2003, Microsoft's public relations team decided that Gates should visit a number of college campuses to address audiences of computer science, science, and engineering students. It was, after all, from this pool of students that future Microsoft employees might come. Perhaps even more important, these student audiences comprised some of the most significant molders of public opinion toward Microsoft. Reaching these fresh, young minds, getting them excited about what Microsoft was doing, making them believe that Bill Gates was not the same person whom they had been reading about during all those dark days of the antitrust trial, such was the subtle, unspoken purpose behind these college visits.

The college tour occurred in late February 2004 and included stops at Carnegie Mellon in Pittsburgh; Cornell University in Ithaca, New York; MIT and Harvard in Cambridge, Massachusetts. The meetings with the students were carefully designed. Undoubtedly, a visit by Bill Gates to any of these campuses could have pulled in thousands of students. The organizers did not want such mass meetings. They clearly wanted Gates to speak to a select slice of the college campuses. He spoke to 750 students at MIT, and half that number later the same afternoon at Harvard. Accordingly, there seemed to be no effort to publicize Gates's visits. At the MIT student center, for example, it was impossible to find any mention of the Gates appearance, though it was happening in a building just two hundred yards away. One MIT student, upon learning that Gates was speaking in a few minutes, was disappointed to learn that he would not get to hear one of his idols.

Gates dressed for the two Cambridge appearances as if he were just another college student—black sweater, open-necked shirt. At each stop he spoke for nearly an hour. He then answered the students' questions. The speech that Gates gave was one that he has given countless times before. He took the students through a brief history of the personal computer and his own role in helping to found the personal computer software industry. He then offered the students a glimpse into the future of personal computer software over the next five to ten years. He pointed to the brand-new SPOT watch that he was wearing and explained that it operated wirelessly and gave him access to real-time information plucked from the Internet. It contained Microsoft's latest piece of software. He proudly observed how much more powerful the SPOT watch he was wearing on his wrist was than the original IBM personal computer of the early 1980s.

He was distressed, he said, to find that excitement about the field of computer science had waned of late; and this seemed odd, he believed, because computer science was on the cusp of remarkable software breakthroughs that would transform people's personal and business lives. With growing excitement in his voice, he spoke about the efforts at Microsoft research that had produced the software for the SPOT watch and that was currently working to perfect voice- and print-recognition as the next major advances in software.

In his view, the major issue facing Microsoft and all others in the software industry was computer security. Just that week, he noted, Microsoft had announced a "caller ID" of sorts for incoming spam, designed to significantly reduce the amount of incoming spam.

The students were given a chance to ask questions of Gates. Some wanted to know how Microsoft hoped to cope with the rising threat of free software (Gates insisted there would always be a place in the industry for commercial software since it would likely be of a higher quality than the free software).

Some asked personal questions. The audience, especially at Harvard, was amused that the man speaking to them had dropped out of their school and gone on to become the richest man in the world and one of the brightest minds of his era. One MIT student asked Gates what he would have done had he not dropped out of Harvard and co-founded Microsoft. He replied that he would probably be pursuing some aspect of computational biology and/or artificial intelligence, two pursuits he had grown to love. He expressed no regret about his time at college or dropping out: "There were very smart people to talk to. They fed you every day. You didn't have to go to classes." Perhaps because he wanted to be kind to the Harvard audience—and did not want to appear to be encouraging them to drop out as well—he put the blame for his dropping out on the constant pressure that his friend Paul Allen had put on him in order to leave the school and help him found a software enterprise. "We're going to get left behind," Gates quoted Allen as saying to him all the time, until Gates finally left school. Gates was conscious of not making it sound as if the way to success was by dropping out of college. He said that only if someone felt he could come up with a "paradigm shift" should he even think of leaving school.

At Harvard, one student asked what Gates would have done if Microsoft had not succeeded. Had there been a contingency plan in his mind? Yes, said Gates, his backup plan had been to return to Harvard. "When I left Harvard, I went on leave. I'm still on leave." The audience roared in laughter at that one. Gates admitted that he had never felt very nervous in trying to get Microsoft off the ground because he had banked $80,000 from previous work experiences.

During Gates's appearance at MIT, at various times, students got up and exited the auditorium, one of those rare occasions when people actually walked out on a Gates speech. But the students had no choice; they had to run to their next class. Gates took their departures in stride. He seemed unaffected by the exiting students.

In general, it was clear that most people who heard Bill Gates that day at MIT and Harvard had relished seeing him in person. Afterward, some expressed some mild disappointment that he had dwelled more on the world of commercial software and less on their own academic-oriented pursuits. But, from Gates's viewpoint, the college tour appeared highly successful, if only because he had, even for a brief few hours, brought these young computer science students into the world of the new Microsoft. And given all that had happened at Microsoft in the past five years, reaching out to such people could yield important positive results for the company and for Gates down the road.

There were some signs that the outside world was responding positively to Microsoft's efforts to refurbish its reputation. When *Fortune*'s list of America's Most Admired Companies appeared in March 2004, Microsoft had inched up from seventh (in 2003) to sixth (in 2004). It had been number three in 1999, number two in 2000, number five in 2001, and number four in 2002.

To some within the company, the changes that Microsoft was undertaking were monumental. "We are undergoing the largest cultural shift right now in the company that I've seen in the last fifteen years," said Mary Snapp. "It's a move from being Redmond-centered to understanding that we are a corporate citizen in an industry and in the world," and an understanding, she said, that Microsoft had a different role to play from the days when it was small and when many fewer people were using PCs.

To others, it was way too early to assess just how monumental the changes might be.

Undeniably, the process had started; the rebooting of Microsoft was under way. But it was new. Two years was not a long time to make such sweeping changes, not a long time to turn cynics into fans, not the amount of time needed to change the company's image from predator to benefactor, and not enough time to make the world believe that reforms had indeed been put in place. Still, Bill Gates and Steve Ballmer had definitely begun the process of reinventing their company.

Afterword

This book began just as a major legal case confronting Microsoft was coming to a close, that of *United States v. Microsoft*. That legal case, which ended on November 1, 2002, and revolved around antitrust charges, set in motion the recovery process and reforms that are the centerpiece of *Microsoft Rebooted*.

As the book closes, a second important legal decision brought by the European Union's regulators also involving antitrust allegations, was announced seventeen months later, on March 24, 2004.

The American legal case precipitated the need for Microsoft to undertake a vast reinventing of its culture and its approach to the outside world. The European Union case will in all likelihood cause the company to make an even greater effort to embed the new reforms within the company.

At first glance, the European decision appeared a harsher verdict on Microsoft than the American one, if only because the American case ended in a settlement while the European Union case concluded with an actual verdict and the imposing of serious punishment on the company.

The European regulators decreed that Microsoft had broken European law by exploiting its "near monopoly" over the Windows operating system to prevent competitors from selling other types of software. The decision affects only Microsoft's operations in Europe.

Some obvious similarities existed in the American and European cases: Both challenged Microsoft to demonstrate that it was not abusing its position as a monopolist; both questioned Microsoft's practice of bundling a certain piece of software (the browser in the American case; media-playing software in the European one); and both did serious damage to Microsoft's reputation.

Key questions surrounded the two cases: How serious would the damage to Microsoft's reputation be? How would the company deal with the implications of the legal cases? I've spent a good deal of time answering these questions as they relate to the American case, and the book concludes just as Microsoft is beginning to tackle the implications for the European one.

Specifics of the Decree

The specifics of the decree from the European Commission, the executive arm of the European Union (E.U.), were that:

- Microsoft had ninety days to offer a version of Windows with its media-playing software taken out. Microsoft could still sell a version of Windows with Media Player in E.U. countries, but this bundled version could not be favored in any way over the unbundled one. The bundling, or tying, as the European Union preferred to call it, harmed competition in the European Union's view, because it kept numerous high-quality alternatives from becoming available. Media players were considered by the European Union to be separate products from operating systems, as there was separate demand for them.
- Microsoft had 120 days to disclose the necessary information about Windows to competitors who made software for computer servers in order to permit those competitors to design products that would work as easily with Windows as Microsoft's own server software.
- Microsoft was fined $613 million. (For Microsoft this was a mere drop in the bucket, less than 1 percent of its total available cash; still, the fine was considered a substantial one by any standard.)

The reaction to the European Union decision came from all quarters.

Microsoft, declaring that it would appeal the decision and thus perhaps delay its implementation for years, acknowledged that it was quite disappointed—that settlement talks had broken down, that the

European Union had seen fit to render this verdict, that regulators failed to understand the need for Microsoft to be allowed to innovate and to create better products (through bundling, which in the company's view was a great convenience to consumers).

In a public statement, Steve Ballmer said: "There's an important principle at stake in this case. We believe that every company should have the ability to improve its products to meet the needs of consumers. We recognize the special position our company has; but, nonetheless, we think we should have the ability to improve our products subject to the appropriate guidelines. . . . Our research shows that a majority, a very broad majority, of European consumers believe that Windows Media Player should be included with Windows."

Microsoft's top legal man, Brad Smith, called the decision "an unfortunate step and it's an unnecessary step." He received support from a most unexpected source: the U.S. Department of Justice! "Sound antitrust policy must avoid chilling innovation and competition even by 'dominant' companies," said R. Hewitt Pace, assistant attorney general in charge of the antitrust division, in a statement that had the Department of Justice (DOJ) siding with Microsoft. Of course, Pace was reflecting a pro-business Department of Justice under President George W. Bush, which by 2004 was in sharp contrast with the trust-busting DOJ of the late 1990s under President Bill Clinton.

Competitors to Microsoft seemed far more satisfied with the E.U. decision than with the settlement of the American legal case. They suggested that hope existed for the first time that there could be fair competition between Microsoft and its rivals.

Sandwiched in between these two legal decisions was a crucial period of seventeen months during which Steve Ballmer and Bill Gates took the opportunity to reinvent their company in ways that were more broad-gauging than any reinventing ever undertaken within Microsoft. Throughout these pages, I have described in great detail this process of reinventing: the introduction of far-reaching reforms that were designed to present Microsoft to the outside world in a new, positive light.

Throughout those seventeen months of recovery and reform, Microsoft's leaders did not seem overly concerned by the pending decision of the European Union. They showed no outward worry that another crushing legal blow might befall Microsoft. Still, Microsoft's executives knew all too well that another legal cloud hung over their heads and that just because *United States v. Microsoft* had come to a close, it did not mean that the company was out of legal trouble. The E.U. case did not come up in conversation that often; but when it did, Microsoft leaders made sure to caution: *We're not out of the woods yet. We still have this case in Europe.* But no one seemed overly nervous about the outcome.

Meanwhile, the recovery and reform process went forward, in large measure because Steve Ballmer and Bill Gates understood that the company had to put a new, more congenial face on its dealings with the outside world. They may also have believed that the reform program might have the beneficial effect of Microsoft's avoiding further legal hot water.

Regulators Not Impressed

In the end, the European regulators did not seem impressed with Microsoft's reforms. They had been asked to adjudicate many of the same issues and principles involved in *United States v. Microsoft*. It did not matter to the regulators that Microsoft had tried to adopt a softer, more open approach to competitors, the media, Wall Street, and Washington, D.C. It seemed only to matter to them that Microsoft appeared to be up to its old tricks. And if the American legal system could not take tough steps against Microsoft, the European regulators could—and would.

Microsoft could have chosen to interpret the E.U. decision as a crippling blow to its reform effort. After all, the new reform winds blowing out of Redmond had made no impression on the regulators in Brussels. But none of the Microsoft leaders, long-faced and distraught as they were, thought Steve Ballmer and Bill Gates should halt the reforms in their tracks. Ballmer and Gates had known from the beginning of those reforms that the journey would be long and uphill, and that it would most likely take years to win over the cynics and the doubters.

Perhaps that explains why the tone in the voices of Microsoft leaders in the closing days of March 2004 was more relief than bitterness at the outcome of the E.U. decision. They were reasonably confident that Microsoft's appeal of the case would likely put off any implementation for as many as five years. With the E.U. decision now handed down, at least they knew the exact size of the fine and could for the first time safely begin to use Microsoft's billions of dollars of cash on hand without worrying whether there would be enough cash to pay legal fines. They felt assured, too, by the fact that the European regulators had been far friendlier to Microsoft than had Judge Jackson, and that boded well for an eventual settlement of the case on terms that were more favorable than the harsh March 2004 E.U. verdict.

These same Microsoft leaders were, however, at a loss to understand why the regulators had turned down a settlement in the days leading up to the verdict. The terms that Steve Ballmer and his colleagues had offered as part of a settlement seemed, in the view of these company leaders, quite compatible with what the regulators wanted of Microsoft.

Brad Smith, in an interview with *The New York Times,* said Microsoft's settlement offer included bundling two rival media players in with Microsoft's Media Player in the Windows operating system. The company also offered, he said, to divulge all the necessary information about Windows that the European Union was seeking to restore fair competition in the server software market.

Still, on the whole, Microsoft seemed more at ease with the E.U. decision than they had with the American one.

After the American decision, company leaders had to scramble to put together a package of reforms that might encounter stiff resistance from the Microsoft community. But by the time the E.U. decision had come down, those reforms were in place, a new culture was functioning at

Microsoft, and the company's leaders had overcome whatever resistance had cropped up within Microsoft to those changes. Certainly, the E.U. decision was exasperating to Microsoft's upper echelons if only because it brought back, however briefly, memories of the company's darkest days during the DOJ trial. Until the European regulators had their say, Ballmer and Gates and other senior executives were beginning to get comfortable with the new Microsoft. It seemed less jarring for them, less awkward to encourage a company that had once been aggressive, even arrogant, to be open and respectful, frank and quick, in its passing on information to others. It seemed as if the company was finally coming out of its dark days.

Then, with disturbing suddenness, the newspapers were again full of stories about official bodies getting ready to punish Microsoft; full of articles about official bodies finding Microsoft guilty of being a monopolist, or of being an abusive monopolist. It was all too much déjà vu for company leaders. Privately, they acknowledged that the E.U. decision served as another reminder that the company could only withstand so many blows before it lost credibility. As one Microsoft official put it a couple of days after the E.U. decision, "Sure we worry that people are going to wake up one day and say, 'Gosh, I've seen and heard enough. I'm going to take on some other (software) options.'"

Still, given the likelihood that the final E.U. decision is in fact years away, if at all, and given that Microsoft might reach a settlement with the E.U. regulators in the future, a general feeling pervades Microsoft—that the company can move forward without feeling too unnerved.

If Microsoft can stay out of the courts, if it can keep the negative newspaper articles to a minimum, if it can calm its rivals, then the company has a chance of turning a corner. No one can predict whether Microsoft's reforms will succeed or, if they do, how long that will take. But Steve Ballmer and Bill Gates seem pleased that they have put a new Microsoft in place, and although their reinventing of the company is a work in progress, they think that one day (hopefully with them still running the place) the rebooting will be regarded as a thorough success.

Notes

Chapter 1: A Surreal Halloween

page

6   **News reports surfaced . . . :** One report appeared in John Heilemann's long article "The Truth, the Whole Truth, and Nothing but the Truth," *Wired,* November 2000.

7   **"a sense of relief . . .":** Bill Gates Sr., interview with author, November 6, 2003. All Bill Gates Sr. quotes in the book are from my interview with him unless otherwise indicated.

7   **"Though Gates is famous . . .":** "Ending the Paper Chase," *Time,* June 14, 1993.

7   **"[T]he real battle . . .":** "Demonizing Gates," *Time*, November 2, 1998.

8   **"magical software":** Bill Gates, interview with author, July 31, 2003. All Bill Gates quotes in the book are from my interview with him unless otherwise indicated.

9   **"It is deep in the culture . . .":** Pam Edstrom, interview with author, September 9, 2003.

9   **"After the launch . . .":** Bob Herbold, interview with author, September 4, 2003. All Bob Herbold quotes in the book are from my interview with him unless otherwise indicated.

11   **"Whatever happens . . .":** Brad Smith recounted this anecdote in an interview with the author, July 28, 2003. All Brad Smith quotes in the book are from my interviews with him on July 28 and September 4, 2003, unless otherwise indicated.

16   **"The trial matured people . . .":** Jon Shirley, interview with author, April 23, 2003. All Jon Shirley quotes in the book are from my interview with him unless otherwise indicated.

22   **"Providing value to customers . . .":** Bill Gates and Steve Ballmer shareholders letter, 2003 Annual Report.

Chapter 2: The Lawyer Gates for the Defense

page

24 **"The only thing . . ."**: Scott McNealy quoted in Robert Uhlig, "Bill Gates Is Richer Than All African Countries Put Together," April 10, 1999, *globalvisionary@cybernaute.com.*

25 **"I am no antitrust scholar . . ."**: "The Bill & Warren Show," *Fortune,* July 20, 1998.

26 **"Possibly, they were naïve . . ."**: Lew Platt, interview with author, June 27, 2003. All Lew Platt quotes in the book are from my interview with him unless otherwise indicated.

26 **"The image of our company . . ."**: Jeff Raikes, interview with author, August 8, 2003. All Jeff Raikes quotes in the book are from my interview with him unless otherwise indicated.

26 **"Antitrust is among . . ."**: Craig Mundie, interview with author, November 6, 2003. All other Craig Mundie quotes in the book are from interviews with him on June 12, 2003, or November 6, 2003, unless otherwise indicated.

28 **"In other words . . ."**: Gary Reback quoted in "In Search of the Real Bill Gates," *Time,* January 13, 1997. All Gary Reback quotes in the book are from the *Time* article unless otherwise indicated.

29 **"Should we improve . . ."**: Bill Gates quoted in ibid.

29 **"pretty relentless . . ."**: Rob Glaser quoted in ibid.

29 **"If we weren't so ruthless . . ."**: Bill Gates quoted in ibid.

30 **"Taken to an extreme . . ."**: Nathan Myhrvold quoted in "Cyber Elite Top 50," *Time Digital,* 1998.

30 **"Microsoft didn't realize. . . ."**: Mike Murray, interview with author, April 22, 2003. All Mike Murray quotes in the book are from my interviews with him on April 22 and July 29, 2003, unless otherwise indicated.

31 **"as close as anyone . . ."**: *The Seattle Times,* February 14, 1982.

32 **"Who is this man?"**: Stephen Manes and Paul Andrews, *Gates: How Microsoft's Mogul Reinvented an Industry—and Made Himself the Richest Man in America* (New York: Touchstone Books, 1994, paperback), p. 5.

32 **"Here was a way . . ."**: Nathan Myhrvold, interview with author, July 25, 2003. All Nathan Myhrvold quotes in the book are from my interviews with him on June 10 and July 25, 2003, unless otherwise indicated.

34 **"The problem started . . ."**: Kornel Marton, interview with author, May 23, 2003.

35 **"So where are my victims? . . ."**: Nathan Myhrvold reported one such conversation with Gates in our interview, July 25, 2003.

36 **"The key message . . ."**: Kevin Johnson, interview with author, June 13, 2003. All Kevin Johnson quotes in the book are from my interview with him unless otherwise indicated.

41 "That's not chocolate sundae.": Bill Gates Sr. quoted in "Behind the Gates Myth," *Newsweek*, August 30, 1999.

43 "Do we have a clear plan . . .": Bill Gates quoted in *Time*, March 22, 1999.

43 To *Time* magazine, Gates's . . .: Ibid.

43 "totally truthful answers . . .": Bill Gates quoted in "Behind the Gates Myth."

44 "supercilious": Judge Jackson quoted in AP Online, November 1, 2002.

44 "I think he has. . . .": Jackson quoted in "Bill Gates," *Fortune*, December 7, 1998.

Chapter 3: The Most Unique Partnership in Business

page

57 "The benefit of sparking . . .": "The Bill & Warren Show."

63 "Work it, work it . . .": Steve Ballmer, speech at 92nd St. Y, New York City, November 13, 2003.

64 "In general, I see . . .": Steve Ballmer, interview with author, September 10, 2003. All Steve Ballmer quotes in the book are from my interview with him unless otherwise noted.

67 "It was fairly clear . . .": Steve Ballmer, 92nd St. Y speech.

67 "We were both kind of . . .": Bill Gates quoted in "You Call This a Midlife Crisis?" *The New York Times*, August 31, 2003.

68 "Even though Steve . . .": Warren Buffett quoted in Brent Schlender, "All You Need Is Love . . . ," *Fortune*, July 8, 2002.

68 "When I took over . . .": Anoop Gupta, interview with author, September 8, 2003. All Anoop Gupta quotes in the book are from my interview with him unless otherwise stated.

70 "Steve's personality and . . .": Mary Snapp, interview with author, December 18, 2003. All other Mary Snapp quotes in the book are from my interview with her unless otherwise indicated.

Chapter 4: Putting the Start-up to Bed

page

78 "the highest priority . . .": Bill Gates, "Trustworthy Computing" memo, January 15, 2002.

78–79 "Computing falls well . . .": Ibid.

80 "Part of the initiative . . .": Scott Charney, interview with author, July 29, 2003.

81 "part of our . . .": Bill Gates, "Trustworthy Computing" memo, July 18, 2002.

89 "advances in chips . . .": Bill Gates, speech at Comdex, November 17, 2002.

Chapter 5: Yes, Mom, I'm Thinking

page

95   **"What are you doing?"**: "In Search of the Real Bill Gates."

96   **"I realized later . . ."**: Bill Gates with Nathan Myhrvold and Peter Rinearson, *The Road Ahead* (New York: Penguin Books, 1996, paperback), p. 1.

96   **"It was hard to tear . . ."**: Ibid., pp. 12–13.

98   **"crazy dreams"**: Ibid., p. 16.

98   **"Computers weren't personal . . ."**: Bill Gates speech, Minority Student Day, Redmond, Washington, February 14, 2003.

99   *"Trey took time off . . ."*: *Gates*, pp. 89–90.

104   **"There is hardly. . . ."**: Peter Rinearson, interview with author, April 24, 2003. All Peter Rinearson quotes in the book are from my interview with him unless otherwise noted.

104   **Oh my God, he knows about this.**: Peter Haynes, interview with author, April 23, 2003.

105   **"he knew exactly . . ."**: Deborah Willingham, interview with author, April 25, 2003. All Deborah Willingham quotes in the book are from my interview with her unless otherwise indicated.

111   **"It wasn't that Bill . . ."**: Corey duBrowa, interview with author, November 5, 2003. All other Corey duBrowa quotes are from my interview with him unless otherwise indicated.

114   **"E-mail is really . . ."**: Bill Gates in talk to CEO summit, Redmond, Washington, May 23, 2003.

116   **"There are better detective . . ."**: "Bill Moyers and Bill Gates: A Global Health Dialogue," Columbia University Mailman School of Public Health, broadcast on PBS, May 9, 2003.

Chapter 6: Meeting with Former African Prostitutes

page

120   **He told the media . . .** : The information in this paragraph comes from "All You Need Is Love . . ."

124   **"such a systematic failure . . ."**: Bill Gates quoted in ibid.

126   **"Both Bill and Melinda . . ."**: Joe Cerrell, interview with author, November 6, 2003.

126   **"hands were shaken . . ."**: "Bill Gates: The Biggest Thing in India Since the Beatles," *The Christian Science Monitor*, November 14, 2002.

127   **"second smartest . . ."**: Ibid.

129   **In 1999, when he became. . . .** : Quoted in "Bill Gates Is Richer than all African Countries Put Together."

129 **"I think your psyche . . .":** "Behind the Gates Myth."

130 **"noticeably older . . .":** "All You Need Is Love . . ."

131 **"Those who think . . .":** "Gates Aims Billions to Attack Illnesses of World's Neediest," *The New York Times*, July 13, 2003.

132 **"[F]rankly, one of the best . . .":** "Fighting the Fevers," *The New York Times*, September 25, 2003.

132 **"The buzz among African aid workers . . .":** Ibid.

Chapter 7: Open and Respectful

page

139 **"That's what Microsoft . . .":** Charles Simonyi, interview with author, June 12, 2003. All Charles Simonyi quotes in the book are from my interview with him unless otherwise indicated.

140 **"Steve is a totally . . .":** Jim Allchin, interview with author, July 30, 2003. All Jim Allchin quotes in the book are from my interview with him unless otherwise indicated.

142 **"increased expectations":** Steve Ballmer, 92nd St. Y speech.

146 **"non-commercial software products . . .":** Steve Ballmer memo, "The Microsoft Business Plan," June 4, 2003.

147 **"We've always been able . . .":** Steve Ballmer, 92nd St. Y speech.

Chapter 8: The Discipline Revolution

page

152 **"I told Bill . . .":** Scott Oki, interview with author, June 9, 2003.

157 **"Their instinct is . . .":** Jim Cash, interview with author, June 11, 2003. All Jim Cash quotes are from my interviews with him on June 11 and September 10, 2003, unless otherwise indicated.

159 **"There were only . . .":** John Connors, interview with author, September 8, 2003. All John Connors quotes in the book are from my interview with him unless otherwise indicated.

161 **"I don't know what . . .":** Steve Ballmer, 92nd St. Y speech.

168 **Jeff Raikes found out . . . :** "Microsoft to Unveil Plan to Give Financial Managers New Clout," *The Wall Street Journal*, July 23, 2003.

170 **"This company is . . .":** Elijah Hurwitz, interview with author, July 23, 2003. All other Elijah Hurwitz quotes are from my interview with him unless otherwise indicated.

Chapter 9: Great People with Great Values

page

175   "They wanted someone . . .": Alan Levy, interview with author, March 15, 2003.

177   "No, we're programmers": *Gates,* p. 104.

178   "Microsoft expects . . .": Ibid.

178   "Bill is not threatened . . .": Nathan Myhrvold quoted in David A. Heenan and Warren Bennis, *Co-Leaders: The Power of Great Partnerships* (New York: John Wiley & Sons, 1999), p. 50.

187   "We will never back off . . .": Ken DiPietro, interview with author, September 4, 2003. All Ken DiPietro quotes in the book are from my interview with him unless otherwise indicated.

187   "I tend to go . . .": Rick Rashid, interview with author, July 29, 2003.

188   "Now as the market . . .": John O'Rourke, interview with author, July 23, 2003.

Chapter 10: The New Culture of Being Friendly and Humble

page

190   "I think of Microsoft's persistence. . . .": Robert S. Rosenschein, interview with author, April 2, 2003.

191   "That was symbolic. . . .": Robbie Bach, interview with author, September 8, 2003. All other Rabbie Bach quotes are from my interview with him unless otherwise indicated.

193   "intellectual pissing contest": Chris Bartlett quoted in "Microsoft Reaches Middle Age," *Financial Times,* July 28, 2003.

197   "I'd still say . . .": Steve Ballmer quoted in "You Call This . . ."

198   "How do you really behave . . .": Steve Ballmer, 92nd St. Y speech.

201   "I'm probably apologizing . . .": Steve Ballmer quoted in "You Call This . . ."

201   "It takes so much . . .": Mark Zbikowski, interview with author, July 25, 2003.

202   "That's my deal . . .": Steve Ballmer, 92nd St. Y speech.

204   "It shot from . . .": John Eng, interview with author, July 23, 2003.

207   "Some of the lunch-time . . .": Andrew Wilson, interview with author, July 23, 2003.

215   "We changed in that . . .": Orlando Ayala quoted in "You Call This . . ."

Chapter 11: Has the Revolution Begun?

page

221 "Hey, if I didn't . . .": "Behind the Gates Myth."

224 "I think there are . . .": Steve Ballmer quoted in "Microsoft CEO Wants Company to Broaden Its Reach, Burnish Its Reputation," *The Seattle Times,* February 24, 2003.

225 "We're farther than 20 . . .": Steve Ballmer, 92nd St. Y speech.

230 "All that I see . . .": Eric Benhamou, interview with author, July 7, 2003.

232 "Ballmer has set . . .": Dwight Davis, interview with author, June 12, 2003.

Afterword

page

239 "There's an important . . .": *The New York Times,* Steve Ballmer quoted in "Excerpts from Ruling in Europe and Microsoft's Response," March 25, 2004.

239 "an unfortunate step . . .": Brad Smith quoted in *The New York Times,* "European Rule Against Microsoft; Appeal Is Promised," March 25, 2004.

239 "Sound antitrust policy . . .": Ibid.

241 Brad Smith, in an interview . . .: Ibid.

Index